Get out fast

// Anything goes

Catch out here

Man with gun

⊗ Good for a handout

▽ Tramps here

‡ Officer

Unsafe place

⨅ Gentleman

Good water

⊤ Sit-down feed

Woman

Hold your tongue

Safe camp

Q At crossroads
go this way

Hobo

A Young Man's Thoughts on Trains and Tramping in America

A Young Man's Thoughts on
Trains and Tramping in America

Eddy Joe Cotton

Hobo

Central Pacific Rail Road

Old Emigrant Road

Hot Springs

Old Overland Station

China Camp

Central Pacific Rail Road

DESERT

Harmony Books ★ New York

Grateful acknowledgment is made to the following for previously published material:

BUG MUSIC, INC.: Excerpts from the song lyric "Heart Is Saved" written by Iggy Pop. Copyright © 1996. Published by James Osterberg Music (BMI)/Administered by BUG. All rights reserved. Reprinted by permission of BUG Music, Inc.

AUDIGRAM SONGS, INC: Excerpts from the song lyric "Drifter's Wife," words and music by J. J. Cale. Copyright © 1981 by Audigram Songs, Inc. Reprinted by permission of Audigram Songs, Inc.

PFD: Excerpts from *Hard Travellin'* by Kenneth Allsop. Copyright © 1967 by Kenneth Allsop. Reprinted by permission of PFD on behalf of the Estate of Kenneth Allsop.

Published by Harmony Books, New York, New York.

Member of the Crown Publishing Group, a division of Random House, Inc.

www.randomhouse.com

HARMONY BOOKS is a registered trademark and the Harmony Books colophon is a trademark of Random House, Inc.

Printed in the United States of America

DESIGN BY ELINA D. NUDELMAN

Endpaper map © David Lindroth Inc.

Map illustration courtesy Central Pacific Railroad Photographic History Museum, from the Larry K. Hersh Collection, © 2002 CPRR.org.

Library of Congress Cataloging-in-Publication Data

Cotton, Eddy Joe.
Hobo: a young man's thoughts on trains and tramping in America / Eddy Joe Cotton.
   1. Cotton, Eddy Joe.   2. Tramps—United States—Biography.   3. Railroad travel—United States.   4. United States—Description and travel.   I. Title.
HV4505 .C68 2002
917.3'0492—dc21
[B]   2002017191

ISBN 0-609-60738-3

10 9 8 7 6 5 4 3 2 1

First Edition

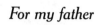

For my father

Contents

Acknowledgments   ix

List of Photographs   xi

A Note from the Author   xiii

Introduction   xv

Prologue: Coconut Road   xix

Part One

1: **Denver, Colorado**   3
October 24, 1991—Sunrise

2: **Fort Worth, Texas**   7
1950s—Summertime

3: **Denver to Wyoming**   25
October 24, 1991—Sunset

4: **Northern Wyoming to Greybull**   43
October 25, 1991—Midnight

5: **Northern Wyoming to Missoula**   59
October 29, 1991—Sunrise

6: **Missoula Yard, Montana**   69
October 30, 1991—Nightfall

7: **Missoula Yard** 89
Halloween, October 31, 1991—Midnight

8: **Idaho Falls to Blackfoot** 95
November 1, 1991—Sunup

9: **Blackfoot, Idaho, to Evanston, Wyoming** 113
November 2, 1991

10: **Ogden, Utah** 143
November 7, 1991—Afternoon

Part Two:

Starlet Las Vegas: The Desert Diva

11: **Winnemucca, Nevada** 161
November 9, 1991—Morning Twilight

12: **Winnemucca, Lovelock, Reno** 179
November 9, 1991—Midday

13: **Highway 95, Reno to Las Vegas** 199
November 12, 1991—All Day

14: **Las Vegas** 215
November 14, 1991—3:00 A.M.

15: **McCarren International Airport, Las Vegas** 235
November 16, 1991—Morning

Epilogue: Sunset Road 241

Glossary 257

Resources 285

Acknowledgments

A sentimental and hearty thank you to the following people:

TRAMPS: Alabama, Chris O'Connor, Solomon Paul Hobbes, Stringbean, Five Livered Larry, Yukon Sam, Billie the Kid, Shortstop, Half-Step, Misty, and Jefferson.

WRITERS: Steven Kotler, Erika Lopez, and Brenda Knight.

WORDSMITHS: Pete Fornatale, Mary Evans, Linda Loewenthal, and Carrie Thornton.

PHOTOGRAPHS: Flecher Fleudujon, Jennifer Hawk, Fred Larson, Justine Gilcrease, Gregory Colebourn, and Al Fetterly.

YARD DOGS: Five Livered Larry, Voodoo Freddy, Micha, Hellvis, Bellpod, Airstream Fred, Lilly Rose Love, Jessica Swords, Phoebe, The Hellvets, The Kissing What Nots, The Twelve Toed Man, P-Dorkle, Madball, and the Goddess of Groove with those platform shoes.

OTHERS: Zoopy Funk, Ashleigh Hayes, Joe Hudson, John Crandall, Cornelia, Dale Hayes (for the title), Grandfather Don, Mom, Pop, Pony, and Xica.

List of Photographs

Title page: Train yard somewhere in Oregon, 1998. Photo by Flecher Fleudujon.

Page 2: My father's friends Bob Dawley and David Willis, aka Oliver (holding popsicle), in Mission Beach, San Diego, 1970. The chopper is a 1965 Harley Davidson Sportster, radical custom. Photo by Bill Recchia.

Page 6: One of my grandfather's first hot rods, 1949. Photo by Donald Moser.

Page 24: On tour with the Yard Dogs Road Show. A 4:00 A.M. bowl of soup. After the show, Springfield, Oregon, 1998. Photo by Flecher Fleudujon.

Page 42: Palm tree, Santa Monica, California. One week sleeping on the beach, under the lifeguard shacks with Chris and Jennifer. No hard feelings. 1993. Photo by Jennifer Hawk.

Page 58: On tour with the Yard Dogs Road Show. Southbound Union Pacific. Portland to Eugene, 1998. Photo by Flecher Fleudujon.

Page 68: Three tramps—Eddy Joe Cotton, Chris O'Connor, and The Bird. Train yard west of El Paso, Texas, 1993. Photo by Jennifer Hawk.

Page 88: On tour with the Yard Dogs Road Show. Portland, Oregon. Stringbean on a Southbound Union Pacific. On our way to Eugene, 1998. Photo by Flecher Fleudujon.

Page 94: Train southbound, tramp northbound. Oregon, 1998. Photo by Flecher Fleudujon.

Page 112: Paradise as seen from a moving train, 2001. Photo by Gregory Colebourn.

Page 142: On tour with the Yard Dogs Road Show. Two hours till showtime. Springfield, Eugene, 1998. Photo by Flecher Fleudujon.

Page 160: Winner's Casino. Polaroid. 2001. Photo by Justine Gilcrease.

Page 178: On tour with the Yard Dogs Road Show. Seven hundred miles in one day. Two hours of sleep. Ten people, one bed. Motel, Springfield, Oregon, 1998. Photo by Flecher Fleudujon.

Page 198: On tour with the Yard Dogs Road Show. On the road one week, pulled over four times. Interstate 5, northbound, 1998. Photo by Flecher Fleudujon.

Page 214: The Hard Rock Casino, Las Vegas, Nevada. Escorting friend from San Francisco to Colorado to see boyfriend locked up in state-run facility. Ninety-nine cent sunglasses. Thirty-five-cent phone call to Buckthorn Superstar. 2001. Photo by Justine Gilcrease.

Page 234: Highway 85 outside of Bakersfield, California. Fun in the sun. Life goes on. 2001. Photo by Justine Gilcrease.

A Note from the Author

If, while reading this book, you stumble upon a word or term you do not understand, please refer to the glossary on page 257. The slang terms in this glossary are derived from many passing sources—most commonly the dirty and poetic mouths of tramps. For clarification of these terms the author has consulted resource books, old magazines, and newspaper articles, for which he would like to acknowledge great thanks—mostly to those who cared enough to preserve America's verbal tradition of debauchery and daredevil poetic recklessness. The author would also like to credit his simple interaction and civic wrongdoings with the American misfits and degenerates aforementioned. These terms were created out of necessity—in order to keep them from their inevitable metamorphosis and eventual decline into less specificity, the author has made a strong effort to maintain the originality of these terms.

Introduction

"A hobo works and wanders, a tramp dreams and wanders, and a bum drinks and wanders."

—BEN L. REITMAN

"Bums loafs and sits. Tramps loafs and walks. But a hobo moves and works, and he's clean."

—WORDS OF AN "EXPERIENCED HOBO" FROM THE BOOK *AMERICAN TRAMP AND UNDERWORLD SLANG* BY IRWIN GODFREY

If a man says he's a hobo—don't believe him
If a man says he's a tramp—believe him
Because every man is a tramp

Waiting on a Train

I looked like Rudolph—my nose was red and hard from the cold. Alabama (the tramp who taught me trains) and me were in Wyoming and there were icicles hanging on the trees. The Burlington Northern railroad tracks sat on a hill of rock— quiet—except for the whisper of an autumn gale that had frozen them solid. I could have tapped those tracks with a hammer and shattered them like glass. In that silence between trains you can hear your toes wiggle in your boots. I had gone a thousand miles on one pair of socks. There was a turkey vulture up in the air, looking for ghosts. On the hills where the tracks disappeared a cold rain fell like needles and the hidden sun glowed silver through the broken clouds. I lay back on my bedroll and closed my eyes.

The luck of the tramp changes as the whistle blows. Under his wool poncho, beneath his metal flask, his heart leaps like a jackrabbit. Out of his sleeping bear slumber a tramp comes running with a bedroll on his shoulder. He is a joker in the deck, this little man with a bandanna around his neck, a trucker hat on his head, and a hole in his boot. I took off running.

I caught up with Alabama. He had his hand on the grab iron of a freight car and his boots were skipping along the gravel. He climbed up the ladder and wrestled himself onto the platform. I grabbed the ladder and it froze my fingers stiff. I ran along like that, my hand frozen to the ladder, until I got my other hand on it, and when I did the train lifted me off the ground—like an angel. I climbed up the ladder and hopped onto the platform. I stuck my head out into the air. The cold wind pushed my hair back. And there I was, steady rolling with icicles hanging on the trees, just like Robert Johnson, the blues singer, sang about. I'd never hopped a freight before, but god-

damn it if it wasn't exactly what God had intended for me. It
reminded me of barreling down the highway in my dad's
truck—looking out the window—daydreaming—counting
mile markers—crossing state lines like they were telephone
poles. Back then is when I first got it, "the fever"—white line
fever, as truckers call it. And I've never been the same since.

Black diesel billowed up from the head end of the train.
There were four monster locomotives up there, pulling boxcars
like sled dogs and coughing smoke out of their big diesel smokestacks. The bark of those diesel engines held the cry of a million pistons and cracked the silence in the Wyoming prairie
apart. A light snow fell on the back end of the train, where the
black oil rigs, flatcars, hoppers, and refrigerator cars wobbled
over the rails like crippled old men. The only other sounds—
a cricket grinding her legs, the lonely sputter of a grasshopper
hopping, and the silence of dust settling—quiet as death.
Above the fire pit we had just abandoned, I could see the ash
of a few smoldering branches.

Alabama said the car we were on was called a grainer
because it hauled grain. On the side of the grainer right above
the words ACE CENTER FLOW (the name of the freight car) was
a hobo tag drawn in white chalk. It was a little sketch of a palm
tree with a Mexican hobo hunched down underneath it. He was
wearing a poncho and a sombrero, and beneath the palm tree,
the hobo who doodled it had written his moniker—Herby. I
went on to see that tag in four trains in four states in four weeks.

After ten hours on that train, the clatter of the crooked
rails and thunder of the slack action had become so intense that
I couldn't hear myself think. The damn western sun was stabbing my eyeballs and the pants I had bought for work were
starting to stink like manure—good old farm cow shit. I cringed
under the brim of my hat and watched my shadow creep slow

across the grainer's wall. We were sitting right above the wheels. When the brakes clamped down on them, the brake pads tore steel right off the top—the metallic flakes sparkled in the sunlight. I rolled up in my poncho, lay down on the floor of the car, and watched rusty paint flakes dance in the corner. I daydreamed of carefree America: casino coffee, fucking under white motel sheets, showers with soap, and shingled roofs. I knew that when those foothills ate the sun our boxcar would freeze solid again, and there wasn't a thing I could do about it.

Riding freight is like riding in the back of a pickup truck down a washboard dirt road in Mexico while smoking two hundred Camel straights and eating fifty hard-boiled eggs like Cool Hand Luke. Most of all it feels like getting the piss kicked out of you in a stone-dark dungeon. I had black hands, and when I scratched my eyes it made me look like a raccoon. But deep down I didn't care much, because I was too busy dreaming about all the tramping in the woods I was going to do—all the burning twigs with wooden matches, dipping my nose in cold Rocky Mountain river water and wearing a fur coat like a kid coyote in the moonlight. It warmed my heart to think about all the dirt I would have to eat and all the pretty ladies I would have to serenade—just to get a kiss and a meal. All on my little journey tramping across the country. I sat up, leaned my back against the grainer wall, and watched the sunset.

Prologue: Coconut Road

Three men's thoughts on the life of the American Misfit:

"Now the power is out — trains aren't running. I'm spending my last two dollars on breakfast. I wanna make sure I'm completely busted on this fine, frosty Tuesday morning. What is there *really* to do anyways?"

—STRINGBEAN

My ditch-camping friend Stringbean said that to me in the summer of 1998. We were on our way to Reno. We were in Big Sky country.

"May spring up new and mongrel races of broken and almost
extinguished tribes; the descendants of wandering hunters and
trappers; of fugitives from the Spanish and American frontiers;
of adventurers and desperadoes of every class and country
yearly ejected from the bosom of society into the wilderness."

—WASHINGTON IRVING, SPEAKING OF THE WILD WEST IN 1836

Imagine that—tribes of misfits tramping around the Wild
West in fur coats with no country—no flag—no place to bring
the bacon home to. This quote reminds me of all my train-rider
friends. I guess things haven't changed much.

"Coconut road is the road out of town because sometimes it's
just easier that way."

—SOLOMAN PAUL HOBBES, PROFESSIONAL CARD DEALER
AND TRAMP EXTRAORDINAIRE

Luckily the coconuts that fall from the tree land close
together. They keep each other company and they walk
together and talk together and protect each other and sometimes die for each other. That's a brotherhood. That's a sister-
hood. That's coconut road.

★

In this business of tramping, it's impossible to hold on to anybody
or anything, and as a result I have become a lonely man. I now
have people around me, but the loneliness from that time still
resonates in my heart . . . like the ring of a Sunday church bell
in Salt Lake City. This story goes through towns and characters
like a war-torn carnival. And before I could paint the scenery of
a town or the portrait of a hobo well enough to use him in this

book, the hobo stood up and went to the smoke shop for a pouch of Top rolling tobacco and never came back again. Or the town gave me the go bye—shooed me away. That is the nature of independence. That is also the nature of this story.

My name is Eddy Joe Cotton and I live in Las Vegas. Eight months ago my girlfriend and I packed twenty-three notebooks into the trunk of my Ford, left Denver at three o'clock in the morning, and drove here—of all places. We rented a room for two hundred bucks a week at a motel called Budget Suites of America—a real nice place with clean carpet and clean sheets. The first day I got here I sat on the couch in the room and looked at the nice pictures on the walls and the pure clean white of the porcelain toilet and the tile—*real tile.* And thought:

> These things don't happen to bums.
> Maybe I'm winnin' the game.
> Must be doin' something right.
> Guess I got a good head after all.

I immediately went to work pulling all of the stories and information from my notebooks. They were the notebooks that I carried with me when I was living my life out in the countryside, tramping around. There were a lot of cocktail napkins of course, a circus poster that I tore off some gas station window, four torn-up cardboard boxes, and a stack of cigarette cartons that I used when I couldn't find anything else.

I was twenty-seven years old. I should have been watering the lawn or taking out the garbage. I had no lawn. I had disappeared for six years and all I had to show for it was twenty-three notebooks and a rented mattress. I was at the end of the road— Las Vegas Boulevard, the Strip. A fine place to confide in. A fine place to discover new words and reflect on the old ones.

I wrote a lot of this book in Las Vegas. It was one of the most beautiful eight months of my life. Me and my girlfriend fought a lot, but there was too much magic in that town—in the desert air—to really let the fighting bother us. I think the fighting just made our love that much stronger.

★

I picked the title "Hobo" because it conjures up an image. Even though I'm not a hobo, I thought it would explain the story the best. I feel more like a tramp. Sure, I like that swimming-pool sky and those butterscotch sunsets, out on the lam, in a boxcar, and I like being free, but that doesn't make me a hobo. Hobo is a title that carries a lot of weight—like a gunnysack full of nails. Some men would say that if you're west of Chicago and you call someone a hobo, it's an insult; and if you're east of Chicago and call someone a hobo, it's a compliment. No man knows for sure the differences between a hobo and a tramp and a bum. Therefore I make no claims on the title. A train rider is referred to as a hobo *or* a tramp. In my experience these terms (hobo, tramp, and bum) are used interchangeably. This is best portrayed in the daily banter of my friend Stringbean: Upon rising after a hard night of drinking, he will refer to himself as a "lousy no-good tramp"; at lunch, with his arms up in the air, he will preach to all the "rubes" at the lunch counter about "the rambling gospel" that only a "true hobo" like himself could ever understand; at sunset he will seek out the company of a young lady and serenade her with his "very personal" tales of a "happy-go-lucky scenery bum." Obvious in this exemplification, these terms are as fickle as the moods of the men who use them.

Hobohemia is an informal and chaotic world at best (as implied in my attempted definition of the above terms). A good example of this informality can be found in most any oral tramp story. Stringbean can tell entire detailed stories and in the end it's up to me to decide which parts are true. I've traveled ten miles out of my way to patron a saloon he told me about, and when I arrived at the address he noted, I was standing at the steps of a cathedral. It's not that he lied about the saloon, it's just that he forgot where it was. He filled in the blanks. In Hobohemia this is the type of reality we are dealing with.

★

The historical definitions of hobo, tramp, and bum can be found in the glossary.

★

Because of these aforementioned uncertainties, it is sometimes helpful (in Hobohemia) to think of oneself as a vaudeville clown. Behind the red velvet curtain at a ragtag vaudeville show, "reality" is in all ways debatable. This is also true of Hobohemia. When a tramp is calling into the jungle, it is very similar to a clown walking onstage. The tramp must have his spiel or his skit prepared. Honestly, it's not this romantic. But a good spiel can go a long way. While tramping in this tradition I find it helpful to think of myself as a Joey clown tramp—loosely defined as follows: Joey is the term for an old circus clown, taken from the famous Italian pantomimist Joseph Grimaldi. Joey can also mean a hypocrite. Back in the day an old road clown learned his business of mugging and the art of his spiel from performing in vaudeville shows and manipulating lowbrow drug deals. A Joey clown tramp will use these same tools of theater to hide his tears and present himself upstanding to the outside or inside world. A clown will ride freight and a tramp will work under canvas. At times the clown and the tramp are one and the same. I think of it

this way because I now travel with a rag tag, or mud, show, called
The Yard Dogs Road Show and I daily use the ingenuity of a
Joey clown tramp to facilitate my entertainment business. Some
of this tramp ingenuity is displayed in this book and is also
applicable to everyday life. A showman will do whatever it takes
to get his show to the next town. A tramp will do the same.

★

When I ride trains I remedy my loneliness with a pen and a
notebook. I write down everything that happens to me. In the
pages of this book I offer information from the countless hobos
I've met on the railroad rock. I have met them in the center of
the most desolate states—sometimes under the blinding halogen lights of an oil refinery or at a Salvation Army picnic for
the homeless in El Paso. And what a picnic it was.

   These oil refineries and picnics come with the promise of
civilization—puddles of mud where people huddle together
and forget about the outside world. The hobos who gave me
this information are the men who walk quietly from one train
yard to another. They pass through small towns, and when they
walk down Main Street, coffee cups stop, traffic slows, and for
one brief moment the town folks are reminded that those train
tracks go somewhere. Portola, California, for example. There's
a river there worthy of baptism. I was baptized there. In fact, I
did it myself—all alone—in the cold spiritual waters.

★

I've been riding trains for nine years, but I still can't tell you
when a train is coming or how long it will take to get you where
you're going. I know tramps who could, but I'm not one of
them. These fellas name their Smith and Wesson revolvers
after pretty ex-wives, drink diesel fuel like it's Big Red, and

don't give a damn about you *or* me. So I'll give them my respect and I'll give you enough information to have yourself a new trade. Your own personal truth will come later, much later, when your summer of hoboing and sleeping in the dirt is over.

★

It would be in my highest interest to for any hoboing man or woman to pick up this book and claim themselves the champion of its pages. It would be okay with me if you showed it to your friends and told them that this story is about you. If the story is not close enough to your own, then tell them I had a reputation for stretching the truth and that I was just a po' boy with no brain. Tell them how green I was. Johnny-come-lately, you might say, but that's okay too.

★

As my story rolled along I decided I wanted to share some ideas—so I put in all of these anecdotes—just little entries from my journals—ideas that I thought were important while I was thinking important thoughts. In one way or another they relate to midnights alone on cold trains. I addressed them to myself as not to forget all that I had learned. They're all ideas that a tramp or hobo told me at one time or another—maybe on a curb in Reno or on a Greyhound bus or on a hangover day over a free donut and a cup of St. Vincent de Paul's special coffee.

None of these journal entries should be taken too seriously. I know that most folks learn from their mistakes, and mistakes are beautiful things; no one needs a book telling them how to avoid them.

★

Here is an example of what they will look like.

Journal Entry #1: The Nail Punch

June 9–July 9 1998
Southbound 5
Great roadside head jobs
call me collect on my C-phone
310-555-1349
false teeth

I stole this poem from the men's bathroom at the Ingram
Creek Diner in Northern California off Interstate 5. The phone
number has been altered in order to conceal the identity of this
wayward man. A woman also could have snuck in the bathroom
and written it. I couldn't tell.

A man I just met in Ogden, Utah, looked me straight in the
eye and said,

"A house is not a home if love does not reside there."

He said he had a home once. This man was what you would
call a "nail punch." A nail punch is a man who rides freight
trains, looking for work. He always travels with a clean set of
clothes called glad rags—to wear while he's looking for work in
a new town.

A nail punch would rather hold his piss for a week than talk
about politics or religion. The usual response to these topics is a
hand wave and change of subject. He will have an affection for
cheese-centered hamburger patties at a restaurant called Embers
in Green River, Wyoming, and every few days he will dream
about having a home. A nail punch has a trade such as carpen-
try, carnival support (carny), gambling, diesel mechanics, or
clowning. And through his trade he will have learned the value
of work.

If the nail punch is not respected, he will quit his job and ride a train to greener pastures. He knows there are no guarantees when he gets there but he'll take his chances. Madness is contagious. I would recommend getting a trade of some kind before you get on a freight train. It doesn't mean you have to stay in one place and break your back for a man that has a nicer pickup truck than you, but it can mean the difference between going crazy drunk and hungry and fighting other drunks like yourself over half a Misty Ultra-Light menthol cigarette and having a good meal or a smoke when you need one. If you have a nice set of teeth—real white pickets that catch the sunlight good—and you want to keep them, it might be better if you stay home. Most tramps have had a home at one time or another and even a nice fence running around the yard. Grass that was green and short. Real nice until we got a picket kicked in and then another one and another one until there was no fence left. That's how it happens, too—one picket at a time. One day you look out your window with a tear in your eye because everything you once had is gone. There's nothing complicated about it because once it's gone it's gone. There's nothing holding you in anymore—no fence—no wife—no husband—no nothing. So you set out and go be a loner again—a real misfit who couldn't keep his life together. If you go to the right places and meet the right people you'll be just fine. If you get too drunk and stupid you might find yourself on the bum, in a basket, in an unmarked grave. Bums fight, lose their teeth, and write desperate poetry on bathroom walls. A nail punch has a trade and a prayer and a wide-open mind—with a fire in there to keep his dreams warm and a nice wooden chair, too, to tame his emotions.

★

I told you about a nail punch because that's what I am. I'm a brick mason by trade. A mason can work every day for twenty

years and still only learn one-third of what there is to know
about stone and mud. Riding trains is the same way—you can
know a lot but you can't know everything. Riding freight trains
is the bastard child of all trades. You don't make a dime doing
it, nobody is going to pat you on the back when you're done—
because you're never done—and it's illegal. Maybe you'll fall
on some hard times or get caught up in some good ones or
maybe just get on a KICK and follow it around the world. Or
you might find yourself hunched over a cup of coffee at some
truck stop in Wyoming and you'll have all that wide-open graz-
ing land around you. Maybe you don't even drink coffee. But
this time you will and you'll be sitting there thinking and thinking until your thumb is stuck back into the road, your drunken
compass has forgotten the way home, and you're drifting hard
and heavy—bobbing around this green green land like a
corked-up bottle in the sea.

That's what this book is about—me—cork head, battling the
sea with a broken rudder. I wanted to get to Mexico. That was
it. I ventured into the currents of darkness and sunshine—
walking the countryside, trying to find a place to rest my head,
shamelessly, a place to stab my flag. I had one thing with me
when I left home—a Mexican postcard. My father had given it
to me a few years earlier. I can honestly blame that postcard for
six months of road rash, gin blossoms, and glory. It was a fifty-
cent postcard with a picture of a beautiful Mexican woman on
a beautiful Mexican beach. Those two images fuel dreams and
make kids like me want to go to Mexico. I haven't changed
much since then. I can sit on this couch here in Las Vegas with
these notebooks and cigarette cartons in my hand and honestly
say that I haven't changed a bit. I've tried to mend old ways—

fill my grave with spirituality, integrity, and love—but nothing has proven itself worthy of my resurrection. I once lived in a wash-down by the river with a jar of pickles and peanut butter. So, maybe I am a goddamn hobo—I don't know what it means to be anything—I don't want anything more than my freedom, and anything that gets in my way will be left behind. If that makes me a hobo, then I guess that's what I am.

Right now I'm a cork head in Las Vegas. I have a bed and a roof over my head and a story that I have to finish writing in eight months. If I don't finish it, I won't have that clean white toilet to sit on anymore and my pretty girlfriend with the red lipstick and the platform shoes might not see what it is inside of me that makes the road runner run and the sun shine.

Wadsworth

3

Crossing

Beginning Point

D.Sextion Ho...

Ol...

D.Kauffman's Old Station

Central Pacific Rail Road

Old Emigrant Road

Old Overland Station

China Camp

Central Pacific Rail Road

Road

DESERT

Part One

"Personally I like midwestern towns
I like the girls there and even the clowns
Now that I've been out on the wheel
Out where you're worth what you steal."

—IGGY POP

Chopper: A machine gun or the man operating such a weapon with a gang of racketeers or robbers. A custom motorcycle with an elongated front fork, as well as a "coffin"-shaped fuel tank (usually adorned with a cryptic mural, painted in a high-gloss "metal flake" paint), a backrest or "sissy bar," and highway bars (especially high foot pegs to allow the rider a "laid-back and far-out" riding stance).

Flop: A bed, or a place to sleep. From the fact that one drops heavily asleep, or with a dull thud when falling. Also used to indicate a fall. A failure.

1

Denver, Colorado

OCTOBER 24, 1991—SUNRISE

"You're fired!"

Those were the words I heard while sleeping in the front seat of my father's truck. We were at the Mendoza brickyard in the industrial area of Denver, Colorado. It was late fall and cold. When times get rough between my father and me, I'm usually the first one to go. We've worked together since I was twelve and that wasn't the first time he'd fired me. But as I walked out of that brickyard, I realized that it would be the last. My hands felt stronger this time, better prepared to take care of themselves. I had my down Ford jacket, a couple dollar bills, and a good pair of work boots, so I figured the rest would be up to me.

Sometimes things fall from the sky, things like fortune and shame. The fortune is that the first thing I found along the highway was a pen, the shame is that it was my birthday and someone told me you weren't supposed to spend them alone. It also wasn't the first time for that and it probably wouldn't be the last. The only thing different about this time was that it all felt right, the breeze from the passing trucks felt pretty good. The bare trees on the side of the road, the piles of leaves, the dead brown grass, the pistol-gray air—all of it looked beautiful to me.

I remember my father telling me stories about riding his Harley-Davidson from coast to coast. He'd get so hungry that he'd have to boil dandelion greens he had picked on the side of the road. He had money but it was for gas. For my father, getting to Mexico at that time was more important than eating. Dreams make dandelions taste good, and, like my father, sometimes you have to make sacrifices to go pretty places, you know? Better places, where nobody's screaming and hollering at you all the time. My father's neighbor (a member of the Iron Horseman motorcycle gang) told him that if he went to Mexico, he could drive his motorcycle as fast as he wanted. This neighbor also told him to keep fifty one-dollar bills rolled up in his shirt pocket and that if he got pulled over by the Mexican police, all he had to do was "float 'em that jack roll" and he'd be "good as gone." My father crisscrossed the country six times on his Harley-Davidson. That was back in the sixties, when everyone was on the road. Nowadays you can barely find anyone to talk to, let alone give you a ride.

Survival has and always will be *full throttle down city streets any way you can.* If I had grown up any other way, my boots would have been on their way home, but that's not how life goes. Things become important when you go out and see them, and I've seen a lot of things firsthand, growing up with work power and chapped dungarees.

"There is no romance in poverty, just the lesson of our independence."

That was what my father told me once. We were sitting on our front porch in Rhode Island. The next day we had our bags along with our tools and furniture packed into the back of our truck. We had a full tank of gas and a half bag of groceries. We went on to look for work in five states before we found another home in Colorado. See, my mom wasn't always around and we had to take care of each other, just like a couple of kids traveling around, trying to find a good life.

There is a certain twitch a man gets in his stomach when he's not sure about his next meal. That twitch can make a man crazy. I have only been hungry a few times in my life, but each time I learned something very important about myself. I learned that I was stronger than my stomach, and strange as it may seem, after three days my thoughts cleared and I had become God. And I think that's funny.

I was walking down the side of the road completely busted and unsure of where I was going. I wasn't hungry yet—but I knew I would be soon. I had many options, but it would be a few days before I could clear my head enough to decide. I wasn't concerned at that point. I was looking ahead and seeing car after car, and I knew I wouldn't get picked up unless I stuck my thumb out.

Fort Worth ★ Dallas

TEXAS

China Camp

Central Pacific Rail Road

Emigrant Road

DESERT

Player: One who schemes or gambles on success. A race car driver or speed competitor who tests his skills and his machines against rivals, either on or off the track. "Race car spelled backwards is race car" is common philosophy of said enthusiast. A man who frequents the company of more than one woman at any one time.

First of May: Properly, anyone newly employed by the circus, where the season starts about the first of May. By adoption, any tramp, but one newly arrived in a "push" or new to tramp life and as yet inexperienced.

2
Fort Worth, Texas

1950s—SUMMERTIME

Fast Tits
How the hell did i get here?

When you're waiting on a ride you don't have anything but time. When I first started hitching I got impatient—didn't know what to do with myself. When you're sitting in a drainage ditch or in a boxcar somewhere, you're supposed to use that time to fix your life. But before you can do that you have to answer for yourself one question:

"How the hell did I get here?"

I did it ten times in three weeks and this is the answer I came up with:

"Hot rods, Powder Puffs, tornadoes, transvestites, merchant seaman, magic mushrooms, Papa Pistolero, Providence, and pool halls."

Hot Rods

My grandfather Don was a mechanic. When he was fifteen he and his friend Gordon bought a wrecked Model B
roadster. They pulled out the straight 4-cylinder and dropped
in a Ford flathead V8. The 4-cylinder put out 40 horsepower.
The V8 put out 85 horsepower. After milling the heads,
installing a quarter stroke camshaft from a '46 Mercury and
two rejetted intake carburetors, it hopped up to over 100. Then
they lowered the body and took off the fenders and that was
it—they had themselves a hot rod. The first of many for my
grandfather. For him it was all about fixing them up and making them go just a little bit faster. Don and Gordon were lucky
if they had that thing on the road for three days total. Most of
their time was spent under the hood.

Don loved to work on cars, so when he was in high school
he worked the graveyard shift at Tim's Industries, an airplane
manufacturer, in order to finance them. He worked on the wing
section of low-range fighter planes. He also worked at Lock-
heed Aircraft, building Superstar four-prop passenger planes.
Don was either under the hood, in school, or at work. He
didn't sleep much.

After high school Don joined the air force. They trained
him as an electrician and stationed him at Karswell Air Force
Base in Fort Worth, Texas. He only had to work three days a
week. So with his extra time and money he rented an old service station and opened a speed shop called California
Customs. He built customs and hot rods. He chopped tops,
leaded creases, installed Carson Tops (a top specially designed
for chopped convertibles that was upholstered inside and out),
installed dual exhaust with glass packs, and lowered bodies,
using shackles for Ford and lowering blocks for Chevy. The
kids, greasers and punks, wanted to be cool—dual exhaust,

glass packs, and lowering blocks did this cheap and easy. The point of using glass packs instead of mufflers was the sound. If you pulled out the choke at the appropriate time, like when the bobby sock girl and her giggling friends were leaning against the popcorn shack at the drive-in, you could really make them think you had something freaky under the hood.

Don had two racing partners: Al and Roy Beterly. Al never had any money, but he was the best goddamn mechanic in Texas. Roy did have money and he took care of the finances. Don, with his affection for long hours of labor and custom, took care of the bodywork and a lot of the race preparations. Together the three of them researched national speed records for the quarter mile and determined which one of the fifteen classes they had the best chance of winning. They decided on the sport-car class. The record stood at 117 mph. Their goal was to have a car ready in ten months—for the nationals in Oklahoma City. The year was 1957.

They started with a '51 MGTD—a small English sportster. The first step was making it as light as possible, so they stripped it down and drilled out the frame. The second step was waiting for someone in Texas to wreck one of the new '55 Chevrolets. The '55 had a 265 cubic-inch overhead valve V8, which was the hottest motor at the time and the best mate for the MGTD. They called junkyard after junkyard and had to wait until one came up. The third step was mounting the V8 on the MGTD's frame. At first they bolted it seven inches higher than normal; this transferred more of the engine weight to the back wheels, which gave the car better traction and acceleration. In the end the motor was mounted a full twelve inches off the frame, which meant cutting out the fire wall to make room for the transmission. The fourth step was installing a Ford stickshift transmission and mounting fat rubber on the back.

Because of its low gear ratio, they kept the MGTD's rear end. They put a hotter cam and a lightweight flywheel in the V8 and topped it off with a trio of Stromberg '97 carburetors. When they were done they had a spirited little horse—a real kicker.

The local test track was an old WWII air force training runway in the desert—alone—in the middle of nowhere. In the summer it got hot as hell. When the motors wound up and the exhaust mixed with the desert heat, the cars became a mirage. The heat rising from the blacktop, out of the tailpipes, the sun, hot rubber, and loud-ass engines—all of it making a riot out in the desert—some kind of hot rod music and insanity.

Powder Puffs

My grandmother Gloria and her friends were out there on that track in Texas. They pranced through the muscle and heat in high-heeled shoes, tight jeans, and cute little pink jackets. They called themselves the Powder Puffs. They threw flags, sat on the corners of car seats, and gave emotional support to all the players. The boys didn't drive for nothing—keep a Powder Puff impressed or she'd hop the door and trade you in for a real contender. Sure, it was all cute and funny like that on the surface, but what it really came down to was the blacktop. The Powder Puffs were at the track for one reason: to drive. In fact, my grandmother's point of pride was tweaking that MGTD on the quarter mile—making her hop, squeal, and rocket into the big Texas twilight. Turn on the fire and shovel the coal—old Gloria and the Powder Puffs are gonna tear shit up.

The MGTD had an ET (elapsed time) of 12 seconds—crossing the finish line at 125 mph. This track speed made it the second-fastest car in the state and also put it 8 mph over the existing national record. The fastest car in Texas at the time was a rail job called the Scorpion. It topped out at 136 mph. Since the MGTD was in the sports class, it had to have fenders and room enough for two people—the fenders could have been postage stamps, it didn't matter. The Scorpion was a rail job, which meant it had no body or if it did, it was a small handmade aluminum one. So rail jobs were always lighter and faster. In the top eliminator the Scorpion was the only car that could beat the MGTD. Two weeks before nationals the MGTD blew up.

For some reason men have the ability to spend hours and hours under the hood—tweaking motors. They spend more time wiping blood from their knuckles and oil into their boots than they ever spend behind the wheel. This is because when he's driving he's feeling it, not the speed or the scenery but the motor itself. There's a cartoon of the motor's moving parts firing in his head. If it feels right, he feels right, and that's the glory, but sadly it doesn't always work that way. If a man hears a skip or a bog, he's back under the hood crucifying the poor thing until it bleeds from its brake drums and bows its head to the master. Like a damn wild horse.

I know that some people care what's under the hood, so I included it, but the most influence those moving parts had wasn't on the track as much as it was in the hearts and spirit of my family. It didn't just move them across the country, it inspired them to go. Speed is the prize at the bottom of the box. It's the Tootsie at the center of the POP. It makes you do things you wouldn't normally do—like disco dance or ride a freight train. My grandmother got a buzz of pride from driving that race car. It was a milestone for lady power. It was tough talk and fast tits.

Tornadoes

One Texas afternoon my grandmother Gloria was barreling down the highway in a '54 Cadillac Coupe de Ville with her best friend, Billy—two bleach-blond bombshells—fast and furious mothers of the road. My mother was five years old at the time and she was sitting in the backseat, working on a lollipop. The sky was gray as a gunboat and ominous. The wind blew gently at the cigarette windows. Lightning silently hit the ground and huge tumbleweeds tumbled across the road. The radio played busted up AM love songs while the Cadillac drifted. All was well and quiet. Two or three raindrops sat on the windshield. A tornado touched down on the desert floor and swam through the sagebrush—tearing the world to hell. It passed the Cadillac, tore up two power lines, and disappeared down the road. My mother worked on her lollipop and smiled.

★

After the tornado, Gloria and Don decided to move back to Hollywood. In California, Gloria cleaned the house in a purple miniskirt and silver go-go boots. In the morning she cleaned and in the afternoon she sat by the pool in a lawn chair sipping pink Bali Hai wine out of a tall glass. She mixed it with Bubble Up soda, stuck an umbrella and some fruit in it, and called it a wine cooler. This type of pool sitting was called self-medicating and a very popular pastime in fifties space-age LA. It required one lawn chair, one discontented housewife, and one swimming pool. In the afternoon Gloria drank coffee and cooked dinner for the family. I think they used to call this housewifing. Sadly, Gloria died young—before I was born. And not from drinking. They buried her in her favorite outfit—the sparkly purple miniskirt and silver go-go boots.

Transvestites

When my mom was nineteen she hitchhiked from San Francisco to Key West with a drag queen named Spencer. It was the summer of 1974. Spencer danced with a chorus line called the Cockettes. Getting to Key West took ten days—considering they stopped in New Orleans for two days and Mexico for one, this was record time. Spencer was wearing white satin hot pants that were slit at his waist, a red velvet vest, and flip-flops. My mom was wearing a French-cut backless zebra-striped swimsuit and flip-flops—she had a mohawk. They both carried an Indian bag that contained a scarf, makeup, and a clean pair of panties. They got rides from long-haul truckers, washed their panties in gas station sinks, and fell madly in love with each other. They wore those outfits for the entire trip—which explains their prancing road-dog efficiency in getting to Key West.

In El Paso they decided to get married. They couldn't pay a priest, so Spencer gave blood and my mom pawned a gold bracelet that her grandfather had given her. Their profit came out to forty bucks. They crossed the border into Mexico but failed to find a priest who would marry them for less than sixty. Spencer bought my mom a white linen dress with roses embroidered on the collar and himself a white linen peasant shirt. They stood on the church steps in the cool Mexican night and declared themselves man and wife. This was the closest my mother ever came to getting married. The rest of the trip went smooth. No ill propositions or sleaze—just a romantic journey across the country.

Merchant Seaman

My mother and father met on Venice Beach. One week later they shoved six people, ten gallons of Red Mountain wine, a pound of grass, enough mescaline to turn a donkey into a unicorn, and a sheet of blotter acid into the door panel of a 1968 Dodge van and hit the road. There are five letters in Dodge—

three were missing—the two left were an O and a D. About eight hundred miles down the highway they decided to have a baby. That baby was me.

They moved into a nudist colony outside Providence, Rhode Island, called Dire Woods. There was a small lake there that froze over in the winter. The residents of Dire Woods cut a hole in the ice every winter and jumped into the water. One of my first memories is jumping through that hole. I remember holding my breath, looking into the black water, and seeing the blades of sunlight shoot through the surface. When I came back to the top my dad fished me out, dried me off, and stuck me in the wood stove sauna on the side of the lake.

My mother and father built a house, hidden in the woods outside the nudist colony. I was born in it—naturally—the first intentional home birth recorded in Rhode Island in fifty years. My mother learned home birthing from an eighty-seven-year-old man who lived in a barn by the lake. We called him Grandpa. He was a retired merchant marine—a seaman. The inside of his barn was covered in old photos from his travels— Hawaiian girls in grass skirts standing beside sailors with tat-tooed arms, and big seafaring ships that had the names of women painted on the bow. He was a self-taught scholar. Grandpa pilfered his knowledge from a huge personal library that littered the walls of his barn. He let my mother read the books whenever she wanted. He was wise enough to hand her a few on the subject of home birth. Two days after I was born, she brought me to the barn. Grandpa held me in his arms and asked if he could give me a middle name.

"Well, he's a beautiful baby," he said. "So I think his middle name should be Beauty."

And that's how I got my middle name—from an eighty-

seven-year-old merchant marine who lived in a barn in a nudist colony in the backwoods of Rhode Island. Joe isn't my real
middle name. It's short for Joey clown tramp. Beauty was what
Grandpa saw in me and I'm sure that when I was a baby I saw
the same in him. I love the sea, the drunken shuffle of port
towns, and the scent of spiced rum. I think Grandpa might have
given those things to me.

The house that my parents built was a quarter mile into
the woods from the lake. It was a one-room wood structure with
a small loft. Most of the wood for the house was scavenged from
construction sites and abandoned houses. My parents would
find houses that families, through some hard times or broken
hearts, had simply walked away from—leaving everything as it
was—clothes in the dresser and dishes in the sink. This is what
our house was built of—the ruins of scattered lives—some hill-
billy mystery that we would never fully understand until it
floated up from the floorboards.

We had a few ducks and a garden and an outhouse with
a crescent moon cut into the door. There were two other houses
nearby. My parents' friends lived in them with their children.
The air was good. The minute I could crawl, my mom put me
in the dirt and let me go. I scrambled into the woods and spent
hours talking to the trees, chewing on sticks, and watching the
leaves fall. When I got hungry or cold I screamed and my
mother came and got me. This is what my father told me about
my childhood.

Magic Mushrooms

My father loved to tramp through those woods. About a
mile into the trees was an old gypsy wagon that had been consumed by the forest. It had a small peaked roof that was circled

in long ago broken glass. Inside was a rotted floor and growing up out of it was a berry bush that sprouted red pods. There was gypsy blood in the skin of each one of those pods. I'm sure that wagon had a beautiful story. It was the kind of wagon you could look into and feel the magic of a spoon dropping, or hear the content snore of a star gazer or crystal-ball reader—old spells for love and money and laughter at the naive wish for such treacherous and beautiful things.

My father told me a story about the night he ate magic mushrooms and disappeared into those woods behind our house. He was batting through the trees and stumbled into an open field. The moon was full and bright. In the field he saw a village. There were six hill-shaped cottages. All the lights were out and the people were sleeping. He walked up to one and touched it, smelled it, and realized what it was—a haystack. There was a small cabin on the edge of the field with a kerosene lantern burning in the window. Inside there was a shadow reading a book, and a painting on the wall. The shadow was an old-timer who baled his hay like he had always baled his hay. My father disappeared back into the woods. I think he admired that man in the forest—his solitude and dedication inspired him—away—that's all—away from the world of machinery—somewhere quiet where a man can think.

If my dad had been born a hundred years earlier he'd have been a cowboy. His possessions would've included one horse, one bedroll, and one saddlebag full of books. All he would've cared about was finding a quiet shade tree to sit under and read his books. My father found religion in solitude, and the only time he felt at home in America was when he was on his Harley-Davidson, full throttle in the wind, with his beard pushed back and his sunglasses on.

Papa Pistolero

One day when I was four or five my dad tied me to his back and we went for a hike. We followed a set of railroad tracks that snaked through the trees. We followed them to a road. We walked two hours down the road to a town. It was a single-pump gas station town with a single man and a single dog. We bought some snacks.

We met a hitchhiker who was dressed like a Mexican cowboy—I called him Papa Pistolero. He was probably just a boy about my age now. He wore a black cowboy hat. He slowly tipped it as we passed. In the blue afternoon light he looked like a saint—standing there, on the white line of no man's road.

"Don't worry," he said, "everything is gonna be just fine."

If it was any man I wanted to be, it was him, in that black Stetson hat—greeting the world with an easy smile and laughing at it with his nowhere eyes. He was looking down that road and seeing something that I couldn't see. There was probably a gold rush somewhere in those hills, and out there on the horizon he could see his dimes changing to quarters and his old ways finding retribution in the pinecone air.

Our hike lasted for three days. We stayed with people we met and people we knew. We drank water when we were thirsty and ate sandwiches when we were hungry. It was simple. And I think it was these little trips with my father that gave me my guts to ramble.

Providence

When I was two years old my mother left Dire Woods in Rhode Island. Both of my parents have a story about how and why this happened. They loved me dearly and when it came to a separation I guess my father just ended up with me. Like I

said, they both have a different story about it. And I can't say
I really cared about it till I was much older. I was too young to
understand what was going on.

A little boy like that doesn't have to care, but if a man
doesn't care he gets beat down and let down and his blood gets
so hot that it boils through him like hot oil. That's how it was
for my pop. He had a rough life, and when my mom came
along I don't think he was ready for it. He was almost twenty-
seven and my mom was just a kid, sixteen years old, when they
met. She gave birth to me when she was seventeen, and to tell
you the truth I don't know a seventeen-year-old on this planet
who can make heads or tails of it. That takes experience and
my mom was just a kid. She may have thought herself more
than a kid and I believe that she was, but sometimes no matter
what you think, no matter who you are, the relationships in your
life just don't work out. When this time comes you have to let
go and move on—even if you're not sure it's the right thing to
do. And believe me—walking out your door and down the
road like that is probably one of the hardest things in the whole
world.

★

After my mother left, my pop and me moved away from the
lake and into Providence. We lived in a tired ghetto on Baker
Street. My best friend was a little black girl named Lynette.
She and her family lived across the street in a large wooden
house that tilted to the south. Their yard was all dirt, just like
all the other yards in the neighborhood, and there was always a
tribe of kids running circles around it.

One afternoon Lynette's big sister came running out of
the backyard. Her arms were wailing in the air and she was
screaming. She stopped on the front porch, sat down, and

cupped her hands over her right foot. She didn't have any shoes on. When we got close enough we could see the problem. She had a tenpenny nail sticking right out the top of her foot. Lynette looked at it for a second, then pulled it out.

Me and my pop had one floor of an old Victorian directly across the street from Lynette's house. In the center of our apartment was a potbelly wood stove. Buying a cord of wood every winter was cheaper than paying the gas bill. That stove was the heart of our house. We never had a TV because my father was convinced they were no good, and I can't say that I cared. My evenings were spent close to the stove with scissors, glue, construction paper, and scotch tape—building things. I was an artist. We were poor but life was good.

One day I was running around the neighborhood with my brown wagon. I was alone and having a good time. I turned the corner to my house and three black boys, two feet taller than me, stopped on the sidewalk in front of me. The tallest one reached into his pocket and pulled out a big shiny coin. I stopped when I got to them and looked up at him.

"Where you goin'?" he asked.

"Home."

He put the coin in his palm and put it up to my face so I could see it real good.

"I'll give you this for that wagon."

I looked at the shiny coin and then I looked at my beat-up wagon.

"You'd give me that coin for my wagon?"

"Sure would."

I thought about it for a second. That coin had to be worth a lot more than my wagon. It was brand-new and probably made of some kind of precious metal—silver, even. I reached into his palm and grabbed it before he changed his mind.

I shook his hand, handed him the handle, and ran home. My pop was in the kitchen washing dishes when I got there. I was out of breath. I put the coin up in the air and walked over to the sink.

"Look what I got!"

"Where did you get that?" he asked.

"Those boys down the block—they gave it to me."

"What for?"

"I gave them my wagon."

"You gave them your wagon?"

"Yeah, but I figure I could buy another one, maybe more with this."

He wiped his hands off on a towel, took the coin from my hand, and looked at it under the light of the window.

"That's a mighty fine coin there—a nickel—very rare."

"A nickel?" I grabbed it out of his hand and looked at it real close. "What do you mean a nickel? That's silver or gold or something, look how shiny it is."

I sold my wagon for a nickel. I always did shit like that. I was a money illiterate. I never had much affection for the dollar. I think my father considered this a virtue, because he never did anything to discipline me otherwise.

Pool Halls

We packed up and moved to Denver when I was eight. There are two streets in Denver that host true American culture—Broadway and Colfax. Colfax runs east-west and Broadway runs north-south. They cross at an intersection in downtown and then slingshot into Denver's rolling suburbs.

Colfax is better known as "the Cold Facts." Broadway starts out with Wedgel's Pawn Shop, the 404 Saloon, Famous Pizza, then dissolves into car dealerships and strip malls. Near the 404 and Famous Pizza, there used to be a pool hall—I don't remember the name of it. It closed down years ago. Me and my pop used to go there and shoot pool. It was a gaming hall—all right for kids, I guess. It was the only place in town where a man could bring his kid drinking with him. Each pool table had a thick cloud of cigarette smoke over it. And a pack of tired old men holding themselves up with pool cues. They could sleep standing up, like a horse or a hobo in a soup line. The place was quiet—there was an argument every couple hours, maybe the crash of a hard break or the sound of a cue ball landing on the wood floor. But for the most part it was tranquil. My father bought me a pool cue. It was three feet long and I kept it by my bed. He figured that if I learned to shoot a good game of pool, I would always have a hustle to fall back on. Those nights— silent and thick—made me. I talked my dad into buying me a suit from Sears Roebuck. Most of the guys in the pool hall wore suits—they were sophisticated men—men of stature who drove Lincolns and Cadillacs. American men. We bought a baby-blue three-piece. I liked having a three-piece because when I got to the pool hall I could take the jacket off and show off the vest. I always wore a white shirt with it. I got pretty good at pool, and whenever a lady of the night walked in I was the first to get a smile and a blink. After a couple of times I got used to it—so used to it that ever since that day I haven't been able to live without it.

When I was a teenager I passed by the pool hall on my bike one afternoon. The men in suits came stumbling out of the door, drunk and covered in smoke. That's when I realized that they were just a bunch of tramps—a pack of wild dogs in shark-skin suits. They certainly didn't drive Lincolns or Cadillacs. They couldn't even afford a hug from a hooker.

There was Broadway Forty, who would change his name to Colfax Forty when he was on Colfax, and Arky Dan, a train rider from Arkansas, and Tex, who always had a Coke can with a dime and a teaspoon of gold spray paint sitting in the bottom of it. He'd shake that can, stick his nose in it, take in a deep breath, and come out laughing. Some of those guys were good and some were bad—no matter what they were, they lived in truth, walked Denver down, and crashed through Colorado's powder-blue skies like Bigfoots. If my pop had said bad things about these men I probably wouldn't have jumped on my first freight train. He trusted me—that's all. He knew I would take care of myself, and if I didn't I would learn from it.

My dad and me were sitting in Mary and Lou's Diner on Broadway one afternoon when I was twelve and this tramp walked in. He was wearing a suit that had been chewed up by a dog. The pants had a piss stain running down the leg. I wasn't sure it was piss so I asked my pop about it.

"He pissed his pants," was his reply. "That's what happens if you drink too much."

I looked at the man's face and sure enough he was piss drunk. I don't drink much—didn't really like the looks of that piss stain. I'm still on the trains, though.

And Now, Me

My father learned brickwork in Denver. When I was fifteen I started working for him in the summers. After three years I was a pretty good mason. When me and my dad worked together things got hard. Life was already slim and that just made it worse.

When I walked out of the Mendoza brickyard I was tired of life. So I had to go. When I run like that—I do it and don't know why. I do it because something inside makes me do it—that's all. Maybe I needed to get away and make my decisions with a free head.

I won't jabber on about my sob story. I was on my own a lot of the time when I was a teenager and it wasn't going to do me any good to think about the old days back in Rhode Island. Me and my pop fought so bad that the things we said to each other hurt. That morning in the brickyard I decided that I wasn't going to hurt him anymore and I definitely wasn't going to let him hurt me. All I could think to do was walk away. I just had to. If he had known I wasn't going to come back he would've ran a hundred miles up that highway. But he didn't know, and I barely knew myself until I stopped walking and put my thumb out.

White Cross: Amphetamine or methamphetamine. Over-the-counter ephedrine tablets. Identified by the cross stamped into them. Referred to as copilots or black Cadillacs by truck drivers. Also the name of a drugstore on the Strip in Las Vegas.

Black Strap: Coffee, so called from the black-strap molasses with which the beverage is sweetened in logging camps and on tramp ships in lieu of the more expensive refined sugar.

3

Denver to Wyoming

Two hours after I left the brickyard and two hundred cars later a man in a cowboy hat pulled over. I tapped my boot on the chassis of his Tornado and climbed in.

"Must not be going far?" he asked.

"Not too sure. If the weather holds, who knows, could make it to the moon."

"Well, you best be careful out here, you best be careful."

He reached into his briefcase and handed me a bologna sandwich, then poked his hat into the backseat. It fell on the floor with the cigarette butts and the scented ash of a long drive. It was damn near the best sandwich I ever had. My first taste of freedom.

He turned his head from the road.

"You ever hear about those German carpenters? As part of their apprenticeship they send 'em out with a bedroll and a pair of black bell-bottoms and they have to go see the world, for three years. Damn near lose yourself out there if you ain't careful. Ha! Then those Buddhist people . . . all they give ya is a damn flute."

"That's more than I got."

"Yeah it is, but there's one more. Them Cowries, they run around in the Outback of Australia with nothin', absolutely nothin' but a prayer. Just like Jesus."

"A prayer, huh? Well, maybe that's my answer."

As we drove through the evening rain, I watched the drops spread silently on the hood, then disappear over the windshield. We were going northbound on I25 toward Fort Collins. In the fall that part of Colorado gets hit with wicked thunderstorms. They roll in late afternoon, drench the foothills with sweet-smelling rain, turn the blue sky into a bubbling vat of gray clouds and lightning, then disappear into the east. That afternoon the rain was hitting hard. We were doing about 90 mph in the tailwind of a tractor trailer.

"These truckers batch up like this and keep a steady speed, one ear on the CB radio and one ear on the 8-track. Running the front door! Yup! Long and hard with some good speed, keeps the chin off the steering wheel, then it's megaroll all the way home. Yes sir! Yes sir!"

My driver put his trigger finger on the dashboard and tapped the vinyl, then pulled a small white bottle from his shirt pocket. He drank down two pills and threw the container out the window. I had the feeling I would be spending a lot of time in fast cars and lonely truck stops. There ain't much else to do out there in that part of the country but drive. The careless truck-driving men sweat on the steering wheel while candy pills dance in their blood. They pry a woman[1] from the parking lot so they can feed on her sins, then wake up to nurture the gas peddle, like a proud man.

---

1. In truck stop parking lots these women are referred to as "Lot Lizards," defined as prostitutes who frequent truck stops, sometimes "servicing" up to ten trucks in one lot in one night. An old tramp term for prostitute is "Bat," defined as a prostitute—possibly since they are more often seen about after dark, perhaps since they flit about in such a furtive manner much of the time.

We passed the Wyoming border in the middle of the night. At sunrise I waved my friend good-bye from an old truck stop. I was somewhere in the center of that state and didn't know exactly where—didn't really care. The windows of the truck-stop diner were foggy from the steaming eggs and home fries. From behind the glass a woman in blue stalled a coffeepot over a mug and looked up. She smiled through the cotton reflection and looked out past the farmland. The wind slashed a cloud from the sky and dropped it over the horizon. The sun was putting its nose above the hem of green when the earth opened its eyes and smiled.

I pulled the door open and walked along the windows. I found a spot at the counter and placed my last dollar on the counter. I sat down and watched the passing trucks and transparent slingshots of heated road. A horse across the way jumped the fence and ran along the pavement with a mane of wind and startled eyes. The trucks lay on their horns while they swerved in the dust. They stopped for coffee anyway. A trucker stepped down from his cockpit and hobbled through the doors with his hat off, wiping his brow.

"Nearly blew off that stallion."

A few men waved him hello as he hobbled into the bathroom. He took short steps with his right leg. There was something wrong with his foot. I turned back to the counter. The waitress smacked her gum and pulled a pen from behind her ear. She had auburn hair and a movie-star mole above her bright red lips.

"What can I get ya?"

"Some toast, please."

"Sorry, honey, that's not enough for toast."

"What will it get me?"

"Coffee."

"I don't drink coffee."

"Look, honey, these men hold that cup of joe more than they hold their wives, so you better get used to it."

"You must be married," I said.

"Not anymore, I ain't. Last man I had, wanted to take him out with a five-hundred-yard scope."

"What do you do when you love a man?" I asked her.

"I love him too much."

She brought me toast anyway and I ate it slow. I turned my stool to see the bathroom doors open. The trucker paused awhile, then closed the door. A cold breeze followed him to the counter. He tilted his hat from the neon lights and tapped his cigarette on the ashtray.

"Coffee, please."

He slid the silverware aside and placed his hat upside down on the counter. He took a few half-breaths, then choked into a napkin.

"You all right?"

"Yeah, just my asthma acting up." He crumpled up the napkin and threw it into the trash.

"How are the feet?" he asked.

"The what?"

"The road, how's the road?"

"Bright as Sunday morning."

"Where you headed?"

"Not really sure. Probably just start walking north and hope the weather clears."

"That's a beautiful thing, you know, not too many people get that chance."

"Chance? I don't know what you're talking about, seems pretty lonely to me."

"You're damn right it is, spend enough time out here all

you're gonna see is loneliness. And most of it ain't gonna be to your liking."

I rubbed my eyes and looked outside.

"You're making my old trailer seem real warm," I said.

"Your trailer? Don't you even think that thought. See that?" He turned his stool and pointed out the frosty windows to the freeway.

"That could be the last safe place in all of America. You're young, and believe me there aren't many young folks out there. I'll push your ass out that door before I let you go home."

"What the hell are you talking about?" I asked.

"I'm talking about a healthy young man going places he's never gone before."

He leaned over the counter, then leaned back and stirred his coffee, moving the oil slick below the rim.

"Are you trying to tell me some kind of advice?" I asked.

"I'm not trying to *tell* you anything. I'm just asking you to be patient, that's all."

I looked around at some of the other truckers. He was the only one in there that didn't look tired. He had a little spark in his eyes. I took a napkin from the counter and started to write. At first everything came slow, but once the ink melted into the napkin it felt nice. It felt pretty natural.

"What are you writing?"

"Just a journal, I guess, figure my kids might be interested in what all I did."

"I tried writing once. Didn't work. I'm much better at talking. Figure I'll just talk my kid's ear off. That's if I even have kids. I'm getting older and to tell you the truth having kids scares the crap out of me."

"Why?" He fiddled with his hat, dusting the felt.

"'Cause of my dad, I guess. He never did much traditional. Everything was always on the edge. You know? He had a rough time, growing up in the fifties. Then Vietnam came along and after that he didn't stand a chance."

I thought about it for a second but couldn't understand.

"What do you mean he didn't stand a chance?"

"He got hurt. His jaw, his pride. I don't know, I guess when he got back we all expected things to be the same and they just weren't."

I finished off my toast and wiped the counter with a dirty napkin.

"So where are you going next?" I asked.

"Actually, I'm here to meet my father."

"He's a truck driver?"

"No, he's riding trains."

"Trains, huh? Is there a train station around here?"

"Not those kinds of trains."

"Oh . . . I see."

I looked around like I knew what he was talking about.

"Freight trains. He rides freight. That's what I meant by untraditional."

"When's he coming in?"

"Soon, real soon. You can't really tell with those trains. I've waited at this stop for days, spelling my name out on napkins, sleeping in the truck."

"He must come through here often?"

"Only in the fall. He likes to think he don't run a schedule, but I can tell you where he's at any time of the year. Follows the sun like any right-minded bird. In his words, 'As long as a person's got a full belly and keeping warm, shit, the rest is all spiritual.'"

"Yeah, I guess that makes sense."

I turned back to the swinging door. The last customer was ducking into his car. The weather outside was coming in through the power lines. It made the lights dim for a moment, then rattled the cook from his chair. He looked at the gas station clock and walked toward the door, turning the lock and twisting the sign. The glass door had a few raindrops sitting on it.

"They close early here, don't they?"

"Yeah, they call it a siesta, everyone goes home and takes a nap."

"Did you ever ride trains yourself?"

"I grew up in those train yards. I learned how to fight before I could spell. Not that it's all that dangerous, just that some people are always looking to take advantage of you."

He looked down the counter and spun the spoon in his coffee.

"I remember my dad used to put his hand way up in the air and wave his finger. He'd do that every time we left a town, then he'd brush off his shoulders and then brush off my shoulders and we'd walk back to the train yard. He had a way of putting his spirit under things. And whenever we left a place he would pull that spirit out. People wouldn't even know we had passed through. He liked it that way. He thought it was safer. He was just like an old Indian erasing his trail."

He stood tall and tipped his hat to the waitress. She poured his coffee into a Styrofoam cup and walked us to the door. I fell in love with her for a second. Then he put his arm around her and smiled back. I could see he was much older in his graces. I didn't stand a chance. She locked the door behind us, just in time to stop the wet breeze that would bring in the night's storm.

Coconut

I zipped up my jacket while we walked around the building. I put my hand in the pocket and felt something between my fingers. It was an old Mexican postcard that my father had given me. I stopped to look at it. It showed the serene Mexican landscape. For a brief moment it gave me a reason to live, a warm breeze to look forward to. Maybe I would make my way to Mexico. I thought that if I walked long enough I could make it down there. The border must have been at least a thousand miles away, and how the hell do you go a thousand miles without any money? Maybe I would try anyway or maybe not. As it ended up, I didn't have to make the decision—the next two days did it for me. Shotguns and tortillas have a way of changing a kid.

When we got to the back of the restaurant the trucker pulled two rusted buckets from behind an old Lincoln. He sat down on one, took his hat off, and placed a rock on it. I sat down beside him and put my hand out.

"My name's Eddy Joe Cotton."[2]

He took my hand and shook it.

"Half-Step. Lost four toes falling off a train."

He smiled.

"Or Jack, whichever you prefer."

Jack sat on the bucket and combed his hair. The wind would come through and mess it up and he'd comb it again . . . and again. He was a charming man. I think he was nervous, because he didn't talk much once we got outside. We sat there quietly and I thought about asking him where we

---

2. When I arrived at that truck stop in Wyoming I saw the reflection of soft white clouds in the window. They reminded me of cotton. It was a nice feeling—soft—heavenly. I wanted to live up to that. That's where I got Cotton from. Joe came from "Joey," meaning clown, and I have no idea how I thought up "Eddy." I don't really know why I chose to do this. I was new to the push and thought that it was appropriate to change your name. Which isn't necessarily true.

were—what town we were in. The weather wasn't much different from home, except the rain came earlier and it was colder and felt more like snow, and from the looks of it it would be in a couple of hours. I figured we had to be pretty far north.

★

There were still a few stars out and I was scared. I had left Denver in such a huff that I didn't have time to think about it. At home things weren't perfect, but at least I had a place to keep warm.

First you get mad, then you go crazy, and when you combine the two you've gone mad. I didn't just leave home mad, I left empty-handed and that was the scary part. The only food I had was in my stomach. America is the land of milk and honey, right? I sure hoped so.

My only other option was to go back to Denver. Denver isn't all that bad, but all the old folks there had told me that I had only one year left to be irresponsible and after that I would have to settle down. That proposition left me unsettled. I didn't abide by the old folks' philosophy. I was convinced that I could do whatever I wanted, whenever I wanted, and that if I was any less stubborn I would have to give up my freedom. I didn't know that being free meant being hungry too. I couldn't pay my lunch tab with faith. If you don't have money you don't eat. It was very simple.

I didn't want to get old, but I decided that night with Jack that if I had to, I would become a "Gentleman of the Country." A tramp. A man who could break codes. A man who does what he says he's going to do. I might catch a few colds. I might trespass a fence or two. I might sleep in the dirt. I might sit behind a truck stop in Wyoming waiting for a train. I might get on that train. No matter what I did I would do it with honor.

Maybe I'd go to Mexico and contemplate the Northern Star and after a week or two maybe then I would feel settled.

Sometimes life is just plain sad. Sitting on that bucket I remembered a weekend me and my pop spent on Malibu Beach. Everyone around us had fancy umbrellas and shiny hair. We were the only ones at the beach with our jeans on and the only ones without an umbrella. When I walked away from Denver I thought about that sand and that Gidget surfboard paradise. In Malibu that paradise glowed on the billboards like a priority, like something we should all have. When my dad and me finally got to Malibu I realized that we didn't belong there and that we never would.

★

I contemplated Jack's missing toes. I was sure he would rather have those toes than anything else. I liked my toes.

"About your toes, Jack."

"Yeah?"

"How did it happen?"

"I was drunk. I tried to get on a train that was going too fast. If you grab one of those ladders at a certain speed you'll get thrown right over the top."

"That's a good thing to know."

"Yeah, I'd say that's probably a good thing to know."

Three hours later an old beat-up train lassoed the horizon. The light from its locomotive cast long shadows on the dirt. Jack stood into the wind and saluted the engineer and conductor. They waved back. The train had two dirty locomotives on the front end and a line of hobbling broken boxcars on the back— loaded down with scrap metal—old car parts and junk. Most of the boxcars were empty except for stacks of splintered wood crates and torn-up brown packaging paper. Fifteen cars later the train slowed barely enough for an old hobo to jump off. A little skeleton man with a blackened face flew from the train and rolled a few yards on the rock. He laid there for a second, shaking his head. Jack ran over and pulled him up from under his arms.

"You know you ain't supposed to do that!" Jack said.

"Well, shit! I wasn't gonna miss this stop again, took me two days to get back here last time."

The train continued to slow down until it was almost at a standstill.

"See that! They stop for you, hell it's a junker, they don't give a damn about stopping and you know damn well they always stop for you anyway and you always have to jump off right before they stop."

"Hell, that ain't no fun."

Jack threw his hands in the air and walked back down the tracks to get his old man's bedroll. His dad chased him down and grabbed it out of his hand. It was an old duffel bag tied to a roll of blankets. He unzipped the duffel and pulled out a big brown nut.

"Look here, look what I got you."

"What the hell is it?"

"What do you mean what the hell is it? It's a damn coconut, straight from Mexico."

"What am I gonna do with a damn coconut?"

"It's for your asthma. Look, see that dowel in there. I drilled the thing out and filled it with honey. Then made sure there was no air in it. Then I buried it at the Missoula yard, let it sit from full moon to full moon. You drink the honey and it's supposed to be good for your lungs."

Jack took the coconut and walked over to me.

"Hey, Pop! This here is Eddy Joe Cotton, he just started trampin' himself."

The old man patted down his clothes and put out his dirty hand. He smelled like a trout two days caught and left to rot. He wore an oily engineer's cap with tenpenny nails sticking out of the bill and he was short—I swear he wasn't an inch over five feet.

"A fellow drifter, I'll be, and a young one at that. Well . . . they call me Alabama and this is my home. It ain't much but it'll do."

"Your home?"

"Camp, home, whatever you want to call it. This is just one of them, I've got camps in four states, they ain't all as nice as this but it don't matter, long as you can see the moon and smell the air."

He lifted his nose and stretched his arms.

"What's for dinner, Jack?"

"I've got some cans in the truck."

"Any of that chili?"

"Yeah, I got your chili."

Alabama rubbed his hands together while Jack walked away.

"Been a few days since I ate."

"A few days, why so long?" I asked.

"No money and the last shelter I ate at nearly poisoned me."

"I could use something to eat myself."

Alabama walked over to the old Lincoln and sat on the hood. I followed him and sat back down on my bucket.

"I get a check for being a vet once a month, but that only lasts two weeks. After that it's dumpsters or shelters or anything. You can go anywhere in the world and make a living if you use your head. Just look around you, look at the poor people, then work your way up from there. They know how to survive. The most important thing is to pray. I don't know who or what God

is but there's somethin' out there and if you believe in that somethin' you'll always eat. Sometimes like a king, sometimes like a
bum, but that's good, keeps everything in line."

"In line? What do you mean?"

I quickly figured out that Alabama liked to talk a lot.

"I mean, if you're feeling like a king all the time, then you
forget what it's like to be a bum, and if you feel like a bum all
the time, you forget what it was like to be a king. Neither of
them make any sense. It's the place in the middle that makes
the most sense, that's where we all belong, right in the middle."

He pushed his finger from his nose and pointed out
toward the moon.

"Sure is pretty, isn't she."

"She sure is, Alabama, she sure is."

Cold Breeze

In a few minutes Jack came around the building with an
armload of wood and a wrinkled paper bag. He took three cans
out of the bag, then crumpled it up and threw it in the fire pit.
It landed on top of a blackened tin can and some broken glass.
He kneeled down, picked up two rocks, and placed one on
either side of the bag. Alabama gathered up some kindling and
made a pyramid over it and lit it with a match.

When the fire got going, Alabama took out his buck knife
and put the point of it on the top of the chili can. He hit the handle once with his palm. It pierced the tin, then he ran the blade
in a circle and opened the top of the can. He licked the blade
and placed the can on the two rocks, over the small fire. He sat
there and stirred it until it was hot. He did this with all three cans.
His teeth were half gone and the ones that were left were stained
black. He looked like he had been chewing on rocks. We sat by
the fire and talked about trains while the last can of chili warmed.

Two hours later an eighteen-wheeler pulled into the parking lot. The bug guard on top of its grill said RUNNIN' AGAINST THE WIND. A fat man dripped out of the driver's seat one leg at a time. He walked to the back door of the diner and tried to open it. It was locked.

"They're closed," I yelled.

He looked at the three of us, then waddled over to the campfire.

"Did any of you see the little redhead leave?"

"She left hours ago."

"FUCK!" he yelled. "She was supposed to wait for me."

The area around his mouth was all dirty. It was soda pop with bits of diesel exhaust stuck to it. He stood there with a frustrated smile. That was when we all noticed his teeth. The front two were broken halfway off and the nerves were dangling there. He would shift and curse when the wind blew.

"FUCK!"

The cold wind would pass.

"SHIT!"

He finally closed his mouth and pulled himself onto the hood of the Lincoln.

"Where did you come from?" Jack asked.

"West. That last flat was a bitch. I reckon it'll be solid ice within a few hours. It's that fucking wind, freezes the road."

"How was the pass?"

"About the same. If you leave now you'd miss the freeze. Any later and it's going to take you twice as long."

Jack shook his head.

"Shit, I'm deadheading too."[3]

---

3. Deadheading: Driving a truck (an eighteen-wheeler) without cargo, an empty trailer.

"Hauling a load of dispatcher brains, huh?[4] Well, unless you want to leave midday tomorrow I'd say you should get on it. FUCK!"

A nice breeze ran across the fire. I turned around and warmed my back.

"When do they open again, anyway?" I asked.

"At five."

"That storm will be here before that."

Alabama looked at Jack and smiled. "You better get a move on, son. You've got work to do."

"What about you two?"

"We'll be all right. I think we got enough wood here to keep warm."

Jack stood up and walked around to the front of the building. The fat man got down from the Lincoln and warmed himself by the fire. He smelled like gin and cigarettes. He pulled a flattened Twinkie out of his pocket, unwrapped it, and ate it in one bite. He didn't lick his lips.

Jack came back with two wool army blankets and a furry hat. The hat looked like a Chihuahua. He put the Chihuahua on my head and handed me the blankets.

"That will keep the chill off. Be careful. Don't start drinking and don't stop traveling."

"Thanks a lot, Jack. I do appreciate it."

Alabama grabbed him and gave him a good hug and smiled. They didn't seem bothered by the quick good-bye. I think they had done it that way a million times before. It reminded me of my father and me. The way my father always

---

4. "Hauling a load of dispatcher brains" is a more derogatory term for "deadheading." Possibly refers to the foolishness a dispatcher displays when instructing a trucker to travel long distance without a payload.

let me go without concern. It wasn't that he didn't care about me. It was that he knew I could take care of myself, and he knew that if he didn't let me go he'd probably have a fight on his hands. My father and me grew up more like brothers. There was an understanding that we both took care of ourselves, and when the day was done we had a hearty meal and congratulated each other on a good day's work. We watched out for each other but we didn't worry about each other. The worry in our family ran so deep that it didn't bother us anymore. The worry was there, but all it did was provide a backdrop for a beat-up Chevrolet truck and a wayward father and son.

Jack stuffed a twenty-dollar bill into his father's shirt pocket.

"A double sawbuck for the old man," he said, and walked around the building.

Alabama, the fat man, and me sat around the fire. The fat man shared his Twinkies. Alabama told stories. I kept the fire going.

"FUCK!"

The wind blew.

It got very cold.

"So, what do we do now?" I asked Alabama.

"Get on a train."

"All right."

"SHIT!"

Journal Entry #2: Vices and Drags

Coffee and cigarettes—two vices that cost money. Coffee isn't cheap, so it's better to cook it yourself. It can be boiled on an open fire—just put eight to ten cups of water in a coffee tin and balance it on the flames; when the water boils, throw in a cup of coffee grounds, let it boil for a minute, then take it off the fire.

Add one cup of cold water to the top and the grounds will settle to the bottom—pour off the top. They call this cowboy coffee. If you rub dishwashing soap on your cooking cans before you use them, the carbon from the fire will wash off easily. If you want to buy tobacco, it has to be Top or Bugler—these two brands are especially cheap. In fact, hand-rolled cigarettes in general are cheaper. Smoke enough of these and your fingertips turn yellow from the nicotine. If you have no money at all, you have to look for cigarette butts on the ground. Especially near restaurants, bars, or office buildings. Office workers take ten-minute smoke breaks and can't suck it all down when it's time to return to work, so they discard unfinished cigarettes—look in the gutter or on the sidewalk for these. They're called snipes—the same name as the fictitious bird kids go hunting for with potato sacks following the manipulative request of their weirdo uncle. The act of picking up a cigarette butt is called snipe shooting.

A drag or a junker is a local work train. A junker's main purpose is to pick up and deliver short-range freight. Which means they stop at every grain elevator, refinery, and factory on the line. They have low priority and spend most of their time in the hole (on the secondary track or out of service)—if you don't have anywhere to go in a hurry a drag is okay. It's better to ride the back end of a junker because cars on the back end are less likely to get cut out. On most trains, not just junkers, cars slated to get cut out are usually in the front. A junker has three characteristics: they're short, slow, and ugly. They won't have more than three units and the units they do have will be nearing the end of their life. The boxcars on a junker are usually beat to hell and half of them are usually empty. There's nothing wrong with a junker until you're drinking rainwater out of some ditch because the junker left you and the grainer you were sleeping on at a grain elevator in the middle of nowhere while the wheat was still standing.

Greybull

WYOMING

Evanston   Cheyenne

...pring Station

China Camp

Rail Road

Flip: To board a moving train. The act of a rider being flipped or flirted against the side of the train as he boards it.

Lump: A package of food given a tramp. A proper lump, to a tramp of discernment, is one that contains not only the food for sustenance but some pastry or cake as well; hence a "bald-headed lump" is one with nothing but bread and meat.

4
Northern Wyoming to Greybull
OCTOBER 25, 1991—MIDNIGHT

The rain turned to a thick wet snow. The flakes fell into the light of the fire and melted into the flames. Alabama used a stick to spread out the coals. He took what was left of the wood and arranged it in a neat pile and took one can of Jack's chili and placed it beside the pile. That can would rust and the label would fall off before anyone got to eat it. But I'm sure some hungry tramp eventually did.

I ended up in that camp two months later and the wood was gone and the can of chili had been replaced with a can of corn. It was sweet corn and it was good.

A train came in with the storm. Alabama gave me some twine to tie up my bedroll. I wrapped it twice around my blanket, then used what was left for a strap. I threw it over my shoulder and followed him to the side of the restaurant. We poked our heads around the building and waited for the locomotives to pass. A dim light slid across the engineer's face. He had a big mustache and a mouth full of chewing tobacco.

How to Catch a Goose

When morning came, the train was stopped in wide-open farmland. We were on a Burlington Northern in what Alabama called "the Powder River Division" of northern Wyoming. The weather had cleared during the night. The morning sun poured over an eastern hill. There were mounds of dirt in the field that ran in perfect lines over the hills and into the fire of the sun. No trees. There was a shelter made of sticks and torn fabric that sat on the edge of an irrigation ditch. I couldn't see what they were picking, but far into the field there were twenty or so Mexican men and women bent down in the dirt. They howdied from under their straw hats. A brown-skinned woman with long braids placed a metal pot above a small fire, then ducked into the shade of the shelter. The irrigation ditch squished mud between her toes. She bent down to rinse them in the water. Her dark breasts hung like sweet plums. Her dress fell away enough to show the bumps on her nipples and the moisture on her chest.

"Must be harvest time. All the Mexicans are moving in. Look at the moon."

Alabama pointed at the morning moon.

"It's getting full."

"Looks like a harvest moon," I said.

"So be it."

He stood up and leaned against the door of the boxcar.

"You can ride these trains all the way to Acapulco, get some of that tropical sun, just like the rich folks. That moon means a lot more down there than it does up here. That's when the poor folks harvest the palm leaves. They use them for a roof."

"Why on the full moon?"

"That's when the termites come down from the trees. I'm not sure why, but the little critters stay on the ground for a couple of days and if you pick your palms on the full moon you're guaranteed not to have any holes in your roof."

"Do palm leaves really keep the rain out?"

"Better than a shingled roof."

I sat down and looked at the sky. There I was on a freight train in Wyoming, thinking about the Mendoza brickyard back in Denver. I had old pictures of Mexico planted in my memory. The entire point of my father and me working together was to save enough money for a trip to Mexico. We were going to drive down to the great Baja peninsula and see the great Baja 1000 cross-country race. What a great plan. I probably shouldn't have been sleeping in the front of my dad's truck. It was a cold day and I could see that winter was approaching, and I had given up on Mexico. I knew that when the snow came, the work would run out and the money we had saved would be used for food and firewood. My father kept throwing bricks in the back of the truck. He wasn't going to give up. I should have been helping him.

It was that damn postcard that started it all. A picture of heaven. I pulled it out of my pocket and showed it to Alabama.

"Have you been here before?"

He took it from my hand and put it right up to his face. I could see a long scar through his beard. It went the entire length of his jaw.

"Where is it?" he asked.

"Mexico somewhere."

"Where did you get it?"

"My dad gave it to me a long time ago."

"It's a pretty picture. Blue water, palm trees. Shit, could be anywhere."

"I just need to know if it's really that pretty down there."

"Why?"

"I don't know. Thought I might go."

"It's pretty, all right." He smiled with his broken teeth. "Yup, pretty as that picture."

He put one heel in back of the other and started to dance. A little jig. He made a buzzing sound with his lips and swaggered back and forth behind me. He sounded like a bumblebee.

"This is the kind of dancing I do down in Mexico."

He looked at his steel-toe boots and started swinging his arms. One foot in front of the other. One hand to the right and one hand to the left. Five steps to the right, a hop, a hack of the lungs, a shake of the butt, and five steps back to the left. He did his dance. He might have been Fred Astaire or Ricky Ricardo—the leader of a conga band.

"When I built my hut down in Mexico," he said, "there'd be someone by every day to see me. I had a whole family of friends to drink with. I gathered stories in Spanish and kisses in bright red lipstick. Just like these folks here." He pointed out the door.

"They might be working for a mule's pay but they got their family, they got their company. And I'll tell ya something, I'd rather be stuck on a mountain with a mule than in a valley with a fool. A mule looks and thinks before he steps. He'll get you down slow but sure. All retirement will get you is lazy."

He put his hands on my shoulders and gently shook.

"When you work, work smart. If you play your cards right

you'll stay retired your whole life. Retirement is for the young. Vacations are for the poor. And a slow hand . . . well, a slow hand will always be strong. If you use 'em right you'll be able to use those hands till the day you die."

He gasped for air and lay down with his feet out the door. Today's lesson was over.

When I looked back to the road there was a little girl in pink plastic sandals. Her mother rolled some steaming tortillas in a cloth and pointed in our direction. The little girl ran up the hill followed by a trail of crumbs and a parade of small birds. Alabama jumped down from the car and kneeled in front of her.

"Buenas días," he said.

She put her face into her shoulder and unwrapped the tortillas. The steam found her face and a bead of water slid down her forehead. The wind flew into her dress and covered her face with black hair. My eyes followed her back down the hill and into the working fields, where her brothers and sisters were bent over the lines of dirt. The tortillas were made of corn and had bits of wood ash mixed in. The best tortillas I ever had. They tasted like the prairie.

I lifted my legs and leapt out of the boxcar. I could tell Alabama was getting bored, because everything he talked about didn't make sense. He jumped down beside me and said:

"Wish there were some geese or something around here."

"Geese?" I said. "They ain't pretty birds, I'll tell you that."

"They make good eating, though," answered Alabama.

"Good eating, shit, even if there were some geese around here I don't know how you'd catch one."

"Like we do in the park. First you get some fishing line and a hook, then you get some corn and put it on the hook.

Those geese really like that stuff. So you throw the line down on the dirt and wait for them to bite."

"Then what?"

"Well, then, when they bite you pull on the line."

He made a fishing motion with his hands, leaned against the boxcar, and shook his boots.

"And just reel them in and turn them on a rotisserie. You cook them slow.

"Hell, that ain't nothin'," Alabama went on. "One time I was stuck out here for three days. I was gonna eat the first thing that came along and that's what I did. A stray sheep came walkin' up the tracks, so I crept up behind it and cornered it in some barbwire. Took out my knife and he jumped. Thing nearly squeezed out from under me, but I got his throat good and had a nice dinner. Yup, ate like a king that night."

The sun heated his face as he bowed to the ring of dusk. The breeze stopped and the sun kissed the western horizon. As we walked we were getting closer to winter, the days were getting shorter—in fact, I had never seen a day come and go so fast—might have just been the circumstance. It was my first sunset on the road and it was a good one.

A flatbed truck came by and picked up some of the field workers. They held onto their straw hats as the truck bounced down the washboard road. The rest of them waited for the cloud of dust to settle, then walked after it. They had their hands on their stomachs and the scent of tortillas on their minds. I sneezed from the dust. The train jerked to life. The sound of braking metal came pounding from the front of the train, passed and stopped at the last car. I grabbed the door of the boxcar, climbed back in, and we slowly pulled away. The countryside turned to a pleasant blur and a small bird flew alongside the train. I could have reached out and grabbed him. He stayed beside us until he got tired, then turned west and faded into the sun. Alabama threw out his dirty hand and yelled.

"We made it to the country, boy, we made it to the country! I was born out here in the prairie. See how wide open it is. Lots of critters. Makes for good thinking."

"It sure does, Alabama . . . it sure does."

He turned back to the fields and dangled his boots out the door. I imagined that Alabama was plenty old enough to retire. It was too bad that he never would. While he monitored the full moon from a boxcar in Wyoming, there was a man in Acapulco spending his retirement check on Long Island ice teas and diesel for his Winnebago. A Tecate umbrella shading him from the sun. As for Alabama, well, I imagined he would probably spend the rest of his life keeping a little food in his stomach and looking for a dry place to stay out of the rain. He'll just keep running and running because deep down inside he knows he's going to make it to Acapulco anyway.

★

"Some things are more important than shame and better seen through pain."

That's the most important thing I've learned, because I can remember it just like my dad said it yesterday. It's tough and sad, but that's what makes up any right-minded drifter, a past filled with bad memories, bad days, and no pay.

The wheat leaned back as the train passed—a solid scream through the soft prairie. The iron slammed on the crooked rails and the somewhat quiet became louder as we gained speed. Alabama continued to talk, but all I could see was his moving lips. His silent words were accompanied by gestures and laughter. I think he was telling himself jokes.

Double-Barreled

That night the train slowed down and stopped at a railroad crossing on the main street of some small town. I read the sign on a nearby store and it said Greybull Liquor and Drugs. We were in Greybull, Wyoming—about thirty-five miles south of the Montana border. It was late at night and there were only two cars left on Main Street. One of them was parked in front of the saloon and the other was parked in a dirt lot. I could see the silhouette of two kids making out in the front seat. The train pulled into the yard and stopped. Alabama was craving some meat, so he gave me the twenty-dollar bill and I ran down the block to a convenience store. The clerk sat under the orange light of a Marlboro sign, smoking a cigarette. She was reading a *Penthouse*. I grabbed a few marinated hot dogs and some beef jerky, put the money on the counter, got my change, and walked back to the train.

On my walk back, a black step-side Chevy truck slowed down beside me. The man inside was beet-red and fat. He had a gun rack with two rifles on the window of the cab, and across the top of his windshield was a sticker that said NO FAT CHICKS. He rolled down his window. I was wearing the Chihuahua hat Jack had given me. I took it off and immediately said a polite "hello."

"What do you think you're doing around here, boy!?"

"Oh, just getting some marinated hot dogs for my friend."

I showed him the hot dogs.

"Are you on that train?"

"Nope, just walking through."

"If you're on that train I'm gonna call the police."

"Nope, just walking through."

He continued to drive alongside me. I thought about running, but I knew that would just trigger his excitement. So I put the Chihuahua back on my head and kept walking.

"Where you going?"

"South."

"Where's your friend?"

"By the road."

He was getting irritated. I think he was expecting me to stop and salute him. It was tense. His fuse was burning. It had been burning long before I got there. I turned away from the truck. He jammed it into park and I heard him reach for his gun rack. I decided I had had enough of his fooling around. I ran before he opened the door. I was about fifty feet away when he stepped out of his truck and yelled.

"Damn homeless son of a bitch!"

He said it so loud and so mad that I couldn't help but turn around. His belly hung out from under his jacket and he held the rifle like he didn't know how to use it. It just dangled there like a soft penis. I felt sorry for the poor pork pie.

He didn't raise the gun. We both stood there under the beautiful Wyoming stars. I pulled the crisp air into my nose and let it out of my mouth. I could smell the fields of buffalo grass and the sage and the burning diesel.

I bolted for the darkest part of the yard. I ran past a brakeman's shack and a Burlington Northern crew truck. The yard was as quiet as road kill. I found a safe spot between two grainers and jumped over the knuckles. I crept along the back side of the train and kept ducking down to see if his feet were on the other side. I saw his boots crunching the gravel. He had a flashlight and was using it to search all the empty boxcars. I was about twenty feet from him, but he couldn't hear me over the engine noise of a slow-passing locomotive. The diesel exhaust was coming down on my head and I was shaking like a cold rabbit. Alabama was at the end of that train waiting for me and I had to get to him before Pork Pie did.

I snuck up the line to our boxcar, jumped back over the knuckles, and stood quietly between the two boxcars. I couldn't hear anything, so I peeked around the corner. Pork Pie was four cars down, yelling into an empty boxcar.

"Fuckin' homeless people!" his voice echoed across the yard.

I waited till he stuck his head in the next one, then I crept to the door and climbed in. Alabama was lying back on his bedroll, telling himself jokes. I walked over to him, grabbed him by the arm, and whispered into his ear. He jumped up, put his bedroll over his shoulder, and walked to the door. I did the same but it was too late. Alabama grabbed me and pulled me back into the dark. He knelt down and pulled a little fishing knife out of his boot. A little hobo with a little knife. I crouched down beside him.

"Fuckin' bums, get out of there!"

His light shined against the steel metal wall.

"Come on, you fuckin' bums, I know you're in there."

We held our breath. Pork Pie tried to jump into the car but got stuck on his stomach. That was our chance to run but Alabama didn't move. Pork Pie fell back down, then jumped up again and this time he made it. I couldn't believe it. He stood there in all his glory. His soft penis dangling there. He was wearing yellow shooting glasses and a camouflage hunting jacket weighed down with ammunition. His face looked like the swollen, boiled hot dog I had in my hand. Alabama put his knife down and showed Pork Pie his hands.

I'd never felt so hopeless in my entire life. Shit, we had more right to be in that boxcar than he did. Poor Pork Pie had made the great mistake or maybe his parents fucked him up. Now he was fucking with me and Alabama and it didn't feel very good. In fact, it was the worst feeling I'd ever had. Alabama leaned his shoulder against mine. I felt his body heat and it calmed me. I had to let go, let go of my life and my future . . . everything. I didn't have a choice. The thing that scared me the most was that I also felt a freedom in that moment that I had never felt before. I stopped shaking. Pork Pie lifted his gun and walked straight up to me and chiseled it into my rib cage.

"You lied to me, boy, said you wasn't on this train."

"Said you'd call the cops."

"Don't you ever . . . ever lie to me again, boy, you hear?" He shoved the gun in my side until I winced.

"You hear?"

"No, nope, never again," I mumbled.

That was it. That was all it took to make him feel better about himself. He proudly jumped out of the boxcar and strolled back to his truck. He started it; drove out of the yard, down the street, into a driveway two blocks away; and killed the lights. He lived in a mobile home only twenty yards from the railroad tracks. I finally took in a full breath and sat down in the corner. I felt my chest shake as the tears jumped out of my eyes. Alabama stood out the door and waved his mangy finger through the air. He dusted off his shoulders, then dusted off my shoulders and knelt down beside me. He smelled like a beer bottle filled with cigarette butts and trout.

"Idiot!" Alabama said. " 'Don't ever lie to me again,' whatever, you fucking idiot."

He shook his head and kept on poking his mangy finger toward the sky.

"He'd have invited us in for coffee if he knew us at all."

He nodded out the door and twisted the hairs on his chin. I wondered what he was going to say.

"Just part of life, kid. If you're clear there's always some-one there to take it away from you. You know why? 'Cause it makes them feel good about themselves, that's why, not for long, though. After the sun comes up and his mind gets to clearing, he'll be the saddest man alive. I'll tell you, the saddest man alive."

I wiped my eyes with my sleeve. The dirt scratched my skin. The wind outside turned around us and it was quiet. Right where me and Alabama sat it was quiet as Sunday morning.

"See, there's this thing called karma. When life is clear everything is a gift and you're thankful for this kindness, this blessing. But once you start digging yourself a hole it just gets darker and darker until you can hardly feel your way out."

He pointed into the night.

"I killed over two thousand people in Vietnam. People I couldn't even look in the eye. I was a gunner in a helicopter. They put infrared goggles on us at night, then sent us flyin' over the jungle in a Huey with a full rack of M30s and that damn fire in our eyes. It was just like one of those video games. Now all I wanna do is live but my damn past won't let me. You're lucky, kid, you ain't hurt no one yet and I can tell . . . you never will."

He looked at me, smiled, bowed his head, and fiddled with his fat fingers. His eyes were glossy with memories.

"'Yours is not to question why, yours is to do or die.' In Vietnam that's what they told us to do and that's what we did."

I stood up and the train moved. Pork Pie's brown mobile home passed like a tank in the midnight war. He stood under his porch light and waved. He was a sarcastic fuck. He just wanted to live a little. We were probably the most exciting thing that had happened to him in years. Alabama stood at the edge of the boxcar and pissed onto the gravel. It splashed over the railroad ties, the white picket fence, and finally into the birdbath that Pork Pie's wife had put too close to the railroad tracks. I imagined she was a very sad woman.

Cold Rain

It rained a cold, freezing drizzle the entire next day. Alabama and me stood in the boxcar and watched it come down like a waterfall. I thanked Burlington Northern for providing us with a place to hide from the relentless seasons. The scenery was slow. It was a quiet day on the soul train.

It took nearly three hours to travel across the last part of Wyoming and into Montana. It was thinking man's land. The Rocky Mountains took shape through the dense clouds and rain. The train stopped and Alabama decided it would be a good time to cook a can of chili. We jumped ship and went looking for dry wood. We found two outlaws cooking eggs in a tramp camp far from the tracks. They brought us two days of misfortune. Their names were Bobby Blue and Levi Stout and their story is better saved for later. I don't mind sharing camp with a street fighter or a man who smears Vaseline on his artillery, but there's something instinctually wrong about sleeping alongside a murderer.

Journal Entry #3: Mexican Donkey

"Did you know that in Mexico you can pay to watch a lady fuck a donkey? Did you know that in Mexico the strippers will put their pubic hair in your beer? I'd like to go there."

I heard a seventy-five-year-old man say that to my father in a bar one time. They had been talking about Mexico. I relate that man to all of the old men who have not spent their lives wisely. It has nothing to do with manners or morality. It has to do with how you discover new things. You can see new things and know them or you can hear about new things and repeat them.

"I've heard that riding freight trains is dangerous." Everyone I meet says this to me and I tell them that riding freight trains *is* dangerous . . . if you don't know what you're doing. A carpenter wouldn't give a kid a Skil saw and tell him to build a house—he'd first teach him how to use it.

A stopped train is a safe train. If you get on trains that aren't moving, you decrease your chance of getting hurt. This is common sense, but common sense can be elusive after a good day of drinking. I have met many men with missing limbs, and when I ask them how it happened the words "I was kinda drunk" come up often. The funny thing is that they still ride. Evel Knievel landed on his head more than his feet, but he still jumped. It's a simple insanity that can only be remedied by two seconds of airtime and six months in the hospital.

There are two things that put a man on a train—a woman or a war. A bad woman will drive a man mad and have him running under the wheels of the nearest freight train. A war will do the same. Regardless of this we still search for love and we still send the fruit of our restless loins off to war. I was lucky, I didn't get hit by a woman or a war, but most fellows I meet on the trains are ailing from the repercussions of these such activities.

I know men who would be happy as hell to have land mines in their own backyards, just for the thrill of it. To them every day is a war. They get a kick out of it. Some of these men are riding trains, but even more of them are watching football games and eating potato chips and molesting their oldest daughter. It's in the living room of every town and city across the land, a dangerous, frustrated man waiting to kill. The ones on the trains are remedying that pain with loneliness, canned food, and cheap beer. They only jump when threatened. Most of these tramps go to Tijuana once a year—buy tequila shots for Mexican hookers, pull jet-black pubic hairs out of their teeth, and watch ladies fuck donkeys. I wouldn't consider this a purely noble rite of passage, but whatever journey that tramp took on the way to that cantina might have been.

On a freight train there *are* safety measures that should be taken. Don't get in a boxcar with someone you don't know. Every tramp has two men inside of him—a sober one and a drunk one. You might meet a tramp and the two of you might get along famously. But three hours down the line you see him changing. He started drinking two hours earlier and before you know it you're stuck in this sardine can, going 65 mph and running from one end to the other playing Red Rover, Red Rover with a Vietnam vet from Tulsa. He's yelling something about the Viet Cong and he has a very blank look in his eye. The poor man had his heart pickled and was left out to dry on the clothesline of Middle America. This isn't your problem. You want to live another day and there's no sense in eating another man's shit.

I'd say that your problems off the train will almost always outnumber your problems on the train. There are bad train riders and it *is* better to ride alone. But believe me, there are boys with guns and bad intentions living down the block from you, too. They have football and beer cans pouring out their windows. They don't mean any harm and they won't do any harm until someone they don't like the looks of walks across their yard. They might poke a little fun at first—maybe say something that will make their buddies laugh—but if you happen to be that fellow walking across the yard you better keep your mouth shut. And sometimes even that doesn't work. I tried it. It didn't work.

China Camp

On the Hog: Penniless; down and out; forced to accept and eat anything, much as a hog roots for whatever it can find.

C, H, and D: Cold, hungry, and dry. The tramp "calling in" at a jungle fire will declare he is "C, H, and D" to indicate he wants food and drink, with an opportunity to warm himself. A play on the initials of the old Cincinnati, Hamilton, and Dayton Railroad.

5
Northern Wyoming to Missoula

Aah . . . the beautiful contrasts of the American landscape. It was another good, sunny morning. We were crossing a bridge. The old wood trusses shook under the train and way down below was a river that held two men's irreversible sin. Alabama stood on the opposite side of the boxcar door with his beard blowing in the cold wind. His eyes were half shut, blocking the sun. His hands were dancing around in his pockets, sorting through the few quarters he had in there. His work jeans flapped and his jaw popped as we climbed into the scented mountains of Montana.

In the last light of the moon we crossed the northern border of Wyoming and veered west through southern Montana. The night before, we had a run-in with a couple of yeggs who lived by a muddy river, so we hopped a train that now rolled over the last of the flatlands and foothills and into the tall Rocky Mountain ponderosas. The trees there stood like soldiers on both sides of the line and inside the woods there were a few homes with wood-shingled roofs and nicely painted front doors. Two kids popped out of the forest and ran alongside the train. They had swords made of sticks and they wore big tore-up overalls. The older one ran ahead of the younger one until he was right up close to the train. He stopped and looked up at me while our boxcar passed. He had a little hobo in his eye. He started waving and yelling and he took to running again. His friend saw us too and they both ran together alongside the train, waving and screaming.

Alabama walked to the center of the boxcar and started to jig. He threw his feet in the air—one up and one down—and he spun around and put his arms in the air—one up and one down. He looked like the bear in a traveling circus. I went up behind him and did my own jig. We danced long enough to make true asses of ourselves. I guessed that it was okay because you don't really get a chance to be an ass that often and when you do, you should. The kids loved it. They were running so fast that they began to lose their footing, and the younger one tripped and fell into the railroad rock. The older one stopped to help him. We watched out of the boxcar door as they gradually got smaller and smaller and finally disappeared around the corner of a batch of evergreen trees.

Alabama leaned against the back wall of the boxcar and sang a song. A train-riding song. I stood beside him and tapped my boot.

> I picked my teeth of Montana Mud
> That last six days I was on the hooch
> I burned my boots to set them free
> The last six days still botherin' me

Four hours later the sun went down and the temperature changed. Our train was ragtaggin' through the Rocky Mountains at a terribly slow pace. The air got colder and colder at every rustle of the wind. It began to rain and the rain stopped being rain and slowly turned to snow until the storm outside was just a sheet of white broke up by an occasional factory. We were above tree line, above the protection of pines, and there were huge rocks coming out of the divide. They did very little to block the icy wind. I could see a man inside one of the factories. He was behind a foggy window, pushing buttons. He put his hand against the glass and feathered the moisture, then picked up his coffee and inhaled the warm steam. Those strange factories with their beams of light shooting into the snow and their metal smokestacks pushing steam into the dark sky—making clouds.

I saw the man in his warm office. If I could have put my hands over his little heater for two minutes I'd have been the happiest man alive. I had lost track of the night and my hands began to numb, and it seemed the only thing left to do was run back and forth in the boxcar until the shivers went away. When I looked down at my fingertips I could see the colors changing. I shook my arms around in circles and kept moving. I had to keep moving or hypothermia would set in. I felt the pain. The pain seemed common to Alabama as he jumped up and down, shaking his arms, near the boxcar door.

When we humped the summit the sky opened up and the stars began to shine. The trees were loud with the music of nature in the morning. The sun was rising and in the forest the snow was being broken by small footprints. The evergreens were draped with the gowns of winter. A procession of snowflakes greeted the rising sun. The birds were chanting while they untied the gifts that fell from the tree—little snowballs that rolled down the hill and into the cave of a sleeping

bear. He awoke and I awoke when the snow melted and por-
ridge was hot.

The sun had come out but my fingers and toes were still
numb. It was the coldest and the most beautiful part of the day.
The snow was so sweet I could taste it, and the warmth of the
sun so close I could almost feel it.

Finally the trees stopped and a dirt road emerged from the
forest. The train slowed down enough for us to hop off. We
walked down the road until we could see the neon signs of
Main Street, USA—Missoula, Montana. As the crow flies we
were about fifty miles east of the Idaho border.

We ducked into a neon dive called Cafe El Toro; I think
that's what it was called, that could've been in another town—
I don't know. I looked at my hands, trying to find what I
couldn't feel. Some old hag woman laughed as I stumbled to
the bathroom. I needed to run hot water over my hands.

I stood there for a minute, staring into the mirror. It had
a big daisy flower drawn on it in magic marker and the words
"I love Daisy" scribbled below it. While looking at myself I felt
something coming to the surface, something I never knew I had.
It was the will to stand through so much with so little. It seemed
that through all of my time on this planet I had never had much
more than a strong will. It was stronger than ever before and if
the rain started to fall or the loneliness got too strong I knew
where to go. Right here, right here in my heart where no one
else can find me and no one else could ever understand. I
washed my hands and my face and did the best I could to
straighten my clothes. I tried tucking my shirt in and wetting my
hair back, but it didn't do much good, so I just winked at myself
and walked back to the booth.

I felt the paranoid glance of a sideways waitress. She
walked away to spin the green ticket. The cook poked it with a

greasy finger and dipped his head back to the grill. The locals looked curious and I felt a bit obvious among the shiny pickups and tailored western wear. I greeted every stare with a dingy grin. "Don't back down on your pride, son," I thought.

★

The Cafe El Toro and the child abuse hot line were the only buildings in Missoula with their lights on. I didn't know what to make of it other than the dawning sun must bring out the hungry. As for the tension in the room, I looked away from their awkward stares. I took it to heart that there's a pleasure in the train yards. A place that's only two blocks away. Alabama had a cup of coffee, so we didn't have to tip much, just enough to please. We waved good-bye, split the glass doors, and made our way back to the train yard. It was incredibly warm outside—like an Indian summer. The townspeople were out.

We walked the sidewalk for an hour, looking for something to eat. Alabama dug fast-food containers out of a garbage can and I rustled through the restaurant patios looking for half-finished plates or bread or anything. When I looked up from one of the tables I saw a family eating from plates and carrying on in clean clothes. I stopped and just stared at them until the young lady at the table looked over at me. She was real cute—a princess with big dreams. I turned back to the table, picked up a piece of bread, stuck it in my pocket, and walked away.

Alabama came running up behind me with a half-eaten turkey bone leg. He pulled some string out of his pocket and tied it around his neck.

"Look, I'm a tribal American, a triiiiiiiibal Ammmmmer-iccan!"

The waiters rattled their trays. The manager walked from the patio in flame-red cowboy boots and pointed in our direction. Alabama walked straight to the wishing well, dipped his hand in, and grabbed a fistful of change. He stuck it in his pocket, then leaned down and sucked in a mouthful of water. He stood up and shook his head like a wild horse, letting the water spray all over the place. Everyone got wet. But no one got mad. They didn't have a chance because we were gone before they could think about it.

We scurried down the clean city sidewalks and made our way back to the train yard. The sun was moving between clouds. Shadows passed over the green lawns, shingled roofs, and family sedans. While the children made use of their bicycles and plastic toys, the moms were inside throwing pots and pans around, preparing for supper time. The fathers looked cautiously from their screen doors. After we ran by, they went back to storybook pictures, sifting flour, and birthday cake.

Journal Entry #4: Flowers and Pickles

A hobo will eat anything if it's free.
A hobo will wear anything if it's free.

If you ride freight trains you're going to get dirty. The dirtier the better. If you want to stay clean take Amtrak or run with the jet set. Rich folks love their showers and their flowers and their tiny pickles and their soft beds. I wouldn't deny anyone these luxuries, but if you really want to have a good time you've got to spill a little wine, sleep in the dirt, get pissed off and sad, and run across the great tundra like a castrated bull.

When you're on the fly you find ways not to think about your clothes and your hair and all that stuff because it doesn't mean anything—you're just trying to stay warm—trying to see into the country pastures and over the hills, see if you can make any

good come out of the bad and if there are any changes in the
weather coming and what you're going to do about it when it
comes. That's all—not a dime past survival. A blur of snow
and freezing raindrops over mountain passes.

Water is the key to survival. One gallon is considered minimum
supply for any train ride. Gallon-size orange juice bottles work the
best. They're made with citrus-grade plastic, which is less likely to
make your water taste like rubber bands. I've hopped a train with
no water and watched myself dry up like a raisin on the Nevada
salt flats. It could be cold as hell when you get on a train, but later
on when the sun breaks midday you might find yourself riding
with the devil, creaming through the desert with no shade and no
water and your pores bleeding sweat like a water spigot. Exposure
kills more tramps than anything. That goes for the cold, too. If it's
anywhere in the fall, winter, or spring months, you better have a
good sleeping bag or bedroll and a piece of foam to keep you off
the cold ground and a hat and some leather gloves and some
candy bars or beef jerky—any kind of food to keep your insides
warm—because that train will roll and you might not see another
town for days. Oh, and toilet paper, don't forget toilet paper—
unless you want to use your shirt. Ear plugs are also a good idea,
to save your hearing. If you don't have a blanket you can stuff
newspaper in your clothes and it'll act as insulation. That's called
a "California blanket" because the southern part of California has
a climate that allows sleeping out of doors with minimal covering.
If you don't have anything to sleep on you can use cardboard or
sometimes in the yard you can find packing paper or "thousand-
mile paper" as some folks like to call it. Another method is
kerosene and sand. If you get a small metal bucket or a gunboat,
fill it half full with sand and pour kerosene over it—you'll have a
small fire that will keep the chill off. You can also start a wood fire
in a boxcar if you really have to—just watch the smoke, it could

get you in trouble. The cheapest and most portable blanket is a
bottle of cheap liquor like Night Train or Black Crow. It's a silly
way to keep warm but I've seen it work—it keeps the blood tropical and the mind elevated. It's called a Tokay blanket. Of course,
if the temperature really drops and really blows, all you can do is
wait for morning.

Here's a list of what the hobos used to carry with them back
in the thirties, according to Kenneth Allsop in his book *Hard
Travellin': The Hobo and His History:*

```
His benny or overcoat, served also as pillow or
bedcover, with sidepockets enlarged into pouches
for razor (or a substitute sharp sliver of
glass), soap, needle and thread and patches, bag
of coffee, knots of sugar, salt and pepper, a
couple of onions for the next jungle mulligan
stew, a bottle of sugared water if nothing
stronger could be paid for, newspaper as addi-
tional underwear and shoe-lining, a grain sack
with three holes cut out as a windcheater, if he
could afford it a slicker or macintosh cape, and
a "frogsticker" knife for both peeling potatoes
and self-defense. When he slept he tied his
boots around his neck, for these were the one
possession he could on no account have stolen,
and, if he ever had any to put by, he sewed a
few dollar bills into the bottom of his necktie
or in the lining of his jacket.
```

Whenever you're traveling away from something, you're a
tramp, and sometimes a tramp just isn't prepared. It's not his
fault. He just doesn't care all that much about anything anymore. So sometimes he *gets* cold and he *gets* burned and he has
to take on the world with bull power and cheap cheap wine.
When I was a kid and I fell down I'd get back up again and
keep running and running. It didn't matter how long I was gone
or how bad I got treated or how cold or how tired or how dirty I
got. I was still gonna run over the top of every dirt road and out

the back door of every juke joint, grease joint, and canvas joint in the land. So now I might get dirty, and so what. I might get stuck in a storm and as I travel through it the cold cradles me with its fierce pounding and blowing arms and it licks me hard, man! When the storm is over I'm traveled and troubled, but I still know deep down that I'm going to be okay. I come out of the storm happy to be alive and there's my life—my past the same way it was when I left it. But it's expecting something more from me this time and all I want to do is run away again—back into the storm if I have to. So I decide that I'm not going to do anything but get cold and dirty and I'm not going to make anyone believe in anything anymore because that's not my job. All I ever really wanted to do was breathe the air of freedom, anyway. And that's it. So, when people in one tank town look at me funny, I don't give a damn. All they want is to fit me in, but it doesn't work because there isn't a place to fit me in to. And that's okay.

Jungle Buzzard: A tramp or yegg preying on others of his kind; one who holds up the unarmed men gathered at the jungles, robbing them of food and drink. Also one who begs for food and drink at jungles and makes no attempt to contribute to the communal store.

Heater: A pistol or revolver, perhaps since it is from the weapon that the proverbial "hot lead" is discharged.

6

Missoula Yard, Montana

OCTOBER 30, 1991—NIGHTFALL

Alabama and me got back to the train yard in Missoula at nightfall. Huge halogen lights beamed down on the trains. A yard dog was building up a junker and a brakeman was leaning off the front of it. The beam from his flashlight crisscrossed the tracks. The yard dog rolled out of the yard with two gondolas and an oil rig. There was a Ford Bronco sitting under a light pole. We couldn't see but it probably had a bull in it. We hopped on the rails and wobbled down the track. Alabama ran ahead of me—into the dark. The cars rumbled on the road above us. I saw a book on the ground and picked it up. It didn't have a cover and a few pages were missing. I thumbed through it and read part out loud:

He wrote this terrific book of short stories, *The Secret
Goldfish*, in case you never heard of him. The best one in
it was "The Secret Goldfish." It was about this little kid
that wouldn't let anyone look at his goldfish because he had
bought it with his own money. It killed me. Now he's out
in Hollywood, D.B., being a prostitute. If there's one thing
I hate, it's the movies. Don't even mention them to me.

I stuffed it in my coat pocket and ran after Alabama. I
read that whole book but never knew the title because it didn't
have a cover on it.

When I caught up to Alabama he grabbed my arms and
pushed me into the bushes. I lay there in the dirt and looked
down the ditch and into the trees and saw a wooden crate burning in a fire pit and a 40-oz. beer bottle overflowing with boiling water. There was broken glass, scrap metal, charred wood,
and a blanket of cigarette butts on the ground. There were four
tramps sitting on bedrolls, buckets, and logs and one lying on
the ground with his head up on his hand. He had a pile of
snipes sitting in front of him and he was emptying the tobacco
onto a piece of newspaper. The other four were laughing in the
firelight. They looked like coal miners—granite faces, white
eyes, and diesel blood. It was damn pretty, all those tramps sitting together. They were tossing stories, laughing, and beating
each other over the head with lies. Alabama poked me in the
shoulder and pointed at one of them.

"See the guy with the white beard? That's Yukon Sam.
He's been riding trains longer than I have, probably forty years.
And the guy with the vest, that's Tall Tim, and the guy next to
him, lying on the ground, that's Billy the Kid. He's a street
fighter. Fights every Friday night under the bridge—crazier
than a shithouse rat."

The other two were Carny Chris, a skinny black man from South Dakota, and Bear, a fat white man from hell.

Alabama shook the bushes in front of us, stood up, and jumped over them. He missed, tripped on the bush, and pounded his shoulder into the ground. A cloud of dust went up around him. He jumped out of it with his hands in the air and right there in front of them all he did his jig. He kicked the dirt and shook his hips and all the little critters scurried away and a huge gust of wind came from nowhere and swept across the blazing cinders. When it cleared, Alabama was on the ground resting and the rest of them were laughing and hooting and dancing in the wind.

Yukon Sam barreled into Alabama with a running bear hug. He was wearing a nice tan suede jacket with tassels swinging from the sleeves and around his neck was a leather medicine bag that probably hid his mojo.

"Alabama!" he said.

"Where the hell have you been?"

He thought about it and replied.

"Well," he said, "I've been in Mexico. That's where."

"Well, good for you. Shit, it's been years. It's good to see you. Why don't you and your friend have a seat and we'll get you some coffee."

We walked to the fire. Bear and Tall Tim pulled a crate out of the woodpile and put it up next to the fire. We sat down on it. The air reeked of piss, beer, and burning plastic.

"What the hell is that smell?" Alabama asked.

"Billy threw the lid to the damn cooler in the fire."

I looked at Billy, and sure enough he had his head on a beat Coleman cooler and the lid was missing. He looked half stupid. His sandy hair fell over his eyes like a dirt mop. He drank his beer. He smiled. He didn't give a damn about anybody or anything. I felt sorry for him but didn't care to show it because he was a jungle buzzard—just a punk kid with no place to go and nowhere that would care to have him. That was my impression, anyway, and as the night progressed nothing changed. He got dumber and we just dealt with it. An outsider can't get farther out than the railroad tracks—any farther and he'd be in jail or dead. Billy sat up, grabbed the cooler, and yelled over at us.

"You grunts need a beer?" Before we could answer the whole damn cooler was flying at us. It landed at Alabama's feet. The piss water splashed on his pant leg and he wasn't too happy about it.

"Damn it! Billy! After all this time you still don't get it!" Alabama grabbed two Blue Ribbons out of the cooler, then stood up and threw the cooler back across the fire. The rest of the water splashed all over Billy. He didn't give a damn—just drank his beer and laughed out loud. Alabama shook his head and looked over at Yukon Sam.

"It ain't like it used to be . . . is it, Sam?"

Sam shook his head.

"Nope."

"Shit, don't know what to make of it anymore."

"Me neither."

★

Alabama and Yukon Sam went on to talk about the old days of train riding. How a hobo jungle was a community of men and sometimes women who more or less took care of each other. Everyone in a camp would pitch in for a good pot of "mulligan," and if a man didn't have enough they would share with him—give him food, a bedroll, or anything he might need. They said you could come into a camp and it would all be laid out—pots and pans, firewood, a stash of canned goods, a mirror for shaving, a washtub. I guess Yukon had experienced the tail end of the Great Depression and he took out on the trains because he was just old enough to go and because his family couldn't feed him anymore. This happened to millions of kids and he said the trains were wall to wall with hobos, and as it turned out a few of them never stopped riding. The wandering wrecked them and there was no way they could go back to work or even back to their families. So they took to begging and robbing or whatever it took to get a meal or a bottle; some of them would work if they had to and others—the real blown-in-the-glass stiffs—wouldn't pick up a shovel or a hoe if their lives depended on it. I learned a bit from Yukon Sam. He was old—probably in his seventies. But he looked about fifty and he was a spirited man with no signs of insanity or peculiarity. He lived free his entire life and lived to tell about it.

Sam kneeled down by the fire, broke a twisted branch over his knee, and threw it into the flames.

"I'm thinking about retiring my spurs," he said.

"Stop riding?"

"Yup."

"Sounds all right, I guess, but what the hell you gonna do with yourself?"

"I don't know, 'Bama, I really don't know, but I'm past seventy and I ain't seen that other world more than a day or two most of my life." He pointed his beer to the neon lights on Main Street. "If it's the same as when I left, I imagine it won't be to my likin', but at least I won't get killed out there."

Alabama shook his head and replied, "Don't think so, huh? You think it's safer out there? I'll bet ya it ain't. I'll bet ya it's the exact same as when you left. The folks on Main Street ain't hungry no more. They don't worry about starving to death but they still worry. They still think you're a bum and I'll guarantee that ain't changed. I tried go back and it hurt. Yup it hurt. 'Cause it's not the place for me and if it ain't the place for me, it sure ain't the place for you."

"It can't be that bad."

"Well it is."

"Shit, look at all the pretty ladies and the warm homes and the movies, out there you can go to the movies and I ain't been to the movies since I was a kid."

"Ain't missin' much, that's all I can say," mumbled Alabama.

LSD Taco

The Ford Bronco from the yard pulled up on the other side of the fence, up the hill. There were two bulls in it. Billy the Kid adjusted his overalls and grabbed a smashed brown banana peel off the ground. He walked up the hill and threw it over the fence onto their windshield, then strolled back down the hill and sat down in the dirt. He pulled a small glass pipe and a book of matches out of his chest pocket, lit one of the matches, and passed the flame over the top of the bowl.

Then, Billy's eyes bounced out of his head. He threw his fist into the air, pulled a pistol out of his baggy back pocket, planted his feet in the dirt, and stood there in a shooting stance. He shoved a clip into the handle and fired six rounds aimlessly into the trees. The railroad police left a cloud of dust as they sped away. I thought they might be back, but I must have been the only one worrying, because everybody else carried on like nothing had happened. A few minutes passed and I did the same.

Billy sat in the dirt like a kid in a sandbox. He kept poking through his overalls. He had all of his pockets turned inside

out and the cuffs of his pants unrolled. When he stood up he
tripped on his pant leg and fell face-first into the dirt. He was
a kin to clumsiness. In fact, he had to get up off the ground
three times before he made it back to the fire. He sat down
beside me and immediately started talking. He went on something like this:

> I sat around doing LSD for a week once, down by the
> river. A cop came up from behind and touched my shoul-
> der. I turned roun' and kicked his ass. Got fifty days in
> jail. Learned to fight like a motherfucker. Got out and
> realized I could make money kickin' peoples asses. I'm
> gonna settle down and buy a house and teach Tae-Kwon-
> Do. Teach those little shits how to mutilate. My neighbor
> down the tracks is a murderer. Blew some guy's head off.
> They should hang the fucker or somethin'. Hey look the
> hookers on the bridge comin' home from a hard night's
> work all you do is flash 'em a twenty and they'll do what-
> ever you want. A seagull shit on my sandwich once, went
> ahead and ate it anyway. I was fryin' a groundhog once
> had the munchies. This cop looked over from his car
> "what the fuck are you cookin' anyway?" Told him it was
> an arm I found, just laughed and drove away, could've
> been an arm, wouldn't have mattered.

He stood up and did another cop thing with his pistol—bend-
ing it sideways and making shooting sounds with his lips.
    "Bang! . . . Bang! Bang!"
    Alabama snuck up behind him and grabbed the gun out
of his hand and disappeared around the bridge. Billy ran after
him. I heard random gunfire and a few hollering laughs. Twenty
minutes later they stumbled back around the bridge, drunk

dogs smelling like gunpowder. Billy had a greasy paper bag. He threw it on the ground in front of us.

"I traded two tokes off my pipe for six tacos."

He ripped open the bag and passed it around.

"Here, eat up, they're fresh cooked, there's a camp of Mexicans across the way, they're all lit up now. High as a piñata and a long way from home—ain't no better way to be. And don't none of you worry. I got papers on my .357 Magnum, yup, no worries—we're legal."

He put the gun in his arms and cradled it like a baby. It was still hot. He liked the way it felt against his skin. He rambled on all night about that gun and everything he had done with it. Nobody paid him any attention. He finally stopped talking when he threw up all over himself. He sorted through it with his fingers but all that did was spread it over his coveralls. Most of it ended up in his pockets. He passed out by the fence and a few minutes later a swarm of flies landed on him. They ate well. When the fire went down, the only ones still awake were Sam, Alabama, Tall Tim, me, and this big man named Bear. He sat down beside me and patted me on the back.

"I'll tell you what, boy, if you ride with me I'll take you to a place in the desert where there's some real guns. I got sawed-off shotguns to semiautomatic assault rifles, all buried in a secret spot. All wiped down in Vaseline. You never know when things is gonna get rough. They's got a bounty on this one, jack, it pays five grand. We'll split it. I figure with my half I'm gonna go to this gathering down in Florida, those Rainbow people. Gonna feed the whole lot of 'em, then send the rest to my grandma."

"Why do you wanna kill this guy?" I asked.

"He pulled a gun on my buddy and didn't even have the

guts to kill 'em. He deserves to die, runnin' around like a rabid animal. Deserves to be put out of his misery. Who cares, anyway. It's five grand in my pocket. So you in or what?"

I just sat there with my head down, staring at my dirty clothes. I looked up, shook my head, and walked away. I sat down next to Alabama, Yukon Sam, and Tall Tim. They were looking at Tall Tim's vest. It was all beat up and had hundreds of hobo tags and symbols scribbled all over it. He had a story for every one.

"See this one, that's Light Bulb. They call him that because he fell asleep on a coal train and rode that thing all the way to the power plant in Gray Wolf, New Mexico. When they dropped the coal outta the car he nearly fell to the bottom, but he had his belt cinched on the ladder, so he was just dangling there. When he finally got himself undone he walked over to the plant, his clothes were all black and torn up. When all the workers saw him they took to runnin' 'cause they thought he was a ghost, and before ya knew it all of New Mexico was dark as tar in a tin can. When the police finally got there they found him in the break room with a mouth full of donuts. While the damn crew had themselves locked up in their cars. Ha! That's a funny one."

Tall Tim slapped his knee and smiled his wrinkled face. He pulled a pen out of his pocket and asked me to sign his vest. I was honored.

"Lemme see that." Alabama grabbed the pen and waved it in front of my face.

"Now lemme see, I think your handle is gonna be this here." He scribbled on his pant leg, then bent it toward the fire so I could see it.

"Blackjack? What the hell is that supposed to mean?"

"I don't know."

He put his finger to his mouth and thought about it. "Just came to mind."

"Well, all right."

I smiled and put my new handle right next to the "Mail Box" on Tall Tim's shoulder blade.

"See that one there," said Tim. "That's Mail Box, shortest guy on the rails. Someone went and told him that no one and I mean no one could ride the Gray Ghost. It's the heaviest guarded train in all of America. It's a thirty-six-hour ride from LA all the way to Jacksonville, Florida. Sante Fe catches you on that one, they throw you in the barn for two years no questions asked. It's a mail train and a gold train and all sorts of goodies, only train you'll ever find locks on. Old Mail Box, he heard an old-timer tellin' a story about "riding the rods" back in the thirties, that's when they took a piece of wood and laid it between the stabilizer rods under the boxcar and ride under the train, or "Possum Belly." Anyway, he got this idea that he could build a plywood box and just big enough for him and a few sandwiches, then tie it up under that train. Plain crazy idea, but it worked. He said after thirty-six hours in that box with nothin' but peanut butter and banana sandwiches he saw God twice, and the third time God kissed his feet and told him it was his turn at the wheel. He told me God smelled like an overworked ox and before he could get out of that box he had seen the whole world in his dreams. Now he lives in some old shack on the Yellow Brick Road, that's the name for the old Route 66 in New Mexico. He restores old missile silos into churches, calls it the Pandabloo Underwater World. Just plain nuts, just plain nuts."

I looked him in the eyes and laughed and laughed and laughed. Yukon Sam and Alabama sat down beside me and started to talk. Yukon Sam spoke with a mellow voice and was the only one there with a sober demeanor.

"We're takin' off tomorrow, 'Bama. We're gonna pull food stamps[5] in seven states, then go to that big Rainbow gathering[6] they're havin' down in Florida and feed the whole mess of 'em. There won't be a hungry hippy left in Florida. Gonna have a big ol' supper in the woods."

"Sounds good, Sam, sounds good. I haven't been to a Rainbow gathering in years."

Morning Beer

Billy jumped out of his stupor and shook off the flies. They scattered around him in confusion—buzzing, hissing, and colliding into each other like a house full of drunks. He clapped his hands.

"Boys, let's go, the bar's about to open!" It was six in the morning.

---

5. A hobo can eat rather well by collecting food stamps in more than one state. In this case Yukon Sam figured he had seven states to go through before he got to Florida. Most likely he was already registered for social services in all seven states and could simply "pull" his reward as he passed through each one.

6. The first Rainbow Gathering took place in Colorado in 1972. The Rainbow family's objective is to promote peace and well-being among earth's creatures. On the fourth day of the national gathering there's a prayer circle where up to twenty thousand people meditate and pray for world harmony. There is no money exchanged at the gatherings. All commerce is done using the barter system. Every day a hat is passed and money is contributed. This money is then put into a communal store and used to buy food and supplies for everyone. A tramp can go to a Rainbow Gathering two weeks early to help with setup and stay two weeks after to help with clean up. This process can last up to six weeks, thus providing him with free food, a kind social environment, and a bounty of angelic hippie girls to stare at for the duration. The abundance of his time will most likely be spent at A Camp, or Alcohol Camp, a site in the Gathering designated for men and women who like booze.

"Ha! You're right, Billy." Sam looked over the horizon. "It's about that time."

They all stood up and dusted off their clothes. Sam took what looked like a rearview mirror from a '32 Ford and a bottle of olive oil out of his duffel bag. He positioned the mirror on his bag so that he could see himself in it, poured a dime of the oil into his palm, rubbed it between his hands, and ran it through his hair. Alabama arranged a pile of wood by the fire and put his last can of special chili beside it.

"Well, that oughtta do it, whoever comes by next will be happy."

With that we all walked down to Main Street in search of a sunshine Montana saloon.

Family Circus

On the way to the saloon we passed a porch that reminded me of one me and my father had sat on a couple years earlier, somewhere in Rhode Island or Denver. I heard my dad calling out the window for supper time. I really missed those humble meals. They weren't all that good, but it wasn't the food that was so special, it was the picture of him bent over the stove with a smile. Every time he turned on that gas the whole house lit up, just enough to make me feel at home.

Here we were—four dirty outlaws—old western cowboy bums—trudging down the center of Main Street. The locals in the greasy spoon stopped and looked over their coffee cups. They had a hard day ahead of them—work in their tired eyes and the weekend in sight. It was Friday. Yukon Sam was oiled from head to toe. Yukon Sam was the tallest and kind of the father figure. My Ford winter jacket felt like wet meat and my boots squeaked on the concrete. I had railroad oil on the soles. Billy the Kid walked beside me. He was pulling a wagon full of regret and holding a teddy bear that wasn't really there. He walked ahead of us. Carny Chris had his bedroll with him because he was on his way to the interstate, and Bear took up the rear—hunched over like the missing link and fluttering his lips with some hummingbird song. We were one big goddamn happy family.

We got to the saloon and huddled in front of it. We stepped on each other's toes when we tried to look through the round window in the door. The room was dark and smoky. There was a jukebox bouncing in the corner—blue disco lights jumped off of it. We stood there, huddled up. Finally Yukon Sam opened the door and walked in. I caught my toe on the doorjamb and fell on the floor. Billy the Kid grabbed me under my arm and helped me back up. I got on my feet and my heart stopped. Sitting at the bar was the little princess from the Cafe El Toro. At the restaurant she was all smiles, white teeth, pink sheets, and flowered wallpaper—a girl with ballerina dreams. But sitting on that bar stool with her vintage whisky and her devil-red boots—thigh-high and stacked—she was a "God Damn!" Hot, full-fledged dame.

Her chaser fizzed. I stood in the doorway with my mouth gated—a fool in sad rags and boots. She reached over and stole a pack of cigarettes from her boyfriend's shirt pocket—stuck one on her lip—looked at me and smiled. Her boyfriend shook his head. She stepped down from her stool—one temptation at a time. The bar glass rattled—she passed under the neon pulse beer signs, out the front door, and into the first drops of a light morning rain. I sat down at a stool and put my head down in my arms. She stood on the sidewalk, looking down the barrel of a soggy cigarette.

Her boyfriend was twice her age. He put out his last fag and closed his eyes. He shook his head again and mumbled to himself.

"Like Ray Charles said, 'Women are a sometimes thing.'"
And he stood up, put on his leather jacket and walked out the back door.

I looked out the window and across the street there was a housewife hanging her morning laundry under her carport. Three rays of sun shot through the clouds. I turned back to the bar and grabbed a couple cocktail napkins out of the cocktail napkin stand. I borrowed a pen off the register and scribbled down a few sentences.[7]

Ten minutes later I looked back out the window. The housewife's husband walked outside in his bathrobe, picked up the news, and inspected the grass. I could smell the bacon. Hot bacon in the morning, man! Sitting in those three rays of sun at the breakfast table with five boxes of cereal, biscuits, gravy,

---

7. I found the napkins from Missoula burried under all the cigarette cartons. Napkins are last resorts and sometimes fall victim to odd, but at the same time heartfelt, script, such as follows:

"The sun is burnin' all of my mistakes into memory—when all I want to do is forget about them—forget about what beat me down, what made me open the bottle and climb in—turn into a corkhead drifter who's guided by nothing—directed only by sin and sunshine and all that could possibly be. It's gettin' to the point where I'm walking down the road or rolling down the line— maybe coasting seaward after humping the Continental Divide and in my mind and heart I'm just a chicken scratch ahead of all my troubles, one teardrop away from remembering my past. I have problems and they're on my heels like a pack of mighty bloodhounds and if I don't cross the right river or climb the right tree, that big pack of slobbering dogs is gonna catch up to me and if they do I know they're gonna push me down—face-first into the dirt . . . but it don't matter 'cause I ain't gonna let them catch up to me—ain't NO WAY in hell. I'm a scenery bum with too much to see, too many picnic table conversations and right-time milkshakes to keep my mind off that. THAT. All of it disappears on the midnight ghost train—that highballin' stingray train of manifest that's bringing me farther and farther away from any one of those towns where my heart got crucified and any other place where they didn't care enough to understand me or they weren't patient enough to let me be myself. In the end I hated them for hating me. All I wanted to do was accept myself and my life and my mistakes but they wouldn't let me, so I lost everything and everything that wasn't lost I broke into tiny pieces. Now there is only one thing that will keep the dogs off my heels—the rhythm of ramble—the possibility of the Golden Gates that never come."

curtains, and soap. There was a painting tacked up beside the barroom window—a kid and his dad sitting in a boat, fishing in a lake, cattails blowing in the wind and lily pads floating in clear green water. The housewife across the street draped a pink sheet over the clothesline and fastened it with two wooden clothespins. Her husband sat on the front steps of their house and read the paper.

Alabama and Billy were in the corner by the jukebox, finishing someone else's half-finished Millers. Billy was poking his finger through the ashtray, looking for something to smoke. A fourth ray of sunlight came in through the window and shone upon them. The ash from Alabama's used cigarette floated around his head. They were two stiffs in tenpenny crowns and diesel—kings of separate kingdoms sitting in the castle and discussing matters of the land.

I was on the great divide—between home and the road. It had been seven days since I left, one week that felt like three months—not in a bad way but in a way that makes you think. The moments last longer, they're stronger, thicker, more meaningful out there. Easy would be no way to explain it—this book is no way to explain it—you just have to see those days forcing themselves into your head like religion—like gospel—to really get it. I saw a perfect world outside that barroom window— pink sheets and sunshine. A nice white picket fence—two people living together in a little house in a little town in Montana. It made me a little homesick.

In that saloon I heard the pounding of broken hearts, the whisper of desperate lips, and the waltz of tired footsteps—and it haunted me. In a good way. Behind me was home and ahead of me was a fantastic railroad of opportunity. I had the golden ticket—gifted me by my friends, the tired and ancient knights of the American railroad. If I used that ticket wisely I would flower. The lady of the land would open her front door. Old-man winter would resist for one more week and I would have the time I needed to get down to Mexico. And that is exactly what I had to do.

The jungle tramp lives every moment as his last breath and looks for nothing more in life than a hotshot to haul his sorry ass out of town. Going home is not part of his journey. The strings that pulled Alabama's heart were the same strings that pulled mine. Home is where the heart is, and the pain, and the fear that cradles newborn eyes. I felt the tragedy in that saloon and the only place it could end was on the candy-red lips of a sure thing. I joined the little princess on the sidewalk in front of the saloon. She pressed her red curls against my shoulder. We watched raindrops fire out of the sky and crash through the branches of a sycamore tree that God built. In the end, love is the only sure thing, to be hopelessly in love with life as it's lived in America's armpit—sipping her ginger ale over a lipstick-stained glass and getting kissed by the candy-red lips that laid down the heat on that Friday morning fever. The little princess leaned over and kissed me. Sitting on that sidewalk, I felt love like a boy does—before he gets old and bitter—before he lands on his knee with a diamond and a promise—before all of that—in the age of innocence, the sun shines.

★

Later that evening I gave Alabama a hug in the corner of the bar and told him that it was time for me to go. He knew as well as I did that the fastest way to travel is alone. Besides, he was a loner just like me, so he patted me on the back and said:

"That's what a drifter does, he drifts."

I felt every line of that man's face when he spoke and I could see all the world's sadness in his eyes. There's a word for

that . . . honesty. When life's sun is in your eyes seven days a
week, 365 days a year, you can't help but feel sad. I swore I
would feel that sun in my eyes for another hundred years. I
could just keep walking, walking till I was weathered from head
to toe and sad, just like 'Bama.

I told him about how I wanted to go to Mexico—maybe
find the place where the picture on my postcard was taken.

"Shit," I told him. "I don't have anything else to do."

And to tell the truth I was sick of being cold. The postcard was warm. The postcard gave me a bosom to lay my head
on, an ocean to bathe in, and a destination. A place to go. In
two weeks the last of the leaves would fall from the trees and if
I didn't get south before they did, I'd be stuck in the cold. The
only warm place I knew besides Mexico was home and I'd
already decided I wasn't ready for that.

"Things become important when you go out and see
them," I thought.

I gathered up what I had acquired, my dirty wool blankets, my Chihuahua hat, a seashell from Yukon Sam, a plastic
soda bottle filled with water, a few bits of fabric and a roll of
thread to patch my pants, a pair of brakeman's gloves that I
found, and a piece of foam for my hip. I rolled it up and
cinched it with the twine, kissed the little redhead on her cheek,
and walked back to the yard—alone.

Journal Entry #5: Hobohemian Vaudeville

The place where hobos and tramps gather and camp is called
the jungle. A jungle is usually near a railroad yard, crew
change, or a fuel or water tank—any place along the line where
it's easy to board a train. The jungle is the center of a hobo's
social life, a place where drifters and vagabonds meet and com-

pare notes on conditions along the road. A jungle is like a class-room. Instead of a chalkboard there's a fire. One hobo sits, pokes the fire, and talks about "hot" train yards, homeless shelters where the food is cold and the beds hard, the weather in the Northwest—from where he just came—apple-picking season, and which pullman he prefers in the prevailing weather conditions. The jungle is where clothes are washed and boiled to kill bugs and where a train rider can cook and eat a meal or enjoy a good bout of drinking before he swaggers off to dreamland. On heavily traveled routes and in popular city centers, well-established jungles are always easy to find. In the old days tin pots and pans, used for cooking and washing, were carefully hidden where they could always be found by those who followed. Buzzard indeed was the tramp who failed to clean up after he had cooked or in other ways made use of the jungle. On a good day a tramp will find a tribe of stiffs huddled up in the trees and priming for a party—building a fire, collecting money for beer, and rummaging around for a good log or bucket to plant himself on for the night. If you find this you've found home. Take advantage of it, because when the train comes the dirt will fly.

The jungle is Hobohemia's vaudeville. A stage for hobos, tramps, street fighters, hustlers, fakers, drunks, and two-bit pimps. It's a place to tell stories of close-truth, think simple thoughts, and cuddle up with the stars and wood smoke. A jungle is for waiting, and whatever you learn in that classroom, sitting on that milk crate, you take with you on the next train.

In the old days most jungles had a big cooking pot or gumbo that was used to cook mulligan stew. Mulligan was kept continually replenished by contributions from all tramps in the jungle. Hoppins: vegetables, gumps, and meat of any form or description—butcher's scraps, bacon rinds, and the occasional "appropriated" chicken—were boiled down into a slop that might vary in savoriness but that was always hot. Mulligan was served up in anything that would hold it, including a salvaged tin can or a large leaf. Nowadays mulligan comes back to life at more organized hobo gatherings. But these days if you're sitting near the tracks, the most you're going to see is a can of chili in the flames or a can of tuna in oil.

In this primal dirt-floor gathering it almost seems that the American melting pot works similar to the communal ritual of the mulligan's pot—boiling its miscellaneous ingredients. Whites, African-Americans, Mexicans, and Indians live and mix in mutual support. In the jungle no credentials are required and no questions are asked about a man's past. You have to be strong in the jungle but you don't have to be white.

Hobos know their place—in the trees—out of sight—a whisper below the breeze. Many jungles, including the one in Missoula, are in the same place they were one hundred years ago. That's a good, strong culture there—as old as steam locomotives but longer lived.

Bull Horrors: A morbid fear of the police, usually the result of a previous ill-treatment at their hands, or from the realization that an arrest would mean a long term of imprisonment.

7

Missoula Yard

HALLOWEEN, OCTOBER 31, 1991—MIDNIGHT

Thorn Belly

I went back to the yard, sat on the crate, and waited. The bottom half of the cooler was still leaning against the fence. I was the only one there, so I sat back on my bedroll, closed my eyes, and rested. I decided that I would come back to Missoula someday and pay a visit to that little redheaded girl. I also decided that if a boy can't find the beauty in every town he passes through, he should just stay home and eat pork rinds and get pork grease on the sofa.

When a train finally came it was bitter cold, so I decided to ride a locomotive or a unit. Alabama told me that units had bathrooms and chairs and everything. The train stopped to change crews. There were two brakemen talking under a cone of light. I walked slowly behind them and climbed up the ladder of the last locomotive. I unhitched the unit door and crawled onto the floor. I held my breath until the train twitched, rolled a hundred feet, twitched again, and stopped. They were building her up on the back. A bull's spotlight passed over the top of the cabin along with the low roar of his truck. If he climbed up the ladder he would surely see me, so I crawled into the bathroom and just waited for what seemed like an hour. Then the train moved for the last time and it faded into a continuous speed. I could feel the outside changing and by now I knew we had to be out of the yard.

I climbed out of the bathroom and peeked out the window. I couldn't see anything, so I stood up higher, too high. The bull was sitting on a bluff on the service road and spotted me with his light. I ducked down backward and slid onto the floor. I felt the train slow down. I grabbed my bedroll, walked out the platform, and ran to the end of the unit. He was driving alongside the train and talking into a megaphone.

"Get off the train now!"

I looked down the tracks and saw that his road was about to end at a bridge and behind it there were a bunch of bushes. The train was going slow enough to get off, but I didn't want to go to jail, so I lied and yelled back to him.

"I ain't jumpin' off this train, it's movin' too fast!"

He got on his radio and a few seconds later the train slowed down. I acted like I was about to get off real slow, keeping an eye on the bridge and the bushes the whole time. Then the bridge crept by. The bull stopped his truck, opened his door, and stepped into the dirt. I stayed on the last rung of the ladder until the bushes came and I could see a path disappear into them. I jumped off and ran. But they weren't soft bushes, they were thornbushes with spikes at least an inch long. They cut my jacket up good. If I kept running I knew I'd get cut up too, so I laid down in the dirt and let his spotlight sift over me. It swept to my right, stopped, and swept to my left.

A big bang came from the train. I knew it was going to pull away and didn't want to miss it, so I crawled on my hands and knees under the thorns. When I reached the tracks the train was moving heavy, so I ran as fast as I could until my hand found the ladder of a grainer and grabbed it; it swung me off the ground. The train was stronger than me, but I held on anyway and reached up with my leg and hoisted myself onto the platform. I climbed the ladder to the top of the grainer. It was picking up speed good, so I stayed low until the city faded into charcoal and the sky was clear. Every star was out just like my first nights in Wyoming. I was alone and it felt good because I still had that breeze to keep me company and I was starting to think in a hobo drawl. I didn't care about anything but the air I was breathing and all my dark thoughts just passed overhead—like lonely black crows.

Journal Entry # 6: The Bull

The bull is an armed private employee of the railroad who is hired to protect the railroad's land, equipment, and freight. They refer to themselves as "railroad police," "special agents," or "railroad detectives." The term "bull" was coined in the old days because of the bullying attitude many of these men had toward tramps. It's important to know that a bull will rarely get out of his car or truck. If he does, that means he has seen something that warrants his attention. If you see a truck and it has any tools in it or is carrying anyone with a hard hat or a three-day stubble, it's most likely a work truck or a crew truck. These folks rarely pay attention to anything but their work and usually

aren't a threat. The bulls tend to be more refined and rarely
wear coveralls. It won't be long before you can tell a brakeman
from an engineer and an engineer from a bull. They each have a
distinct style and walk. If you know the swagger of a bull, you
can identify him in the dark and from far away. If they can't see
you, they can't fear you. A younger engineer might not want
you on his train. On rare occasions he'll call the bull, but most
of the time he'll let it slide. It's considered good luck to have at
least one hobo on your train. The old engineers know this.

If a bull gets a hold of you he can rearrange your life rather
easily, but most of the time all he'll do is write down your name
in a little notebook, tell you yours is not a life worth living, and
send you on your way. This is what happens most of the time.
Sometimes a bull will radio you into the local police station to
see if you are in any trouble. If you have any warrants or are
wanted by the police for any reason, it's best to say you don't
have any identification and give him a fake name, preferably of
someone who matches your description. If the bull does tell you
to get out of the yard, just wait till it gets dark or until his shift
is over. If the same bull catches you twice, there's a good chance
he'll put you in jail. The penalty varies depending on the railroad and the town. Santa Fe is guaranteed jail time. They trans-
port military cargo and are very protective of it. A military
boxcar is unlike any other. It's usually dark maroon in color,
very tall, and has no doors. If you see anything like this on any
train, it's best not to ride it. It's important to remember that
nothing on a freight train is for sure—nothing. I've seen a bull
get a van, fill it up with tramps, and cart them off to jail, and
I've seen a bull give a tramp a bottle of ice water on a hot summer day. I think good thoughts and respect everyone I meet—
badge or no badge. That works the best.

A bull in the jungle is a bad situation. It usually means he's looking for someone. They turn up the heat when something in town is wrong and a tramp is suspect. So you should know if the town you are in is ill at ease (this information can be easily acquired at any homeless shelter or by simply asking the first tramp you see). Other than that, a bull will never come into a jungle—probably for fear of his life. Not that anything would happen to him. It's just not a place for a man of rank and stature to be seen. Plus there ain't no donuts in there.

Dingbat: A bum or tramp of low degree.

Can Moocher: A tramp or bum, filthy, lost to hope and ambition and often demented, an exile from everything worthwhile. Originally the tomato can was used as a container into which were drained the dregs from beer kegs outside of saloons; later the same receptacle came to be used as a catchall for begged or salvaged food.

Plush: A stuffed animal, specifically a carnival "prize" of the cheap and stuffed variety.

IDAHO

Idaho Falls
Blackfoot

Central

Old Over

China Camp

8

Idaho Falls to Blackfoot

NOVEMBER 1, 1991—SUNUP

It was one of those fall mornings when the prairie grass is covered in frost—weighed down—hunched and broken under the weight of ice and wind. The prairie would soon freeze three feet deep, winter would force himself into the marrow of her bones and sit there until spring. There was a small herd of buffalo in the fields. They snorted clouds of smoke into the cold air. I felt like there should have been more of them.

I was riding a southbound Union Pacific out of Missoula. If all went well I would pass out of Montana, coast into Idaho by early afternoon, and be in Pocatello by sunset. Pocatello is one of Idaho's biggest train yards. When I got to Pocatello I planned to stretch my legs, wash up, and catch another Union Pacific southbound into Green River, Wyoming. Green River is a crew change on the Union Pacific and an interstate town—which makes it a good place to make decisions.

I reached into my pocket and pulled out the Mexican post-card. There she was, the candy-lip señorita in a red and white polka-dot dress. She had coffee skin and black hair that fell into Caribbean blue skies. She was fixing her hair and dancing around the base of a coconut tree. I put her in my shirt pocket—beside my winter day blues. I whistled a cold song and tapped my shoes.

Country Squire

Three hours later the train stopped in Idaho somewhere between Idaho Falls and Blackfoot. The sun was high noon and the frost had melted. The railroad rock was wet. I jumped off the grainer, found an open boxcar three cars down, and climbed into it. Ten minutes later an old bonehead man with a burnt beezer stumbled up from the back of the train. His feet made hard work of the railroad rock. He'd been riding the belly.[8] His skin was probably burned from what looked like three weeks in the sun and his legs were splintered from walking on the railroad rock. He put his half-cocked eye on my shirt pocket, rolled out his hands, and dropped his torn blankets on the ground.

"You got a cigarette?" he said.

---

8. "Riding the belly" is a derogatory term—partially derived from "riding the rods" (see glossary). A tramp with low spirits and seemingly exhausted mental resources will "ride the belly"—or, in a sense, be barely holding on to his wits, as an old-time tramp would barely hold on to the "rods" under a boxcar. Related to this term are the terms "belly of a drag," the underside of a freight train, and the carny term "possom belly," a storage box attached to the bottom of a passenger car or work wagon to carry things such as cable, stakes, and rigging. Also, at times, a place for a quick nap by a worker or temporary homes for unauthorized women. It was a common place for tramps to ride, and at one time it was common practice for cheap carnival bosses to require some of their laborers to sleep in them while on the road.

"A cigarette? The last thing you need is a cigarette."

There was no way this guy should be smoking—drinking, maybe—he looked like he needed a glass of water but not a damn cigarette.

"Look." I held up what was left of my water jug and handed it to him.

"There ain't much left but it'll wet your throat, anyway."

"Fuck you," he said, and gathered up his things and tromped past me for the front of the train.

"Yeah, well fuck you too."

I watched the old fool stumble down the tracks. The units were on a curve, so I saw everything he did from where I sat. It took him ten minutes to make it the length of two boxcars. When he finally got to the first locomotive, he climbed up the ladder and barreled through the cabin. He pulled the garbage out of the can and threw it all over the floor. No cigarette, so he busted out of the front door and stumbled up to the second unit.

At this point the engineer and conductor saw him coming. The conductor grabbed a bottle out of the garbage can. The bum kangarooed over the knuckles between the two locomotives and landed hard on his shoulder. He stood up and started stumbling toward them. The conductor climbed up a ladder on the side of the unit and ran along the top of it. When he got behind the bum he climbed back down, walked up to the bum, and raised the bottle. The old bum threw a drunken punch, missed, and folded onto the platform. I was getting nervous watching all this. I decided that if they got real mean with him that I would have to intervene. So I crept up the side of the train and put myself close enough to hear them talking.

"What do we do with him now?" the engineer asked.

"Shoot, I don't know."

The conductor walked into the unit and opened a toolbox. "Do we have any rope in here?"

"Rope, what are we gonna do with rope?"

"I'm gonna tie him to the railing in case he wakes up."

"Let's leave him here."

"No."

"Why not?"

"He don't look too good. We'll drop him in the next town."

They eventually found some rope and used it to hog-tie the old guy to the railing so he wouldn't fall off.

"Blackfoot! Here we come," I thought.

I hopped on the last unit and sat in the sun. The train crept back onto the main line, reached speed, and we were on our way again. A funeral procession drove alongside us. I thought maybe they were laying to rest all the poor bonehead bums who couldn't find what they were looking for. I kept an eye on the old coon's rope.

The hearse stopped at the liquor store. The driver walked in with a fistful of dollars and walked out with a case of Budweiser and a bag of ice. He threw it in the back with the vacant man and rumbled down the dirt road. All the mourners looked surprised, but it was too cold to complain, so they turned up the heat and followed the hearse over a hill and into the peaceful orchard of bones.

"On to the next town," I thought. "Where a dead man can live again."

I walked into the cabin of the unit and looked in the seat cushions and found half a Camel and pack of matches with three matches in it. I tore the filter off, lit the end, and crept out the front door. I held it between my lips and made my way up the platform to the bum. He was shaking his head and drooling on his shirt collar. I knelt down beside him and stuck the cigarette in his mouth. He fumbled it in his lips, took a long drag, and smiled. The wind blew around us, the diesel smoke passed overhead, and the old bonehead man didn't say a word. The lady with the powder-blue hair, who had used five gallons of gasoline to set his trailer home ablaze, came back to him. In his dreams. Youth hung on his neck like a ginger-blossom lei. His days in the sun. His vacations to Hawaii. His nights on stage and his mornings on top of the bottle with a Camel and a grin.

The train reached speed and the wind picked up. I looked at the back of the train and saw a line of freight rolling around the corner. I remembered one of Alabama's famous quotes about freight-train riders:

"Let me tell you what a tramp is Eddy. Tramps like to lie down on their sides a lot. They like to be in the shade and the only way to lie in the shade is on your side. You're a lucky tramp if you have a hat, that's good shade, but if you don't have a hat you're gonna have a sunburn and not just your face and your arms but your eyeballs, your eyeballs will get beet-red because lots of times there just ain't anywhere to go to get out of the sun. A tramp ain't gonna have a cigarette or a drink when he wants one and he don't think about getting old, he just thinks about getting by, and if a drink of bourbon replaces a drink of water and he's in the desert, well then he needed that bourbon more than the water, but he'll take the water with him, case the bourbon dries up. So do yourself a favor and get a good hat and don't start building those habits, 'cause as sure as the sun's gonna

*shine you're gonna find yourself stuck under it itchin' for a cig-
arette and plain pissed you ain't got a drink. Stay clean and you
just might find a nice home someday."*

I sat there on the train with that burned-up bum blowing
in the wind. The drunk smoked what was left of the Camel and
opened his eyes. He looked at me and turned even redder than
he already was. Then he clamped his eyes shut and dropped
his head back down. I looked back at the fields. The icy wind
was getting on my neck, so I flipped up my collar and laid back
on my bedroll. Something was itching me and I couldn't figure
out what it was.

I closed my eyes and thought about it. "That's it!"

I sat back up. I knew him. I had seen his face across
a campfire in Montana. The fuck-nugget was Bobby Blue.
That's who it was. The man who Alabama and me had spent
that horrible night with in Montana.

IN MEMORY OF BOBBY BLUE AND LEVI STOUT
OCTOBER 27 AND 28, 1991

Earlier I mentioned that Alabama and I had met "two
yeggs cooking eggs" and they lived beside a "river way down
below that held two men's irreversible sin." The man tied to
the railing of that locomotive was the worse of the two—Bobby
Blue. Alabama and me were riding that Burlington Northern
northwest out of Greybull when we met him. I remember it had
rained all day. Alabama wanted to cook chili, so when the rain
slowed we hopped off the train and went looking for firewood.
The fog hung low. There were no leaves on the aspen trees and
all that was left of them was an army of old white ghosts. We
pounced through their shadows with our big boots. Alabama

always looked at the ground when he walked. He was a treasure hunter and he claimed that he could live on the trinkets that fell from people's pockets. The ground out there was cluttered with mulching leaves, stale condoms, Barbie doll parts, and little girls' panties. The air smelled like baby powder.

We hurried through the dark branches until we heard a fire crackling and could see shadows on the snow. The frying pan was frying eggs and two men huddled around it. That was the first time I saw Bobby Blue. He looked across the fire and I saw his life roll over his eyes like a crystal ball. It was no fairy tale. It was a Molotov cocktail.

Alabama saw it too, but it didn't bother him like it bothered me. For him it was just another night on the trail. To me those two were downright dangerous. I could smell it.

I was still dreaming of Mexico—white sand beaches, palm trees, cabanas, and big-eyed señoritas. I didn't want to risk my ass on anything less than that. Those two reeked of compromise.

We sat and talked and ate their food and drank their whisky and even whistled an old Popeye song. Levi Stout and Bobby Blue had a liking for cartoon music and warm beer. They spent an hour singing everything from *The Jetsons*, "Meet George Jetson!"

to *The Flintstones*, "They're a modernstoric fama-leeeeeeee!"

to *The Addams Family*, "They're kooky and they're spooky, they're altogether ooky, they're The Addams Family. Da Da Da Dom! Da Da Da Dom!"

They put their arms around each other when they sang. They sang because they only got one station on their battery-powered television. The station broadcast twenty hours of old cartoons and four hours of some basement preacher sky pilot. He was a middle-aged man who did a live sermon from his basement. His pulpit was a pool table and his robe was made of wood paneling. His words brought faith to a small western town. Levi and Bobby were hiding from the law, so this was all they saw of the outside world. Levi told me that he would send Bobby into town once a week for batteries and whisky. The rest of the time they spent in what he called "the bush."

"I like it out here," he said.

"The air smells like war. The nearest town is two miles away. No roads, just tracks. No one to bother us." He chugged on his bottle of Black Crow and handed it to Alabama. Alabama grabbed it and stood up and pointed across the fire.

"A toast to today's good fortune and tomorrow's rattlesnake freight," he said.

Bobby Blue grabbed the bottle out of his hand and threw it into the bushes.

"There ain't no tomorra'!" he sighed.

Bobby's bad mood caught Alabama off guard. The cartoons had just ended and the preacher was mumbling a prayer on the battery-powered TV. Bobby plain flipped out for a split second, then calmed down and went right back to tending the fire. Alabama walked over to where the bottle had landed and sat down and finished his drink. He lay on his back with the bottle on his chest and looked up at the sky.

"It's gonna rain again tomorrow," Alabama said.

"It's been rainin' every day for two weeks," Bobby mumbled, "don't take no genius to figure it's gonna rain 'gain tomorra'."

"No, don't take a genius. But it might take some twine."

"What you gonna do with twine?"

"I'm gonna build a raft."

"What the hell you gonna build a raft for?"

"That river's 'bout to swell and you fellas might need a raft to keep dry on."

"Hell, that river ain't goin' nowhere and even if it does we ain't gonna need no help buildin' no raft."

Alabama stood up, dusted himself off, and walked over to the television. He had had enough of Bobby's nonsense. He sat down with Levi and learned how to shoot pool with the reverend on the old black and white.

Bobby poked at the fire and glared up at me every now and then. He wasn't a happy man and he wasn't a proud man, but he was a strong man, and as the fire died down he started to talk about what it was that was bothering him. It was the river. The cold Montana water that was puddling around his feet.

"Hell, if the water gets too high all you have to do is walk up the hill."

I pointed toward the railroad tracks.

"I ain't worried 'bout my boots gettin' wet," he said.

"I'm worried 'bout what's at the bottom of that river."

Later that evening all three of them fell asleep in front of the television. I picked up my bedroll, turned off the television, and walked away. I followed the river for a few hundred yards and found a dry place under a bush to lay out my blankets. I didn't feel like sleeping in the mud and I didn't feel like sleeping alongside two loony tick outlaws.

I was so scared lying under that bush that I couldn't sleep. I just looked up at the sky and I let my thoughts wander south.

I'd have ridden a freight train all the way from there to the base of Mexico if I'd have known that cold gray sky would turn to summer blue when I got there. There are no guarantees except the ones I make, and if that rain continues to fall and if any one of those muddy Montana rivers starts to swell, I better know when to walk away from it or at least know how to build a goddamn raft because that river water won't stop for the weak at heart. I had to get on that train and open those boxcar doors and ride my pumpkin dream all the way to Mexico. Down there they have chocolate-dipped bananas and caramel-coated lips and all the sweetness of a lady's dancing hip. I'd undress her. I'd spread her legs. I'd sink into Mexico like a hundred-dollar bill. I had no time for the gray northern skies. I had no time for wayward men.

That's why I walked away from Bobby and Levi's campfire that night, and that's why I cut Bobby Blue's rope.

I watched him take the last drag of his Camel and took out my pocketknife and cut the twine. The old possum fell to the platform of the unit like a sack of potatoes. I bent down, put my head under his arm, and helped him up. The train slowed down at a traffic crossing. I walked him down the steps of the unit and balanced him on the last one. When the train was moving slow enough I gave him a push. He took one long step, one short step, and fell down on his shoulder in the railroad rock. There was a platinum blond in a Lincoln waiting at the signal. Her lips pinched a cigarette. She exhaled out the window. Bobby Blue lay on the ground and she smiled.

Montana Blue

I woke up beside those tracks back in Montana and rolled up my blankets. The rain was falling and the river was wide. By the looks of it Levi and Bobby had about half a day to move their camp. I figured I'd walk back and help them pack up. The clouds moved in circles. The wind was blowing. I walked into the camp and it was empty. The coals were smoking, the posts for their tarp were still stuck in the mud, but they had gone.

I sat down on my bedroll and waited, and after five minutes started thinking.

I couldn't have imagined Alabama leaving without a word. But then again, I walked off without telling him, so maybe he thought I got discouraged and left. Or maybe those two hooligans went and dragged him into the river. But Alabama was smarter than that. They had to be coming back. Maybe the cinder bull came by and they had to hide, or maybe the goddamn devil himself came out of the ground and wrapped his tail around all of them and dragged them all into darkness and damnation.

I looked around in the dirt and found Alabama's boot prints. I knew them well from following him down so many dirt roads. His tracks led off into the shrubs, so I picked up and followed them back up the hill. I lost him for a minute in the railroad rock but picked him up again further down the tracks. He wasn't alone. The three of them had gone on together. I heard two trains the night before and the second one was catchable. Where their boot prints ended gave me a hunch they had jumped it.

I sat back down on my bedroll and put my head in my hands. I sat there helpless for an hour and every minute after of that hour, I had a different emotion and a different hope and a different sorrow. I stood up and stomped down on my boot and felt tough, then crumbled back onto my bedroll, then stood up and kicked a few stones, then crumbled back down again.

"Fuck this adventure hero road crap!" I yelled. "Fuck this growing up fast crap. I need a fucking car and a fucking suitcase and a fucking motel room and fucking girlfriend who wears too much lipstick. I need some class."

I guess you could say I gave up. I started walking toward the interstate. I turned my back on the trains and hoped to hell

I'd find a shower and a nice lady before nightfall. I had had enough tough tits and cold ground and day-old bread. I was on my way to the interstate where tough tits are warm and easy—free like life is supposed to be.

I made it to the Salvation Army. I sat at their front door with a vintage Mexican man and his vintage Mexican bicycle. He had the bike upside down and was trying to fix the tire. He had no idea what he was doing. He kept cursing in Spanish, then laughing in English. A Texas laugh, the damn Mexican had a Texas laugh. He eventually gave up on his bike, walked across the street, and sat down under a cotton tree. The wind blew shadows across his face. The cotton fell like snow. The clouds parted and the sun fell like a golden egg out of the sky's mighty asshole.

He didn't care about his bicycle as much as his cigar and his silver-toed cowboy boots. I dragged his bike across the street, set it upside down under the cotton tree, and helped him fix his tire. With the few words of English he knew, we talked about going to Mexico. It took him two minutes to remember his hometown sunshine, his hometown señoritas, and his hometown pace. His evenings in the public square where the boys walk to the right and the girls walk to the left, the mariachis trade music for mescal, and young lovers pray to Saint Valentine under the bright Mexican moon.

"Piss on America!" he said.

"Mexico es muy romántico." He lifted his eyebrows and his eyes widened. He walked over to a stop sign and pointed at it. He made a spitting sound with his lips and cocked his head.

"In Mexico, no signs. You just drive. You just walk. No signs."

I thought it would be nice to just drive and just walk and not have any signs. I wanted to do what I wanted to do whenever I wanted to do it, and that would be a lot easier without any signs.

The shelter opened for dinner. The Mexican man and me ate day-old bread and jerky-tough beef and took showers. The shower was filled with dirty bums and cheap soap and way too much hair. I got clean real quick. It was a pity to put my pants back on. I went from feeling fresh as flowers to dirty as diesel. On our way out we both grabbed a book off the free shelf. I got *Midnight Cowboy.*

We sat on the log under the cotton tree and read. I did my best to let Alabama and his wisdom drift away. I had to keep walking—no matter what people do, who comes and who goes—you have to keep walking to Mexico or wherever your heart wants to go. It would be red roses, white sand, and bad disco from there on out.

Play the music fast
Lower the donkey
Burn the trash
We're going to Mexico

Boot Prints

At dusk Alabama came walking up from the railroad tracks. He had his hands in his pockets and he was kicking stones. I stood up and smiled. He looked at the tree and down at me and smiled, too. We hugged and I didn't think I'd see it again, but the old kid got a little tear in his eye. He had done the same thing I had done for the last three hours.

"I found your boot prints. Red Wings, right?"

I looked at my boots and nodded.

"I've been following those boot prints all morning. You walked out so far last night I thought you must've walked home.

I got up with Bobby and Levi this morning when that train
came through. I almost went to Seattle with them, but right
after I hopped in that boxcar I got a real strange feeling, down
in my gut—like I felt you were still here or somethin'. So, I
jumped off the train and started walking, couldn't find you so
I gave up and took a nap back by the tracks. I thought you up
and ditched me."

He sat down beside me and the Mexican man on the log
and cracked his broken jaw. I guessed that I'd have to stick with
the plan and keep my north wind blowing. The people that
teach a boy how to run are the people who set him free, and for
me I was still a three-legged horse with a stable somewhere in
the heart of insecurity. I still needed Alabama. I bid the vintage
Mexican man a fond farewell and followed my dusty footprints
back to the field—to what was left of Bobby and Levi's camp.

★

The next morning I felt like I had run my gut with bad
whisky—like I chugged down all of Montana, all of her mud
and mystery—and woke up the next morning with a splitting
headache. Those hooligans are out there for a reason. The red-
necks cut the charm right out of tramping. They hide behind
the assumption that everyone should be like them, and when
they see a boy crossing their line they jump on him like a free
porno magazine. I thought that Pork Pie in Greybull was as
bad as it would get, but Bobby and Levi's two-mile camp in
the trees was even worse. Pork Pie was a gentleman. He had
been in the military and he had taken his abuse from the ranks
of disgust. That morning, we crossed over that river that held
two men's irreversible sin. While the bridge's old wooden
trusses snapped and cracked under the train, Alabama told me
that Bobby and Levi—out of pure insanity—drowned a man

in that very same water. I imagine some hard drinking led to some hard "discussion," and by the end of the night it was two against one and the one ended up at the bottom of the river.

★

After walking Bobby Blue down the ladder I sat back down on the platform of the unit, rearranged my bedroll, and lay back on it. I watched the town drift by—storefronts and backyards. The train picked up speed and the tail end left town. We were back in the country and in the fields and in the air with the wide-open feeling of new horizons and new ways.

I had cut Bobby's twine after he took the last drag of his cigarette and didn't feel a bit guilty about doing it. It was either that or have him follow me and my train all the way to fucking paradise. I'd rather be alone. Mexico was the only thing on my mind and if all went well, I could still be there by the end of the week.

Journal Entry #7: Padding the Hoof

One thing about riding trains is all the walking. It's called "padding the hoof." You can count on walking a lot. You have to walk to find the train yard. You have to walk to find a good boxcar. You have to walk to find food. You have to walk to find your buddy who had too much to drink and got carted away to detox the night before. You're probably going to walk more than you ride, but that's all right because walking can be a social activity and it's good for the bones.

I think for a tramp there are only two kinds of walking. The kind where you walk in and the kind where you walk out. The most important thing about the walking-in part is to know that you have a choice. Take the jungle, for instance. If you see

someone in the jungle that you don't like the looks of, you don't
walk in. It's that simple. But the strange thing about this theory
is that it isn't always reliable. A man doesn't look the way he is
all the time and if you get to thinking this way too much, you
might miss out on some of life's finest interpretation. Therefore
it's sometimes good to sit down and have a hot cup of jamoke
and tell a few stories. If the fella starts to grind and babble and
all his sentences stop short of common sense, then it's time for
the walking-out part.

There are grifters who survive on wit and there are grifters
who survive on muscle. If they're on the hog, it's usually
because they got themselves there and the only way they know to
get out is to lie, cheat, steal, and fight. These are the grifters
that work on muscle. Of course, this doesn't work in the long
run. They just get deeper and deeper—dumber and dumber.
Pretty soon all a grifter knows how to do is fight and steal and
everything in between. It's a life. A way to get by—until the
tears come and they have nowhere to fall. Grifters walk a hell of
a lot more than anyone else because the trains just don't stop for
them. Bad luck—I guess. And they also don't know when to
walk out. They got trouble and it's deep and it's dark but it
doesn't matter to them because that's just how it is and how it
will always be. A grifter who lives on wit has the same life, only
he can mask it with a smile—a skill developed and manicured
by all of America's finest pitchmen and politicians.

There have always been carnivals and I have met many a
roughy or roustabout who could put up a tent. They travel with
all the canvas joints and rag fronts that swindle America's small
towns of their hard-earned small-town money. All in good fun,
of course. It's the big pink stuffed poodle hanging from a hook
behind the leaded glass bottles who's really to blame. If you

want one of those things, you deserve to pay two hundred dollars for it.

Sometimes you don't choose the walking—it chooses you. It's usually administered by the law and never when you want it. I was riding a Southern Pacific eastbound out of Colton, California, one summer. On the "Sunset Route." I hopped a hotshot at sunrise and by midday was highballin' through the Mojave Desert. I was completely exposed and there wasn't much keeping me from falling off. I had a long leather belt with an extra notch in it, so I weaved it through the footboard grate on the platform and cinched myself down. Two hours into the desert a bull drove up beside the train. He radioed the engineer and had me kicked off in the middle of the desert in the hottest part of the day. He waited till I was two hours out of his yard—probably because he was enjoying the drive—to do this. I had to walk three miles to a junkyard and hitchhike another fifty to the next train yard. Devil Pig Fucker! Took an extra two days to get to El Paso.

Because of unforeseen complications like this—don't get on a train without a tough pair of boots. If you work, your boots should have a steel toe. There are many construction bosses that won't let you work without steel-toe boots. If you don't work, then get a good pair of tennis shoes—that's what most drinking men seem to prefer.

Pirate Stew: Any soup or stew fixed in a gumbo over a small fire, particularly with hoppins of the stolen or pilfered variety.

Ghost Story: A story or long tale of woe to gain sympathy; a begging yarn. Like fashions, those ghost stories in vogue and "just the thing" this year are soon out of date and must be altered to meet changed conditions, and it is a matter of pride with every real tramp to have a good string of stories at his command.

9

Blackfoot, Idaho, to
Evanston, Wyoming

November 2, 1991

Blackfoot

The train stopped in Blackfoot, Idaho, not too long after midnight. It was a small town, so the train yard consisted of a tin brakeman's shack with dusty windows and a few small lights strung up on telephone poles. There was a tree over a nearby fence with a dog sleeping under it. The only noise came from the sound of a shovel scratching rocks—an old fart digging a hole in his backyard. His lips vibrated with a sensible hum and every once in a while he would stop, stretch his arms, and wipe his brow. I sat in the shadow of the shack and waited for another southbound train. If I was lucky I would get out by daybreak, but in such a small yard it sometimes takes a few days, so I rolled out my blanket and made myself at home. I put my hands under my head and made good sense of the stars.

The old fart growled and cursed the dirt. He had no idea I was lying there.

"Goddamn it, this fuckin' soil, ain't nothin' but a rock farm, that's all I got here is a damn rock farm."

He jumped back from the shovel, took off his hat, and threw it on the ground. He pointed to the ground and yelled again.

"It'll be the last night, you hear me, the last night I get to diggin' in this godforsaken yard."

He said it with a decade's worth of conviction and by the way his face burned, it must have been half his life spent figuring that piece of dirt. I stood up slow and walked closer so I could see what he was trying to plant. I made out a potato sack filled with the roots of a sapling. An apple tree. A single apple tree was all he had to plant. I lost interest, turned around, and walked back to my blankets. It was pitch-dark and before I got my direction I ran into a post, not a post holding up a fence or a post that made any sense, just a stick of wood stuck in the ground right at the height of my crotch. By the time I was rolling around on the ground I had let out a good scream.

"Who's that?" yelled the old fart.

I kept my mouth closed and tried to crawl further into the dark. I looked back at him and he was walking in the other direction. He walked about ten feet, stopped, felt the top of his head, and walked back to get his hat. He squinted into the dark and slowly walked backward again. I was holding in ten screams and rolling around in the dirt.

"Make yourself seen!" he yelled.

"All right, all right," I said. "Just let me get up."

I stood up and hobbled into the light. It ran across my dirty face and I stood there hunched over like a gorilla.

"What the hell are you doin' out here?" he asked.

"Nothing, just passing through."

We stood there, silently.

"So what about you, what are you doin' out here?" I asked.

"I'm workin'."

"Workin'?" I replied. "It's gotta be half two. Why are you workin' so late?"

"What's it your business?" he snapped. "I live in that house and this is my yard, I can do whatever I please."

"Never said you couldn't," I replied.

"Then what's it to ya?"

"Nothin'. I just don't see why you're workin' so late." I turned to walk away and shook my head. "Why don't you just do like the rest of the folks and dig that hole during the day?"

He fiddled his hat again, then lowered his head and mumbled.

" 'Cause, if any of my neighbors saw me tryin' to plant something in this rock yard, they'd think me half crazy and I don't want any trouble, got enough as it is."

I turned back around.

"Well, I'll tell you one thing, if they saw you digging in your yard at half two, they'd think you were totally crazy."

"So what, I don't need 'em anyway, they took me for a fool when they sold me this land. I sure don't need any help from any one of them. They can go ahead and think whatever they want, but I'll bet they won't have a thing to say when this tree grows and I've got a whole bushel of apples to show for it."

"Apples, huh? I sure do like apples." I sat down Indian style and took a deep breath, thinking about big, sweet apples. He wasn't as nervous as before and after a few minutes he sat down beside me.

"So, where are you headed?"

"Mexico."

"Mexico, huh." He thought about it for a minute. "So you out here just traveling around? I used to do that when I was your age, you up go anywhere you want, say anything you want, free as a bird. It's good to do when you're young, things change when you get older, you can't just up and leave. There are things you have to take care of."

"Things to take care of?" I asked.

"Yeah, like a home and children and a wife."

"A wife? Shit, I don't want no wife I have to take care of." I shook my head. "No way."

I thought about him and his little land and his little apple tree.

"So why'd you stop here?" I asked.

"I fell in love, what else?" He put his head down and shook it. "It takes a lot to keep a man in one place. There's only two things that will do it. Work and love. You have to work to be strong and you have to be strong to love."[9]

"Strong to love?" I shook my head again. "Shit, love's easy."

He started to giggle, then after a second or two he was laughing.

"What?" I asked. "What are you laughin' about?"

"Well, kid, I couldn't tell your age a minute ago, but you just went and gave it away."

"Gave it away? Why?"

---

9. The old fart was a shade tree philosopher. Defined as: One who resists idle chatter; one who has the ability to entertain or extract deeper meaning or said "philosophy" from any situation, in any setting, at any time of day; a self-proclaimed wise man; a term most probably borrowed from "shade tree mechanic." By nature old men want to help young men (as evidenced by Alabama)— especially young men on the lam or young men who as drifters seem helpless. Therefore, an impromptu sermon by a bored old man on the road is not at all uncommon.

"You just did, that's all."

He lay back and cracked a wise smile, smug is what he was, smug as a sneaky dog. That was enough to get me curious, and I had so much on my mind that I couldn't help but ask him more questions.

"So, if you think you know so much about love, tell me this. You think that if someone that's supposed to love you gets up and leaves that they still love you after they've gone?" I was thinking about my father.

"That would depend if they come back," he replied.

"Well, say they're out doing somethin' that might make 'em a better person. And say they're gone for a long time but they're still thinking about their home and they know that if they went back before they were ready that they would probably just leave again within a few weeks."

He put his finger to his chin and shook his head.

"That's a tough one, kid, but I'd safely say that if that's how you are, then you'll probably be alone your whole life."

"Yeah, you're probably right," I said. "With the way things are right now there's no way anyone could find me. Even if it was the right thing and the only thing they could want, they still couldn't find me."

"That's how it goes sometimes, kid, that's just how it goes."

We sat there quietly in the dark. I leaned back on my elbows and looked at the sky. The old fart gathered up a handful of rocks, stood up, and walked into the light. He threw the rocks at a fencepost. They bounced off the post one at a time. When the rocks were gone he put his hands in his pockets and strolled around in a circle. His eyebrows moved up and down— like he was working on a thought. He stopped and waved his finger at me.

"You know those feelings you're talking about, kid?"

"Yeah?"

"I know those feelings. I spent ten years on the road myself."

He thought about it more.

"Ten hard years. And you know what? I learned something. One good lesson that I'll never forget."

He poked his index finger into his temple.

"It's all right here."

He dusted off his coveralls, looked at the horizon, and straightened his hat.

"Looks like the sun's about to come up."

"Yup."

"I'm going inside before the neighbors get up."

"Aren't you gonna tell me what it is?"

"What?"

"The lesson you talked about."

"You really want to know?"

"Couldn't hurt."

He sat back down.

"Let me see if I can remember it." He closed his eyes. "It was straight out of some spiritual book or something."

He sat there with his eyes closed and put his finger up.

"Okay, I think I got it."

He took in a deep breath and slowly began to speak.

It went something like this:

If a man chooses to live a life of experience, he'll know the purpose of every object that he passes on the road. He'll know the process that object goes through to produce the fruits of its labor. He'll know these things because he will have worked them with his own two hands, and after all this, if he does find a home, he'll appreciate home all the more.

If a man chooses a practical life he will suffer less hardships along the way. His stories will have the sweetness of unripe tomatoes but his home will be without the heartache of so many uncertain days. Everything he chooses to place around him will become a permanent fixture. His life's attention will be put to the task of nurturing his homestead, watering his lawn, building waterfalls in his backyard, and shingling his roof. His life will become permanent and the people who pass through will become his inspiration.

He smiled and took another breath.

"I think that's it."

He stood back up and put his hand out. We shook.

"It was good to meet you, kid, if you're still around at lunch, come back by."

"Thank you," I said.

He walked away. The sun turned the sky green and off in the distance I could hear a car horn. The town was waking up. The dirt my friend had dug sat like a mountain beside the valley below. A little river ran the length of the valley and an optimistic young man left town with a wilted heart.

At daybreak I caught a grainer and it was good because I was out in the air and the air was fresh. It was sunny—not warm but sunny. The frost didn't melt till noon and I could see my breath most of the day. I took out my Mexican postcard and looked at it again. It blew my mind how much had come between me and that picture. Alabama. Bobby Blue two times. That old fart with the shovel and finally, rolling southeast out of Blackfoot, absolutely nothing but morning frost and sun-shine. My train would probably stop in Pocatello for a fresh crew, then roll southeast to Green River, Wyoming.

I gathered up some twigs that were sitting in the corner of the platform and put them in a pile. I ripped an edge off my bandanna and tied them into a little broom. I swept the gravel, grain, and dirt into a neat pile and shoved it out a hole over the wheels. I put my piece of foam down and unrolled my blankets. They had oil and dirt ground into them and they were wrinkled up. I wrapped one around my legs and the other one around my head and lay down. I left my face out in the wind and looked up at the clouds and the baby-blue sky, and closed my eyes and let the hot morning sun sink into my eyelids.

I knew that train would roll for at least four hours, and for those four hours no one in the whole world could touch me. No one knew where I was. There was no idea or notion that could mislead me. No tear that could fall, no muscle that could ache—that wasn't my own. I was alone like a sailor in the sea—problems in my head and no coins in my pocket.

I took in a deep breath of cold air and let it sit in my lungs. That breath had all of America in it. The salt from Pacific seas, the gold from Colorado's aspen trees, the buffalo grass from the thousand-mile prairie, and the burning wood of a settler's dream. Inside all that land was a fortune in mineral and gold, and as I passed over it it caught the sun like an ocean wave—rolling and climbing, rolling and climbing. The train whistle screamed. The sun became a circle above the fields. Two birds flew in front of it, turned and faded into it.

Pirate Stew

After Blackfoot my train picked up a new crew in Pocatello and rolled through a couple national parks, traversed two low mountain ranges, crossed the Idaho-Wyoming border in the middle of the night, and coasted back into the front-range flatlands of Wyoming. The train pulled onto the secondary track and stopped in a small field of onions. By the sun it was about eleven in the morning. The hills were round and in the shady spots behind them the ground was still wet. I was on the cold side of the grainer, so I rolled up my blankets, grabbed my little broom, and walked down the track to an open boxcar.

I looked over at the onions and they were ready to be picked. From the way my stomach turned they looked like a bunch of skinny chickens.

I put my bedroll in the door of the boxcar where I could reach it, zipped up my jacket, and tiptoed into the field. There were so many to choose from. I picked a few here and there so it wouldn't look like I'd been there, stuffed them in my coat, and ran back to the train. The entire field got quiet and the wind stopped, and I got this eerie feeling that someone was watching me. They weren't, though, there wasn't a person for miles, so I got comfortable in the boxcar and unloaded the onions.

At first I tried them raw, but I nearly burned a hole in my stomach, so I laid them in a nice line on the floor. I contemplated them for a second, then stomped on each one. I squished them down with my boot—real good. I'd seen French onion soup in a million diners and it looked like a simple little recipe.

The second step was finding a can to heat it up in. So, I walked along the railroad tracks for a few hundred feet and found an old soup can. It was steel and the inside was all rusted out, but it couldn't have been that old because the wrapper still said Campbell's Home Style Soup and there was even a bit of carrot sitting at the bottom.

When I kneeled down to pick it up I looked under the train. The sky was green and underneath it there were a million ears of corn. They were ripening themselves under the proud sun. I picked three ears, shucked 'em right there in the field, cut off the kernels with my pearing knife, put them in the can, and walked back to the boxcar. I poured half a bottle of water over the top and sprinkled in a pinch of salt I picked up in Missoula.

There was one tree in that field. It was a long ways off and it was the only place I would find firewood, so I tied up my shoes tight and ran for it. About halfway there a pickup truck came rumbling up the road. I stopped mid-stride and dove onto my stomach. I could hear the truck getting closer and closer until it faded past me and stopped. I looked up. A man in overalls got out and walked over to the tree and sat down. That's all he did was sit down in the shade, and after awhile he even started to whistle. He tapped his hands on his knees and moved his head up and down. I turned over on my back and put my hands under my head and looked at the sky. No clouds, no dust, no worries.

The train moved. The slack action echoed. I jumped out of the dirt and ran, but I didn't run for the train, I ran for the tree. My hair was sticking straight out, my face was dirty as coal, and my boots pounded like Frankenstein on the hard ground. The farmer didn't budge, though, he just sat there whistling. I stopped at the bottom of the tree and hopped up to the lowest branch. It was deadwood, so it broke from my weight. I fell to the ground and landed in a cloud of dust.

The branch was taller than me and had dried leaves on it. I tried carrying it at first but it was too heavy, so I dragged it across the onions and finally to the tracks. The train was moving slow but those damn boxcars sit high. So I had to wrestle it fifty feet down the tracks before I could get it in.

Thirty minutes into the ride I had a nice bed of coals.

Forty minutes into the ride I had a nice can of stew. The corn was feed corn, so it was hard as hell. It got stuck in my molars. Took me three days to pick it all out. The farmer went home and I imagined that before the sun went down he put a patch on his left eye and pretended he was a pirate. He'd been robbed, but I don't think he cared because he always knew he had it coming.

Payday

Later that day I passed a little village—don't remember the name. The town was only seven or eight houses wedged between the railroad tracks. The road that went through the center of town had only one person to entertain, a weekend drifter with his thumb set on getting to the next town. The boy looked kind of sickly. The road rolled out of his duffel bag and sank over a far hill.

The next town had an old man sitting on his front porch, one of those hammocks that sits on its own stand, a church with the windows boarded up, and a park with a broken merry-go-round. I stood out the door of the boxcar and in the window of a small house I saw the silhouette of a woman preparing hamburger. She probably wanted steak but the money hadn't come. I could tell by the wrinkles in her face that she was frustrated. There was probably half a paycheck in the till at the El Cortez saloon, half in her son's hip pocket, and somewhere between the two, a bad hangover.

Hillbilly Rattle

The next town had a stucco building painted white. In the peak of the roof there was a clock that had stopped at 4:20. There were no numbers on it, just a rusted picture of a locomotive in full steam. The wind found the corner of every doorway and pushed the leaves up the walls and into the train yard. There was a man sitting under the clock with a tin can in his hand. He shook it, stopped, then shook it again. I thought he was panhandling but there wasn't a towner for blocks—no one to hustle. He busted out laughing and screaming and shaking that can as hard as he fucking could. Every so often he'd put his hand into a bag of cherries, clean off the seed, and spit it in the can. The more seeds he put in there, the happier he got. When he got bored with cherries he fell over and went to sleep. The leaves fell on him one by one until he was nearly covered up.

A Love Story

I thought my train was heading east to Cheyenne. So I jumped off, walked over to the clock building, sat down beside the pile of leaves, and poked the bum with my finger.

"Hey, what town is this?"

He opened his eyes but didn't sit up.

"Green River."

"Can I catch a westbound outta here?" I asked.

"I don't know."

He grabbed the bag of cherries and plopped it in front of me.

"Cherries?" he asked.

I grabbed a handful out of the bag and stuffed them in my coat pocket.

"Do you know what the date is?"

He shook his head.

"No, must be November, though, people been talkin' 'bout Thanksgiving."

I walked up the tracks a few hundred feet and they didn't turn, so I figured they had to keep going west. I sat back down next to the bum and waited in the sun for a hotshot.

A six-pack of engineers and brakemen walked from the
crew room and behind them there was another tramp. He
looked rough—even worse than I did. He was drinking a cup
of coffee. They all sat together at a picnic table on the grass.
One of the brakemen noticed me and waved. I figured "what
the hell" and stood up.

"Thanks for the cherries."

"You're welcome."

And I walked over to the picnic table and said hello.

"Where ya headed," the brakeman asked.

"Mexico."

"Mexico?" He shook his head.

"I heard bad things about Mexico. They put you in jail
and you don't get out."

"You been there?" I asked.

"No, just read the papers."

"Figure I'll go see for myself."

He put his hand on the tramp's shoulder and looked at
him. "This here is Ben and we're all about to get you guys on
the right train."

"The right train?" I thought. "You must be joking."

But he wasn't, and five minutes later all five of them had
their schedules out—trying to make sense of them. Ben would
be leaving at nightfall on an eastbound Union Pacific and then
the next day he would catch a southbound Burlington Northern
from Cheyenne to Denver. The same line that Alabama and
me had taken a few weeks earlier. Ben was real excited because
he was "gonna get there" when he said he would and he had
never done that before.

"I ain't been to Denver in years," he said.

"My old lady got extradited. Cops took her to Denver two
weeks ago. She got locked up for vehicular homicide."

The Union Pacific men were curious. They were well-balanced men. I think it's because of the time they spend following the paths of the pioneers. They look like frontiersmen. They don't get exposed to any of the trash on the outside of the train, and unlike a tramp their closets are organized and clean.

"One day she was prancin' around the motel room, right, and I was paying twenty bucks a night for that room and all she did was pace the carpet. After twelve days of that shit I got fed up and threw the keys at her and told her to go for a drive. Anything but pace the damn room."

"What happened?" one of the UP men asked.

"Vehicular homicide," he said. "She killed four people. Got that Beretta goin' a hundred and thirteen miles per hour on the interstate and took out five cars. Not to mention any hope either one of us had of starting over. I made a deal with her that I would do five things: get sober, get a job, buy a mobile home, get spiritual again, and wash my clothes more. I was gettin' it all done, too, and she had to go and fuck it up."

He got frustrated and waved his hands around.

"Goddamn, do I feel guilty about all that. I'm trying to get to Denver because I feel bad for pushing her out the door like that—plus I talked her into jumping bail and coming out to California in the first place. Now we're both more fucked than when we started. Shit! I'm breaking parole right now. Won't even be able to see her when I get there, but I know the pastor at Denver County and I can slip him a cannonball and he'll give it to her. I think he'll understand."

The balanced men drank their coffee and listened with open minds. I was a little surprised by what he was saying, but not really. I think jumping bail is just a common occurrence out there, just like the planting of spring or a broke-down Ford, it's

all part of the scenery. I asked him how he got this far and if he
had any money with him.

"No, nothing to speak of. I started out with my bicycle in
Oakland. I got to Walnut Creek on that, then traded it for a
burrito and twenty bucks. I spent all of that on drinks that same
night, got real drunk, and took out on foot for the Tracy yards.
Knew if I got there I could catch a train outta California.
Caught a train outta Tracy all the way to Reno and met up with
some tramps. They had all pitched in for a motel room and they
let me use the bathroom to clean up. I left Reno after a three-
day drunk and with only half my right pinkie. See that?" He
showed us his right hand and the tip of his pinkie was missing.

"I spent a few hours in the hospital after that but there
wasn't really anything they could do. One of those bastards bit
the damn thing off. We got in an argument over some stupid
slot machine and that same night he got rip-roaring drunk and
got me in my sleep. I sleep alone now."

He stood up and started digging through his U.S. Army
duffel and came out with a wrinkled paper sack. He pulled a
note out of it and threw it across the table.

"That's a letter she wrote me. She thinks she's fat, but
hell, I think she's beautiful."

There were a couple of Polaroids wrapped in newspaper
inside the sack. They were snapshots of a lady wearing big
glasses, standing in a plot of desert cacti. She looked like that
guy Grimace from McDonald's. She was fat on the bottom and
skinny on top.

"That's her land there. When I got that mobile home, we
were going to live there. I was going to get a job at the quarry
and she was going to get a job at the diner. Now, shit! She'll
be lucky to see anything but concrete for two years. I'll wait for

her, though. She's crazy, angry as hell and she's got that manic-depressive disease, but I'll still wait for her."

Jefferson

The Union Pacific men got me on the next train for Ogden, Utah. They set me up with a "scenic cruiser." That's a boxcar with both doors open. While I waited for them to change crews I noticed a man walking toward me from the back of the train. He wasn't a big man; in fact, the closer he got, the smaller he got, and his walk turned into more of a shuffle. He stopped, put down whatever was in his hand, took a bandanna out of his back pocket, and wiped his brow. Then he folded it up neatly and stuck it back in his jeans. He was a boy, no more than fourteen years old. He looked like the kind of kid who would follow the milk truck in order to steal his neighbor's milk. He walked like a long-legged bird. He kept putting his nose down to the ground and looking under the train. I could tell he was up to no good.

When he got to my boxcar he stopped and smiled. His nose looked more like a beak than a nose and he had a watermelon in his hands.

"Hello," he said, "my name is Jefferson and I'd like to know which way this train is headed."

"First of all," I said, "where are *you* headed?"

"To the beach."

"To the beach?"

He put his head in the car and looked back and forth.

"Travelin' alone?" he asked.

I nodded.

"This is the only open car on the train, is it all right if I ride along?"

I looked him over. I didn't trust him, but he was young

and the worst he'd try to do is steal my shoelaces or talk my ear off. I didn't care about any of that, but I sure wanted a slice of that melon.

"You can come along if that melon comes along with you."

He put it on the floor. I threw him my hand and pulled him in. He fell on his belly, then stood up, straightened his jacket, and dusted his hands.

"Where are you headed?" he asked.

"Mexico."

I felt proud when I said it that time. "Mexico." I felt like a real daredevil. I was now going somewhere that was supposed to be dangerous and that made me proud.

"Mexico, huh? I ain't never been there. Been to the ocean, though, been to the ocean lots of times."

"Everyone's been to the ocean. What's so special about that?"

"Nothin', I guess. I heard that Mexico was on the way to the ocean. So I suppose I might be passing through there."

He picked up the watermelon and walked to the corner of the boxcar and put it down.

"Hey, what's your name?"

"Eddy."

"So Eddy, why Mexico? You got family there?"

"No, just wanna go, just to see it."

"You know where I'd like to go, Eddy?"

"Where?"

"Somewhere nice and sunny where I could eat this watermelon."

I looked over at him and shook my head and spit a cherry pit on the ground.

"How long have you been out here, kid?"

"Out where?" he asked.

"Out here." I pointed to the horizon. "On the road?" "About a week."

"You've been away from home for a week and all you've got to show for it is a damn watermelon?"

"No, I got this, too."

He reached into his pocket and pulled out four pieces of colored plastic. One piece was a red island, the second piece was a brown tree trunk, the third piece was a set of green palm leaves, and the fourth piece was a bunch of coconuts. He fiddled with them for about five minutes, then sat it down on the floor. It was a plastic palm tree, about eight inches high.

"What the hell is that?" I asked.

"It's a tree, like the kind you find by the ocean, friend of mine, he told me that you can eat these brown things here, said they had milk in 'em."

"Well, of course, they're coconuts, aren't they?"

"Shoot, I don't know, they don't have trees like that where I come from."

"But you've been to the ocean, they have 'em there."

"Yeah, but I was just a kid, all I remember is the drive down there, the window down, the wind gettin' in my eyes. I never seen a tree like that before."

"Well, you're still a kid then, if you've never seen a palm tree, then you're still a kid."

He crossed his arms and cringed his eyes.

"I'm fourteen years old."

"I was climbing palm trees when I was fourteen, in fact, I could build an entire house with one of those." I pointed to his tree. "And you know what else?" I thought of Alabama and laughed to myself. "It would keep the rain out better than a shingled roof."

Buddies

At sunset when our train started to move, a potato sack half full of glass bottles came flying in the door and crashed on the floor. And after it an old Indian man with a huge hunkered-down backpack came flying in the door and crashed on the floor. He rolled over on his side and just lay there moaning. I ran over and helped him up. Jefferson carried his backpack and bag of bottles over to the other side of the boxcar. The bag was dripping wet.

"Beer?" he said. "Did the beer make it?"

"If that's what's in this bag, then it made it."

"Thank God. I thought I might have missed the door."

He walked over to the bag, grabbed a bottle out of it, opened it, drank down the whole thing, and wiped off his lips with his sleeve.

"Sure do like Miller, can't stand wine. I get the good stuff. It's either Miller or nothin'."

I put my hand out and he shook it.

"My name's Eddy and this here is Jefferson."

"Nice to meet you guys," he said, "I'm Pollock."

Pollock, Jefferson, and me sat in the last rays of the setting sun and drank Miller from bottles. We were rolling westbound toward Ogden, Utah. I had never met an Indian before—let alone an Indian named Pollock. The beer was cold like Lake Tahoe in the wintertime, and after the train moved we all had a good laugh about our past and how unfortunate our lives had all been. I guess misfortune is to end up in a place where the relief comes in a bottle and the insights are illuminated by drunken eyes. We got wasted. In the sun, under a metal roof with a potato sack full of scenery.

The train parted the prairie like Ricky Ricardo's hair and we felt slow. Slow as an old man's rocking chair. Slow as an uphill train. Slow as a bad memory. Things were good and bad all at the same time, so we sat together and complained for the remainder of the night. Complain is what a tramp does best— no matter how sweet life gets, a tramp will always chat it down, throw a low pitch, or grind some funny ghost story. That way— no one but the Lord can ever say they've got one up on him.

Bird Man

In the morning the train stopped in another field of onions and they smelled good. Toward midday we all wondered if the train was going to move again. We had all had a train stop for an hour or two, but when three or four roll around you start to wonder.

We threw rocks at a mile marker, balanced on the tracks, and looked for fossils in the railroad rock. I found a couple of good ones that looked like dead bugs and saber-toothed tiger teeth. I put them in my pocket. Jefferson got curious around sunset and walked up to the front of the train and didn't come back for a good hour. When he reappeared he was shaking his head and walking slow.

"This train ain't movin'," he said.

"What are you talking about?"

Pollock nodded. "I knew it, they broke the units, left us out here—didn't they?"

"Yup."

"I heard the air brake but I thought they were just putting a new car on."

I walked over to the track and kicked it.

"We're on the secondary."

"That's not the main line?" Pollock asked.

"Nope, there's another track on the other side."

"Shit, we could be here for days."

★

He was right, and two days it was. That evening we had a little fire alongside the tracks. Pollock pulled a cooking kit, three
cans of clam chowder, and some saltine crackers out of his
backpack. He carefully opened the cans and emptied them into
one of the pots. I found two rocks in the bushes, placed them
beside the fire, and Pollock used them to balance the chowder
over the flames.

The moon was a sliver over the field and we could see many
stars. The train sat there patiently. An occasional wind blew
through her open doors and between her wheels—making the
sound of blowing sand on metal. Her knuckles popped and
metallic sound echoed the length of her. She was alive—resting
there like a dinosaur in the tar of a pitch-dark and silent night.
On the road she carried herself like a lady, a mystery to all
men—a diamond in their eye. Much like the memory of old love.
The train had so much weight in its bones. It moved slow—
sometimes resting for days, other times maintaining a steady gal-
lop for weeks on end. And there was nothing you could ever do
to control her. She was just how she was, out there with the
onions and the bums—bumming and laughing and trying to
think good thoughts. We drank all the Miller. Pollock went to
sleep on the ground close to the fire. The flames put a soft light
on his face. He had many wrinkles. His face was a map of his
life. It had every road he had traveled carved into it, and the
roads of misery and heartache you could see under his eyes—a
bit more traveled than the others. The roads around his mouth
were of better days—smiles and dimples from trying to win the
ladies, and red splashes from blushing over a fallen word or mis-
taken lie. As he slept his chest was rising and falling. The fire
crackled and to him, Jefferson and me were a million miles away.

I stayed up all night with Jefferson. At sunrise he got into a philosophical mood and tried to put a handle on his situation. Listening to him talk was like reading a children's book. He was trying to understand a part of life that a man twice his age shouldn't have to think about. There was no reason for him being out there—no explanation that his young mind could fabricate. No matter how hard he tried, he couldn't find an explanation for his wandering. He did have a father with a mean right hook—on the good days. On the bad days he used a shovel. I think all of that made the ocean look like heaven to him.

"The ocean . . . man!" he yelled.

"Think about it, sand and blue water—bikinis and birds."

I kept up with his ocean philosophies for a few hours but eventually got tired and lay down. I heard his little words fade away until I was completely asleep. I liked the little bird man but I couldn't stomach his dreams.

Sober

Pollock woke up and he was sober. He looked like he had never been sober and I don't think he liked it. He walked around the smoking fire pit six or seven times. The fifth time he looked as if a thought had entered his head. He walked two more times around and stopped at his backpack. The sun was at nine o'clock and bright. He used the sunlight to look into the bottom of his bag. I thought he was looking for a book or a bottle of water. But he didn't drink water. He did have a Bible. He took it out, kissed the cover, looked up at the sky with his bloodshot lamps, and mumbled a prayer to San Antonio. He put the Bible away and pulled out two cans of Sterno. He used the rim of one can to open the other one, then the rim of the open one to open the second one. The paraffin inside was hot pink and it smelled like wood alcohol, and I think that's what it was. Next he grabbed the cooking pot that we used for the chowder and placed it in front of him. Than he pulled a red bandanna out of his back pocket and laid it over the top of the pot. With his knife he shoveled the Sterno out of the cans and into the bandanna. He took up all four corners of the bandanna and squeezed the paraffin with his fingers until all the wood alcohol had run out.

"Pink Lady." He grinned.

"Gettin' me through."

He took out a can of Squirt soda pop and poured it over the top. He raised the blackened pot to the sky—toasted the Lord, then drank a third of it down. When he lowered it, his lips were black and bent like pipe cleaners. I think he was smiling but I couldn't tell. He didn't look happy but he did look satisfied. He passed the pot to me. I took it—looked at the bottom of it and back at him, and back at the bottom of the pot again. Clam chowder and paraffin. It looked like Popeye puke and tasted like the ocean after an oil spill. But it did the job. I gave the pot to Jefferson. He took a sip and handed it back to Pollock.

The next day Pollock dried up again, got sober real fast, and turned from a babbling idiot to a wordless monk. Poor guy got so hungry he was eating raw onions and throwing them all up. And worse than that, he got the runs and was shitting his pants on a regular basis. I felt sorry for him and offered to fix him onion stew, but he refused and went on about his business of throwing up and dripping. Jefferson and me sat at the other end of the boxcar and decided that we would never drink again. It felt good to be young and strong, and that would be enough for us.

Pollock stumbled around the boxcar, mumbling about beer and cigarettes. He went to put on his backpack and the weight of it pulled him over. He lay there like a turtle, mumbling about Miller. We helped him up. He balanced between us, then took a few steps and fell down again.

That evening the precious sound of slack action came from the front of the train. The train moved and for five long hours we all dreamed about pizza crust and grilled cheese sandwiches and what we were going to eat when we got to the next town. Pollock put his head into his shell and sucked his cheeks in and wrinkled up like a raisin. That was the last we saw of him. He disappeared into the streets of Evanston, the next town we stopped in, like a cowboy with worn heels and no click.

Grabbing Scenery

We stayed in Evanston long enough to eat two meals at a shelter and pick up a few loaves of bread. The locals walked slow and the children there stayed out after dark. I guess no one was worried about their kids getting eaten up by a hungry tramp. I know that people are different in different places and sometimes livestock is family and children are left to graze. As a kid I was always left in the pasture to take care of myself, and I wouldn't trade that for anything, not even an overprotective mom who cooked a good steak. I'd rather eat grass.

Jefferson and me sat on a park bench and picked the mud out of our boots and lay down in the grass. At about midnight we packed up and walked back to the yard. We sat in the dark and picked more mud out of our boots. Three hours later we caught a boxcar on a Union Pacific and rode that through the rest of Wyoming and into Utah. Jefferson fell asleep in the corner and didn't open his eyes till sunrise. By that time I was wide awake and sitting with my feet out the door. He got up like a dog and he had a big smile on his face.

"You musta had some good dreams last night," I said.

"Why?"

"Look at that damn smile you got." I turned my head back to the door. "Ain't seen a smile that big in a long time, especially not in the morning."

He just sat there in the corner, looking around at the inside of the boxcar.

"Well, everything's all right, isn't it, I mean why wouldn't I be smiling?"

"I don't know, guess I can't really see the point in it. There ain't a pretty lady or a good meal around and Christmas ain't for a few weeks. There really ain't any reason to be smiling."

"Who said you need a reason, I mean look around, there's nothing around that could hurt us. That's good enough reason to smile, isn't it?"

"I guess, but you won't be saying that when we stop, there's plenty of things that'll hurt us when we stop."

"Who said we're gonna stop, hell I'm not gonna stop . . ." He shook his head. *"Never."*

I thought about that for a second, then stood up and threw my hands in the air.

"What the hell are you talking about? This train's gotta stop every twelve hours, at least."

"Then I'll get off and start walkin', but I ain't gonna stop, not until I get to where I'm going." He shook his head like an old man and for a second I almost thought he knew what he was talking about.

"So, where *are* you going?" I asked.

"Hell, I don't know." He shook his head again. "But I sure know where I'm not goin'. I'm not goin' back where I came from. No way!"

We passed a line of backyards. Behind the short fences were donkeys pulling carts of ore and elves pointing to a pond where a bubble released a goldfish's fart. The flowered chairs sat around the table discussing the politics of the backyard. The flamingos stood at attention as a flock of finch birds passed on to the next town. The next yard, one after another, the fences and lawn chairs breezed by in a streak of greens, reds, and ferryboat blues. The houses ended and the front of the train disappeared into the forest. We were at the base of the Wasatch mountain range in northeast Utah. We would pass through Echo, veer northwest through Morgan, and eventually drop into Ogden. The train was slow moving because of the uphill grade and the winding track.

An hour into the hills Jefferson started to pace back and forth. He walked over to my end of the boxcar and sat down and pointed outside.

"See that road there and those pine trees?"

"Been starin' at 'em for weeks now."

"What do you think's behind all of those trees?"

"Just more trees, I guess, a whole forest probably."

He stood up again and got a real concerned look on his face.

"Suppose there's something more behind there."

"Like what?"

"Like something you'd never expect."

I shook my head.

"There's nothing back there but a hundred years' worth of pine trees and behind that more of the same."

He shook his head.

"Nope, there's an Indian village back there with teepees and everything, and I bet they're sitting in those trees, cookin' a wild boar, dancin' in grass skirts—looking at us right now."

I shook my head. He rambled on about his little luau with dark-skinned Indian ladies in grass skirts and a pig roasting above a fire. I thought about Hawaii being behind those trees, but I knew that Jefferson was just sick with his daydreams about the ocean. Jefferson and me did have one thing in common: we both had a destination, maybe it was as vague as an Indian in a grass skirt, but I had to let it be—at least it was a place to dream about. I really wanted to believe that there was something more behind those trees, but something deep down inside wouldn't let me.

Journal Entry # 8: The Train Yard

A train yard can have three tracks, a shack, and a single light post, or it can have hundreds of tracks, tall watchtowers, and enough light for ten football fields.

Trying to find the yard in a town? First look at a map of the town. If you can't afford one, go to a gas station and neatly unfold a new one or ask the cashier if he has one you can look at. The yards can be located by evaluating the town's terrain. If you're in a flat town with no rivers, any bridges on the map will most likely be near the train yard, going over the tracks. If it's a small town, the tracks will follow the main road into town and eventually branch off. The one resource tramps have is time. If all else fails, sit down on a park bench for twenty minutes and listen for a train whistle.

If the town does have hills, the train yard will be probably be in a valley at a lower elevation. In mining towns or farm towns the yard will be near the mine, mill, or grain elevators. In boom

towns like Denver the yard will be downtown. In factory towns
the yard will be near the plant. In river and port towns the yard
will be near the water.

A freight train can only roll legally for twelve hours before
stopping for a fresh crew and fuel. Many of these crew changes
or "divisions" are in small towns where you can hear the leaves
falling and the birds chirping. Others are in the middle of monster yards. Once you learn crew changes you've got it made. If
you see two guys carrying duffel bags climb on a unit, that
means you're at a division. The train they are boarding should
leave relatively soon. If you're new in a yard, ask a railroad
worker where the nearest division is or crew change is.

The question I get the most is, "How do you know where the
train is going?" A map of the rails helps. You can get one of
these at almost any public library. A compass helps. But asking
a brakeman or another tramp is the best thing to do. A brakeman will rarely know when a train is leaving, but he will know
where it's going. Whether he tells you the truth will depend on
his own free will. A trip to Las Vegas can quickly become a trip
to Reno if you get bad information. Brakemen can swing either
way depending on their mood. They will help you good sometimes and other times not at all. The only thing you can depend
on is yourself and your own experience. In time you'll know
which railroad company runs which line and you'll know where
that line goes. You'll know that the Southern Pacific will leave
Ogden, Utah, westbound and eventually arrive in Reno and
that the Union Pacific will leave southbound, stop in Salt Lake,
and eventually arrive in Las Vegas or Grand Junction.

Once you've left a single train yard in all available directions,
you'll know where to hop on the train and you'll know which
direction that train is going just by the landmarks. There will
probably be an old house with a front porch full of split-up

La-Z-Boy recliners and a yard soaked in transmission fluid and stacked high with dog shit. More often there will be a bridge or a nice shade tree or a barbed-wire fence with a field behind it. There's a field like this in Cheyenne, Wyoming, behind Eagle Liquors. There's two trees below the tracks in a little valley. In the late summer and fall the buffalo grass is just high enough to keep your ass out of the spotlight. Union Pacific does a west-bound crew change there.

There are no road signs on the main line or in the train yards. The liquor store, the dog shit, and the lady with no front teeth, holding a bottle of Miller and coughing up chicken carti-lage into her hand—these are your road signs. A train yard is like a tattoo, you get it when you're drunk—even though you're not supposed to. Besides, when that southbound Burlington Northern hits the high 48 and the lady of the land is rolling alongside you—it don't matter where you're going. She'll be all that matters to you—trust me. It's like true love—when you're holding her, the lady of the land, in your arms, you don't care about much else. If you do get on the wrong train, who's watch-ing, anyway? Nobody, really—just the Indians in the trees and the Huck Finn boys with holes in their knees.

Ring Tail: A grouchy individual. No doubt from
the name of some especially vicious or dangerous
animal that happened to have a tail marked with a
ring of different-colored fur—possibly the raccoon.
Also, "ring tail snorter."

10

Ogden, Utah

"Like as the birds that gather in the trees of afternoon, then at nightfall vanish all away, so are the separations of the world."

—ASHVAGHOSA

A few hours passed and the sun dimmed. Jefferson and me were chugging up a hill through the mountains—into the thick evergreens and golden aspen. Jefferson dangled his legs out the boxcar door and scouted the trees for Indians. Thirty feet down the railroad embankment rocks were turning in a river. The tailings from an abandoned gold mine sat in a rusted mound across the water. I felt a warm chinook wind blow through the valley—a kiss of spring. The approaching winter had lost its bite, and that fierce night Alabama and I crossed over the Rocky Mountains two weeks earlier was a distant memory—a lifetime had passed.

I was hungry. We had been in that boxcar for ten hours and covered many miles. But it didn't do much for the pit in my stomach. Jefferson's melon looked like a steak. I'd rather move hungry than sit fat. But after ten hours things can change. And they did.

"You gonna cut that melon or what?" I asked.

"No."

"What do you mean no?"

"I ain't eatin' it till I get to the beach."

I laughed. The way that train was moving, that melon wasn't going to make it to the beach. I pointed west out the door.

"That ocean ain't for another week and by then that melon will be a raisin and no one will get any of it."

I put my hands out. "So hand it over."

"I ain't cuttin' this melon, I already told ya."

"Look, kid." I waved my fist in his face and gave him a real mean look. "If you don't hand it over I'm gonna have to fight you for it."

"You wouldn't hit me over a stupid melon."

I walked a little bit closer until I had him backed into the corner.

"You wanna bet?"

He put the melon down between us and backed away.

"All right, Eddy, I'll eat this melon with you, but not in here, not in the shade. If I can't eat it at the beach, I at least wanna eat it in the sun."

He danced around the melon. There was a little angel sitting atop his head.

"You ain't that cute." I waved my fist again. "Not too cute ta take a good piece outta."

I chased him out of the corner and grabbed the melon. He ran at the door and didn't stop—just flew out of it. He landed on his feet and fell on his stomach and rolled down the embankment and splashed into the river below. I walked to the door and looked up at the sun. The valley radiated with beauty. The river swam around the trees, cooling their roots. There was a light rain feeding the stream. It fell down the valley in the same direction as the train. I grabbed my bedroll and threw it over my shoulder and jumped out. We were on a slow upgrade. I landed on my feet. Jefferson was about twenty feet down, pulling on a branch.

"C'mon, Jeff. Get your butt outta that river, we've got a train to catch. I'm gonna find you that damn beach and those damn Indians and that damn pig, too."

He jumped up and out of the water. He had a few gashes where his jeans had ripped but he was fine. He'd feel better in a few days. He ran up behind me and followed me along the railroad tracks. He trotted along like a long-legged bird, twitching his nose and dipping his head, looking for more adventure to cool his anxious bones.

I had to steal that melon before Jefferson got all possessive of it. Crazy dreams can suspend whole orchards of sweetness. Let that fruit sit on the tree long enough and the sun will dry up every bit of sweetness that was right there in front of you the whole damn time. The truth is you just can't wait for fucking paradise—because sure enough you'll end up just like Jefferson, dreaming about that damn feeling you had as a kid in the backseat of your father's car. The wind in your hair and your eyes all closed up. Someday a kid has to grow up and realize that life isn't that sweet. It's more sour than sweet and that's just the way it goes.

We walked for a few hundred yards until the train picked up speed. I pointed to the top of a grainer.

"Look up there, Jefferson, there's no top on that grainer." I put my hand on his shoulder. "Jump up there and tell me what's in it."

He scuffled up the ladder.

"Hurry up, kid, tell me what's up there."

He got to the top and looked down at me.

"It's full of wood chips and there's a bunch of grain, I dunno, oats or something on top of it, or maybe it's seed, whatever it is it's starting to sprout. It's as green as a spring lawn up here."

It wasn't a grainer, it was an open hopper.

"All right, then, come down and grab this thing."

I raised the melon over my head and he grabbed it and threw it over the top. It made a soft sound when it landed. The train was moving heavy again. When I grabbed for the ladder my bedroll slipped off my shoulder. I tried to save it but it fell and rolled straight down the hill. It stopped about two inches from the river. I shook it off as a loss, grabbed the ladder, and pulled my feet off the ground. The brakes squealed, the train slowed, then picked up speed again. I sat on the porch and caught my breath. A pair of skinny legs came flying off the ladder and over my head. Jefferson busted the ground with his Willy Walter boots and ran back down the embankment. He fell toward the bottom and splashed right back into the river. He stood up and yelled.

"I got it, Eddy, I got it."

He jumped out of that river like a flash of lightning. He shook off his head, grabbed my bedroll, and barreled back up the hill. By the time he reached the tracks the train was wagging its tail in his face. He was in full haul for the back of it—taking long strides—rocks were flying up from his boots. That was the last I saw of him—running with my bedroll in his right hand and desperately waving with his left. When the train turned the corner, I couldn't see past the third car back. There was nothing I could do, that hog up front was highballing and there was no way I could jump off.

I climbed the ladder, peeked over the edge, and sure enough there was a lawn of thick green grass and a watermelon. I sat beside it. My only hope was that he grabbed the last car, but that train was moving too fast and I couldn't see him catching up to it.

I don't want to admit it but I'm going to—I got a tear in the corner of my eye. It sat there for a second, then rolled down my cheek and splashed onto my boot. It sunk into the leather and stayed there for many months. I put my face in my hands and shook my head.

"I don't want no more," I thought. "I can't take no more. No more fault and no more trouble."

I lifted my head from my hands and looked up. The sky was clear. I was thirty minutes closer to Mexico and I had a watermelon for breakfast. I lay down in the grass and fooled myself into thinking things weren't so bad.

Sun Dog

The tree branches stood still and the train parted the forest like a plow. I looked at the top of each one and inside the needles and branches I could see birds singing. I could almost hear them chirping. The train made uphill sounds. A roll of stinky torn blankets came flying over my head and landed on the grass in front of me. It was my bedroll.

"Johnny-come-lately," I thought, and turned around and there he was—the little tramp with a big mouth and smart-ass grin. Jefferson jumped down from the top of the hopper, chomping on a mouthful of sunflower seeds. He had a red spiderweb in each eye and his funny face had a sunshine glow from some acquaintance he had made on the back of the train. He was stoned.

"Ya old sun dog!" I yelled.

He stood in front of me with his arms crossed, high on his chest.

"Hey, kid," he said, "how long you been on the road?"

"'Bout a week."

"You been out here for a week and all you got to show for it is . . ."

"You smart-ass!"

I hopped up and smiled and patted him on the back. We laughed together and sat down and the first thing that sun did was break back through the clouds. The tops of the trees passed and we had a little watermelon picnic on the top of the train.

"I got your roll for you, didn't I? And look at this." He pulled a rolled-up paper bag out of his back pocket.

"A joint," he said.

"A fine row of Acapulco Gold, all rolled up in a paper bag."

"Where the hell did you get that?"

"Look back there, see that fourth container? There's four Mexicans piled down in the grate on that forty-eight, they got a whole bag of grass and that's it, nothing but a big bag of grass and four big smiles."

I put my hands together and made like I was firing a pistol into the trees.

"High as a piñata and a long way from home, ain't no better way to be."

The sun shined. That warm chinook breeze filled our ears, we sat on that seed car with a pile of feathers, a cast-iron sofa, and a lawn built for two that made like a magic carpet and flew across all of America. The beach has sun and surf and enough tranquility to make a simple boy happy. He'll become a simple man and he'll sit beside himself and travel across the land.

The Swimming Hole: Hot Springs

That evening before sunset we passed a hot springs resort. The main lodge was a log structure with a big front porch. Inside was a desk with folded towels stacked on top of it. A lady in a terry cloth robe sat on a wooden bench, reading a magazine. The porch led to a stone staircase that marched up the hill and stopped at three terraces along the way. There were pools of different sizes on each level. In front of the main lodge was a big swimming pool. It looked like a pot of simmering stew. Two inflated alligators and a fat kid with scuba gear on his head flopped around in the water. There was a snack shack with bags of potato chips nailed to the side of it and small metal signs advertising ice cream sandwiches. Two little girls jumped up to the counter with dollar bills in their hands, shivering and laughing. The hot springs were advertised as "A Bit of Tomorrow Today." These words looked down on the roadway that wound through the wooded hills. The tracks met up with the road where the trees split.

I saw an old man grin over the steering wheel of his Cadillac. He was dreaming about the day the rain turned to gin. He had one too many drinks at the casino, it was time to leave—hit the big time—go to Reno and pierce his Social Security check with a gambler's pen.

★

There were sexy teenage girls sliding down slides and mothers fixing sandwiches of orange cheese and rye at the resort. Me and Jefferson jumped up fast and waved. It was the first time in months that I'd seen a girl in a swimsuit. There was one girl with young breasts that pointed like missiles through her wet shirt. I could see the dark rings of her nipples and below that I could see her pubic hairs crawling out of her panties. She bent over like a housewife and everything slid out from the side and I nearly passed out from the sight of her young flesh.

"Ouch!" I yelled.

Jefferson was staring so hard that he stepped all over my feet and nearly fell off the train. I grabbed him and he started breathing again, then walked back to his corner and sat down.

This little lake of paradise must have been a mirage, because the sun went down and the ladies were replaced with fat men in inner tubes. They were fishing for trout in the calm parts of the river.

Even though the beach came and went like a wet dream, I was sure happy it came at all. The day was good, and as for the night, it was rather quiet and deep and after a while very, very cold. I looked up at the stars and dreamed about sitting beside one of those pretty ladies in tiny swimsuits.

There are a lot of places out there where a man can be truly alone. Not alone places where a monk might live or places

someone spiritual might go to get themselves stoned on purpose. No, just places with wide-open sky and wide-open space.
You find yourself looking for a building or a light from someone's house—anything to break up the night. I had a feeling
the train was going to stop soon, so I really didn't want to go
to sleep. I kept my bedroll by my side and my collar up and
stared out into the absolute darkness. Jefferson lay down on the
floor with his knees against his chest and went to sleep.

A Night at the Fair

We got to Ogden, Utah, before sunrise. We ate warm
soup with Vietnam veterans at the Salvation Army. The church
volunteers gave us each a loaf of bread and a plastic garbage
bag full of scones before we left. I carried that bag around for
a week. I didn't go to the bathroom once—the damn things
clogged me up. We hoisted the scones over our shoulders and
walked back to the railroad tracks. We veered west behind the
Union Pacific building and found a spot to wait under a
viaduct. We cleared away the needles and diapers and sat
down.

There were two tramps huddled around a fifty-gallon barrel—burning bales of hay from the donkey corral. There was
a carnival going on. The fancy rides spun like Chinese lanterns
on the Fourth of July. The donkeys carried children and the
Ferris wheel carried young lovers. There was a pimp pushing
cotton candy and a fat kid popping balloons. He cried when
his prize was too small, and Mom didn't like that. She slapped
him silly. The two tramps got a kick out of it and laughed at
the poor kid. To celebrate they ripped off another bale of hay
and a wooden Indian too. He burned rather well. He kept us
warm for a couple of hours.

Jefferson patted me on the back and smiled.

"I like you, Eddy."

"You're not so bad yourself, Jefferson."

"Thank you," he said.

We sat by the barrel and I tried to make up for what I did to him over his watermelon. I told him what I knew about growing up. The happy days and the hard ones and of course the sad ones.

Jefferson and me had both grown up too fast and fallen down too young, but luckily we found buddies, like each other, out there on the bum, who could show us how to get back up again. Alabama taught me a few things about getting along, and in my own dumb way I tried to do the same for Jefferson. We gave each other shit, we drank together, we looked at naked women, and we traveled together. If that isn't bonding like a dumb kid American, then I don't know what is.

I respected the little shit just because he was an optimist and I can tell you right now that optimism is a young man's game. I stayed optimistic a little longer because I met Jefferson, and maybe I will be my entire life.

Salt Flats

Two hours before sunrise we got on the wrong train. What I thought was southbound Union Pacific ended up being a westbound Southern Pacific. Instead of heading into Salt Lake City we were crossing the Great Salt Lake on our way to Nevada.

At sunrise we were in the middle of hot salt flats. The power lines dipped into the Sahara skyline. I felt like a camel—like I'd seen nothing but sand and wind for a week. A far-off hill brought the landscape into perspective. It was an island in a white sea. Jefferson put his palm tree together and put it in front of his face.

"Looks like paradise to me," he said.

"For a shipwrecked sailor, maybe."

"I like wide-open space," he said.

"Yeah? Well, I like cold beer and kind women."

The sun set and it was pitch-dark. The first light of the night cascaded from an electric fountain. A highway casino town. A gambler's paradise in the middle of the Nevada desert. That meant the interstate was close by, and along with that a good flow of people. I wanted a cup of coffee from a restaurant, a paper place mat, and the smell of air conditioning. I'd been riding freight for two weeks, I was tired, and I was going the wrong direction; I needed to get off the train.

Jefferson was shivering in his sleep and mumbling about his dreams. I untied my blankets, shook them out, and covered him up. I grabbed my little broom out of my back pocket and set it down beside him, threw my Chihuahua hat on my head, stuffed Yukon's seashells into my jacket pocket, and jumped off the train. I rolled down the hill and landed in a ditch. I looked over the weeds and saw the town of Winnemucca, Nevada. A twenty-four-hour paradise. It gave my life new opportunity. It was the beginning of a vicious love affair.

Thoughts on Jefferson

Jefferson ended up being more than a sidekick. He was a reflection of myself. Traveling with him was a huge lesson in self-identity. He wanted to ride. He didn't care where he was going as long as he could prove something to himself by getting there. He is the pride of all stories. A boy with frontier.

Through him I understood the purpose of my own travels. Palm trees, cheap beer, and bronze señoritas had nothing
to do with it. I needed to know that I could build my own fires,
ride my own trains, and focus my entire life on one Mexican
dream. At that point I realized I was young enough to still be
an optimist, and I had learned the skills of the back roads. I felt
complete. I'd almost say I felt like an adult.

Some folks believe that a man has to have a home, a
career, and a debt to have an identity. I had found my identity
the hard way. There was no railroad saint to pat me on the back
when I received my hobo crown. I had to congratulate myself.
You just learn to do that out there.

I needed to see how other folks were living before I came
to any drastic conclusions about my own life. Alabama,
Jefferson, the Old Fart, Pork Pie, Bobby Blue, all had their
own private pitch and business. And none of them were much
like the other. I don't know if it was true or not, but I was
thinking that maybe all that tramping was showing me how to
be a better person. If I would have stayed home I might not
have grown up at all. I figured that after five years of riding
trains I would have a new and brighter personality and by the
time I was dead I would have enough charm and grit to get a
gig in Las Vegas. Hell, Frank Sinatra, Sammy Davis Jr.,
Dean Martin, Peter Lawford, and Joey Bishop became the
"Rat Pack" and none of them even graduated from high
school. Shit, Dean Martin used to run moonshine. If
Thunder Road made him, Thunder Road can make me. The
only identity I had was the one I made up, and to me it was
the only one worth having.

Journal Entry # 9: Hump Yards and Smokestacks

A hump yard is built on a hill. A single track will start at the top of the hill and at the bottom, in the bowl, it will separate into a rake of two or more tracks. A yard dog (a locomotive that is only used in the train yard) will push boxcars up one side of the hill and at the top release them down the other side onto one of the lower tracks. This is called building a train. The boxcars pick up good speed and slam into the train below. If you happen to be sleeping in one of these boxcars, what you'll experience is called misfortune. The momentum has been known to throw a tramp the length of a boxcar and back again. It's a shocker. A real bone shaker. I believe that some people need it. I believe that some people never see it coming. You can prepare yourself for this by sleeping with your feet facing the front end of the train—if possible. This is an all-around good idea for any ride. Trains derail and if they do, this is one thing that might save your neck.

Wherever there are trains and mountains there are tunnels. I left Denver on a Rio Grande westbound one afternoon in the middle of winter. It's a slow train that crawls over the Rocky Mountains—through many small towns and many tunnels. I didn't think much of it—maybe I was too thrilled with the pretty snowflakes and the winter evergreen. The first ten tunnels were short. It got dark for a few minutes and eventually got light again. When I rolled into the next one I was expecting the same, but this time it got dark and stayed dark. I was in the Moffat— a six-mile uphill tunnel. After five minutes I was having trouble breathing. The tunnel was filling up with diesel exhaust. I wet down my bandanna and tied it around my mouth. After ten minutes I thought about trouble and how it sneaks up on me.

After fifteen minutes I thought about fresh air. And how nice it is when I have it and how dumb I feel when I don't—and where does that leave me? In the dust, that's where . . . in a goddamn hole.

My problem is that I don't always see those tunnels coming. They sneak up on me and I might have it good—green green evergreens—a nice wind in my eyes and the next thing I know it's gone, nothing left but regret. So I make a bad decision without even knowing I made a decision at all.

Five minutes later the walls of the tunnel had shape again because the daylight from the other end was touching them. I could breathe again and there I had all the value in life that could ever be weighed in silver and gold. It was there in the evergreens, but this time they were greener and taller and the air was sweeter and the wind warmer. The Moffat was behind me and I was thankful to be alive. Old train riders tell me I had nothing to worry about, but after that experience I would have to disagree.

There are three notable tunnels in North America: In Washington there's Burlington Northern's Cascade tunnel, which is nearly eight miles long and is located ninety-two miles east of Seattle and fifty miles west of Wenatchee. In Montana there's Burlington Northern's Libby Dam tunnel, which is eight miles long and is located west of Whitefish and fifty-odd miles east of Libby. And the Rio Grande's Moffat, the tunnel I just mentioned, is in Colorado, about sixty miles west of Denver.

Many railroads issue gas masks to engineers who work these routes. In the days of steam many hobos died of asphyxiation in these tunnels. Back then Southern Pacific had cab-forward locomotives built especially for these routes—with the smokestacks located behind the crew. Nowadays these tunnels are ventilated.

The railroads have drilled shafts into the tops and sides and equipped them with large ventilation fans. This helps a bit, but no matter what, tramps still choke down plenty of diesel. This is another reason it's good to ride the tail end. By the time the exhaust gets to the back it will have dissipated enough to make the ride tolerable.

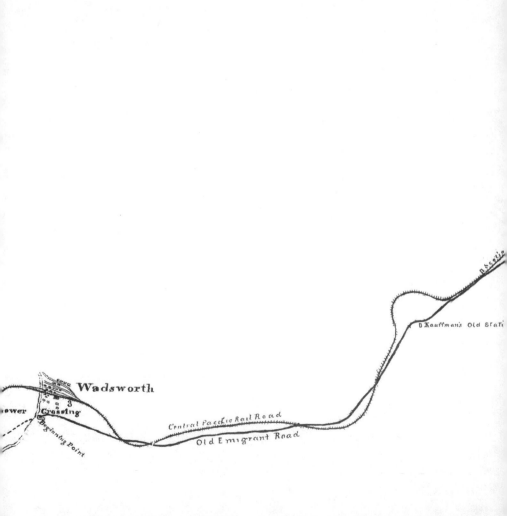

Old Overland Station

China Camp

Central Pacific Rail Road

Grant Road

DESERT

Part Two

Starlet Las Vegas:
The Desert Diva

"Portland Oregon to the Mexican line
Boy let me tell you the women are fine
If you don't hang around there very long
They'll never ever know you're gone."

—J. J. CALE

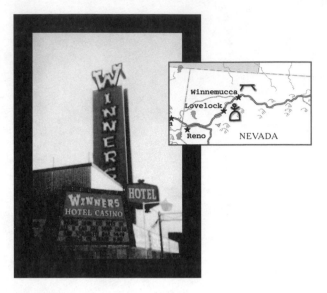

Starlet: A young actress publicized as a future star.

Barrel Stiff: An old, worn-out bum, living in a barrel house, eating whatever may be salvaged from garbage cans or cheap lunchrooms, and absolutely without hope or ambition.

Starlet + Barrel Stiff = "a union born of gasoline and good nature."

Biscuit Shooter: A waitress or short-order cook. The average tramp and migratory worker is not used to restaurants where the food or service is of the best, and the manner in which the dishes are "shot" at the diner is reflected in the term for the person responsible.

Low

Truckee River

11

Winnemucca, Nevada

NOVEMBER 9, 1991—MORNING TWILIGHT

inside the Winner's Casino: Winnemucca, Nevada

Winnemucca is the town after Salt Lake,
Halfway to Reno
And a quarter way down the nearest slot.

The best thing about Nevada is the availability of a neon light in the middle of nowhere. That light signals a twenty-four-hour cup of coffee in a place where everyone is awake. Everyone except the tourists who thought they might stay up till sunrise—but instead passed out around three A.M. The tourists couldn't keep up with the yodeler who screamed "BINGO" at the top of his lungs. He won another stuffed poodle for his wife. She was excited about the first one but the fifth one had lost its charm.

The old security guard stood behind my booth, in that twenty-four-hour coffee shop, monitoring the morning donuts. His pistol was unsnapped and lying in its holster like a sleepy banana. It was a joke. The whole place was a cruel joke.

Then there was the janitor who jingled his keys loud— like sleep was plugged into the sunrise and not the sunset. Those damn hypocrites thought I was looking under the table for change. I wasn't, I was looking to take a nap. The cool vinyl felt good against my cheek.

The night before, Winnemucca had sparkled in the dark like an electric palm tree. My bones were shaking from a wobbly boxcar on a bad road and I was thirsty for a cup of coffee. For the first time in my life I was craving coffee. I remembered the pretty waitress at that first truck stop in Wyoming. She had the cutest mole above her lip and when she talked she cocked her hip and touched her pen to her lip.

"You better get used to it," she had said.

"These men hold that cup of joe more than they hold their wives."

She was right. A good coffee mug has curves and warmth and is a fine place to insert sexual anxiety. Put the nickel down beside her and the spoon in her mouth and she'll lubricate your loneliness. If you're lucky you'll get feisty, overprotective, and jealous and juiced on coffee and tear the restaurant down one waitress at a time. The prettiest one will love you, burn her apron, quit her job, and lie across a Sealy Posturepedic like a Mayan goddess.

My feet were back on solid ground—a paisley carpet with pyramids dedicated to financial distress and stained with the blue plate special that went over so well three years back.

I didn't care. In fact, I was in love with Winnemucca the moment I fell off the train. It had a certain smell, like a closet that hasn't been opened for thirty years. Or maybe the smell was from all the slop that had fallen under the table, or maybe it was me. Whatever it was, it was comforting.

I got a good nap in before the waitress came.

"C'mon, kid, get up."

She poked me with her pencil, then turned the page on her order pad. I rumbled through my pockets and came out with a buck and some change.

"What'll that get me?"

"A shower at the RV park and a cup of coffee."

She sure was cute when she said that. I could tell she *really* cared.

"A shower, huh? How about a shave, will that get me a shave, too?"

She pushed the butter knife off my napkin.

"Here, use that and when you're done get a job and come back for a real meal."

She quickly flipped her pad over and walked away. She left me with a nice cloud of Lilac Bermuda or Caribbean Bile—some kind of cheap perfume. An announcement came on over the elevator music.

"They say laughter is the best medicine. We deliver our dose every Wednesday evening at seven o'clock. Come fill your prescription in the Winner's Lounge."

I bet if I'd had on a nice pair of Bermuda shorts and an American flag on my cap I'd have gotten some respect. I pounded my fist on the table and stood up.

"Damn it, I want some respect."

No one heard me, so I climbed back into my seat. I didn't care, just because no one else did, and the truth is that in

Nevada respect is a tired old dog, long past the years of justice and equality. He's more sunk into the porch swing of honesty and sobriety. His wild years are over. I knew if I was rich I might get better service, but bad service is better than no service and at least this way I wouldn't have to leave a tip.

Plastic Sunset

I stayed at the booth and watched Greyhound drivers order French fries and construction workers eat bacon and biscuits. The construction workers out there in Nevada are mobile men who follow storms all over the country—hoping to rebuild what storms destroy—natural disasters such as tornadoes, hurricanes, and earthquakes, or in this case the fact that someone's uncle decided to build a drive-through chapel in "America's New Love Capital." Yes, Winnemucca, Nevada. A place where you can have a honeymoon buffet with a nail punch from LA and a gutter punk from New Orleans.

The waitress got a little case off the "feelgoods" and brought me a cup of coffee anyway. It was too hot to drink. So I grabbed my Chihuahua hat off the table, put it on, stood up, and walked out of the diner, through the casino, and into the streets. The sun's light left the moon's surface and shined onto my smiling face. There was a fine layer of film over the landscape. With the purple tundra and the banana-toting cowboy security guards, I felt like I was on the set of a spaghetti Western.

Something about the state of Nevada feels foreign, I thought, or maybe lost, or better yet it feels hollow and on top of that it has a sense of resilience.

If a fiberglass horse stays still long enough it'll grow old, and the people that try to ride it will eventually realize that it isn't going anywhere—yeah, I'd say that's how Nevada feels. It's a mighty fine place to push your head underwater and just float until you turn blue, then go buy yourself a Toyota and a small home and plant yourself a yard and build a picnic bench and pretend that everything is all right. If you decide to have children, make sure their birth certificate doesn't say Nevada, 'cause if it does those kids are bound to cheat on their mates, stay up all night yelling at the television set, drink coffee at sunset, put on a polyester matador costume, slap the kids, and go off to work at the casino. That's Nevada pride and it runs deeper than the folks who possess it.

I love Nevada. I might say it a million times while I'm there, "I'm hankering to get out of this state." But I'd just be lying to myself. I can feel that state inside my bones. I can feel the neon enter my veins and the plastic sunset lift my spirits. In front of that casino I realized that the only thing more revitalizing than a Nevada sunset is a Nevada sunrise. It's candy for the soul.

★

I got to fumbling through my pockets and spilling pennies, bag ties, and seashells on the sidewalk. I hadn't cleaned my pockets out in weeks, and since there was a trash can there, I decided it was a good place to do it. I still had a few seashells from Yukon Sam in Missoula and flat pennies from Wyoming and a bunch of crumpled-up notes with chicken scratch all the way to the edge of the paper. I had forgotten about Alabama giving me those notes. They were mostly tidbits on odd towns and train yards in the western states or as Alabama would say, "the western frontier." He wouldn't say it like he was talking about the weather. He'd stand up and scream it out loud and long, "theeeeee weeeeestern frontieeeeeer." He thought there were still places where people hadn't been yet.

I unrolled one of the notes and this is what it said.

PORTOLLA, CA. A good switch yard. A crew change many time a day, going in both directions. A nice river to bathe in and a potato shack diner called Good and Plenty two blocks from the train yard (open 24 hrs.) order the Swiss King Sandwich and eat half there then take half with you for breakfast but make sure you take off the bacon before you eat it cold or you'll be swearin' your way over the Sierras. There's a pub there and they usually leave the back door open so you can lean back from your barstool and see the yard. The locals all think they're pool sharks but that's because they haven't left town for thirty years, be patient and play along. The UP crew is very hospitable and they'll always point you in the right direction. It's a good place to get off and clean up. If you walk west up the tracks a few 3 or 4 miles there is a nice mountain stream (the same one as in town) and a good swimming hole. A good summer fling.

SALT LAKE CITY, UTAH. A shit hole. Infested with half-minded homeless people and old tramps that got lazy. The food sucks. This town has a serious spirit problem and should be avoided at all costs. The best way to get west from there is to get on a public bus up to Ogden. It costs about $.75 and takes about 45 minutes. There you go behind the Amtrak station and veer west. There's a Southern Pacific crew change there and it'll get you to Reno with one crew change along the way. In Reno there's a swimming pool that's painted black and looks like a swamp. There should still be catfish in that pool, can usually catch one if you're patient enough but don't go before dark. You can also catch west out of Salt Lake on the Union Pacific. Out behind the big Union Pacific railroad building there is a curve in the tracks that heads out toward three or four tall smokestacks. You

can catch a piggyback out of there but at that point you could either be on your way to Las Vegas or Reno. I still haven't figured this one out. Vegas is booming and clean. Reno is also trying but better equipped for a dirty fella like yourself.

♠

T-top

I'd need those notes, so I stuffed them back in my pocket and walked into the casino. My booth and my cup of coffee were still there, so I sat down, drank the whole thing, and waited for a refill. The construction workers prepared themselves for a hot day. The waitress powdered her face with another two-dollar tab, unhappy but looking forward to the tanned leather seats in her '85 Tornado—a good break for her feet—a damn good deal for twenty-five hundred dollars. The T-tops made her drive home special.

The wind came in the door and floated through her hair.

I thought how nice it would be to reach up her blouse. Her nipples were hard and her tits had the tough texture of her Sears Roebuck brassiere. Her bra was just loose enough to slide off with one hand and her breasts were just sweaty enough to slide nicely across my chest. I like the feeling of greasy breasts and a workday crotch. She was probably blessed with both and if I'd had my way, she'd have been nicely bent over that table.

I'd have been lucky to get a refill, let alone a ride in her new car.

This waitress had too many flying saucers, over-easy eggs, and half-empty ketchup bottles behind her eyes, far too many memories of fellas like me trying to convince themselves they might have something to offer such a fine lady.

I closed my eyes and lay down in the booth. I was a little overexcited. Just the shape of her cheap bra and the daydream of what was under it made me want to monkey around the place like a chimpanzee. It was those machines that did it to me— those trains. All I'd seen for weeks was backyards and broke-down cars. When a tramp gets off the main line he's damn twisted in the head. Sitting in that booth, I was experiencing a special and rather vicious *exhilaration.* The ground isn't moving, the brakes on the boxcar aren't screaming, and worst of all the waitress at the casino is boiling hot in a devil-short miniskirt. I figured out what it was, it was "sexual anxiety" and it made me sick to my stomach. I was losing control—*rapidly.* "Well, what can I do?" I thought. "It's really pretty simple." I calculated it in my head. "Stay clean, get married, stay home, breed, go to the movies, have a barbecue, get up, go to work, come home, watch TV. I could do that! Yeah, I could really do that!" I jumped back out of my booth and threw my arms in the air. My boots shook the floor and everyone in the diner looked at me.

"I'm gonna do it!" I yelled.

"I'm gonna find love for *every* one of you. And we'll start right here in this casino." I slammed my fist on the table and raised my voice. "We'll all just stay *right here!*—at the Desert Oasis—and be one big happy normal family."

The construction workers wanted to kick my ass. Luckily the security guard was feeling macho and talked them down. The tourists spilled coffee and scrambled back to the slot machines. A kid with a bib pointed at me, laughed, and made gurgling noises. I smiled at him and crawled back into my booth.

The two gutter punks at the booth behind me got all excited and cheered me on. To the point of throwing pancakes across the room. The construction workers took to that like dogs in heat, throwing their hard hats down on the table and pouncing over to the gutter punks' booth. One gutter punk stood up, grabbed a curtain rod, and went into a fake ninja routine. The other punk grabbed a loaf of display bread from the salad bar and swung it around his head. The security guard stood between them. The gutter punks didn't stand a chance. But it didn't matter because they didn't intend to fight. They were just having a little fun. I'd say the redneck construction workers would have won out of pure muscle, but the gutter punks, by making good use of their environment, would have gotten the last laugh. They went back and forth over the security guard. His banana wasn't loaded. I watched about five minutes of it, got bored, and walked back into the casino.

Piña Colada

I sat down at the poker bar. I dumped my coat pockets on the bar. I had a nice pile of rocks. I had been stuffing my coat pockets since Green River and I had quite a collection of fossils from a million years back. In my twisted little mind they were worth millions of dollars. The bartender didn't understand this, to him they were just a bunch of rocks. I asked him for a beer but he wouldn't budge.

"You have enough to pay?"

"What do you mean do I have enough?" I pointed to the fossils. "What do you think these are?"

He shrugged his shoulders.

"Rocks?"

I couldn't believe him. I shook my head and laughed.

"Come on! These here are the teeth of a saber-toothed tiger, some kind of museum pieces are what these are and all I want for them is a cold beer."

He shook his head and got angry. He looked at the other security guard out of the corner of his eye. I wasn't worried about that, no, I was more worried about the state of Nevada. I had a feeling deep down in my bones that the whole state was going to dry up, just like that, just like a raisin, and I had to get a draw before that happened.

"Look," I said, "this whole state is about to change and I'm not talking about the weather or the government. I'm talking about . . ."

He didn't want to hear it. He turned and walked away. I leaned back over the bar and yelled.

"Come on!"

I reached into my pocket and pulled out the wrinkled notes.

"These, here, take these. I'll give you a good bit of advice. I got a whole mess of good advice in these pockets. I got advice from men who've seen more of this world than you ever will. Shit! I got a damn encyclopedia in these pockets."

Then I pointed to my head and whispered to myself.

"Hell! That don't even compare to what I got up here."

I knew he could hear, but it didn't matter, he was fed up and I was pissed off. It took him five minutes to start back my way. He was even more nervous this time. He stopped, looked back, took another step, and repeated the ritual. It took him three minutes to make the length of the bar.

"Look," he said, "I got a tab on this bar for a hundred bums just like you. They come in here off those trains and tell me the exact same thing you do and they grovel for the same glass of Budweiser and you know what I tell them?"

He paused and looked around the room.

"A head full of advice ain't worth a thing unless you got someone to buy it. So make yourself comfortable but don't stay too long."

"How about money, then, what if these pockets were filled with money?"

"Then you'd have a nice meal and a hot shower and after all that you'd probably get yourself a Budweiser, wouldn't you?"

"Yeah, maybe I would, but after that Budweiser"—I pointed outside—"I'd still end up back out there. I might be fat, clean, and drunk but I'd still be right back where I started."

"So what," he said. "You got yourself in that situation. I don't know why you'd be worried about putting yourself back."

"I'm not worried about it!" I said.

I crossed my arms on the bar and put my head down.

"Tired's more the word."

He grabbed a cold glass from the cooler and held it up.

"See that, I bet you don't see these out in that desert."

I looked up.

"What. A glass?"

"Not just any glass, a *cold* glass. The ones we use for a piña coladas."

He put it down on the bar.

"Where you headed, kid?"

"Mexico."

"Going on a vacation?"

"Vacation? No, just going 'cause it's warm."

I reached into my back pocket.

"And 'cause of this."

I put the postcard down on the bar and slid it over to him.

"Supposed to be prettier than that postcard."

He looked at it.

"It is prettier than that and I'll tell you something else." He leaned over the bar and whispered. "It's just like the 1950s down there. I've been there. They paint the trunks of their palm trees white and they have resorts with bamboo bars and bartenders with pencil-thin mustaches, and all the buildings, they're painted bright colors. When you go to church down there the preacher plays red conga drums and the ladies wear pink taffeta dresses. On weekdays those Mexicans just go to the carnival, or if they feel like it they'll take a siesta and just do absolutely nothing at all."

"Nothing, really, and it's okay, they ain't gonna think you're lazy or tell you to move on?" I asked.

"It's different down there, kid. A lot more fellas like you, in fact, they have whole beaches set aside for you traveling types."

"Traveling types? What are you talkin' about? I ain't done a day of traveling in my life. I might be gettin' around but I sure ain't 'traveling.'"

"Yeah, well, if you ain't traveling, then you're full of shit. You had to travel to get here just like I had to travel to get to work last night."

"Traveling sounds romantic, you know? It almost sounds fun and ever since I left home it's been nothing but hard work. I'd like to travel, though. Yeah, that would be nice."

I leaned back in my seat and closed my eyes. "Yeah, I'd like to go on one of those vacations, with a hotel room and one of those bamboo bars and one of those piña coladas and you know what? Bet you if I cleaned up and got myself a new pair of shoes I could even find myself a lady."

He shrugged his shoulders and said, "You bet you could!"

Then he turned a bottle of booze into the blender and whipped it up.

"The thing about Mexico is you don't need much to get by down there, but just because it's an easy place to vacation doesn't mean you should take it for granted. Before you can really enjoy anything, you have to learn to appreciate it, and if you get yourself into the right part of Mexico, you can have that vacation and you can get that respect and you won't need much money to do it. You'll only need a few bucks to contribute, and don't look at it like you're buying something, look at it like you're helping out, and if you help people out they'll help you, even if it's just by letting you have a cheap and peaceful place to stay for a few months."

The blender stopped and he poured the drink into a glass, stabbed a cherry and a lime with an umbrella, and stuck it in the top. It sure looked tasty. He slid it over to me and told me to have a good day and walked away. I hadn't had a drink like that in my entire life. It was fresh and cold and when I took a sip it felt like paradise had crawled down my throat.

Misty . . .

Ten minutes later a lady with curly blond hair put her hand down on the bar and split her fingers in two.

"Two packs of Misty Ultra Light One Hundreds and a book of matches."

She was wearing a jazzercise headband and her eyelashes were caked in butter. There wasn't a thing about her that looked real. I looked up from the bar and smiled, and she blinked and snapped her gum and rubbed her bronze arm up against me. When she retrieved the matches, she ran her ass over my leg. She was firm and Coppertone.

"So where you goin'?" she asked.

"What makes you think I'm going anywhere?"

"Well honey, if I were to be honest, I'd say you've already been there."

"Damn right I have, why did you ask, anyway?"

"I'm goin' to Reno." She shrugged her shoulders and turned toward the door. "I don't know, thought you might need a lift or somethin'."

She grabbed her change from the counter and split. I turned my bar stool past a crowd of onlookers and yelled right when she got to the door.

"How about Vegas?"

She looked back and shook her head. Her hair blocked out the herd of buffalo that were painted across the glass doors.

"I'm goin' to Reno, kid, I'll treat you that far but I'm not goin' to Vegas."

I turned back around to the bartender, who was shifting his eyebrows in her direction.

"Come on, kid, you don't get an offer like that every day."

The doors closed behind her. The breeze came in with the scent of twilight bubble gum. The waitress across the way was still sweating from the hot grill. I figured that if I closed my eyes again I could find the temptation to go to Reno, and if the day turned into night and I was all alone again I'd regret it. So I threw my last two fossils on the bar, ran my hair back in the mirror, and made for the field of buffaloes.

★

I've seen a man disfigure a rabbit, tear it apart bone by bone. He was making a stew. He filled a big pot with cabbage and carrots that grew on the side of the road—in someone's garden. He was a very old man and the road was a story he told when his shoes were too tight. A storyteller talks when he has nothing to say. A storyteller talks just to relieve himself of the day. I've learned this a few times in the last three weeks since I left home. I've learned to disguise my intentions with the opposite desires, simply because it's safer that way. I might walk away from camp in a southerly direction, but that doesn't mean I'm on my way south. It only means I don't want anyone to know where I'm going. The longer a boy keeps his secrets, the longer he stays alone, and I had secrets, pocketsful, but they weren't worth a thing unless I had someone to share them with. Everyone in that casino knew where I was going and I walked out with pride, too. I could shake up a whole establishment if I wanted and leave with a fine woman to boot. That day in the Winner's Casino I had the makings of a role-model man, a hero this country has long been without. I was on my way to Reno.

Journal Entry # 10: The Hobo Holiday

A hobo holiday is when a tramp leaves the train yard and attempts to make good with the outside world. This is an accident waiting to happen, but most tramps still try it at least once a year. Every tramp has his own reason for an encounter with the big straight world. He might try to go see his family or his kids. He might need to go back to his hometown and pick up a social security or a veteran's check. But most of the time there is no reason other than loneliness.

If you're riding a freight train and you see a unit pulled off the main line—sitting on the secondary—it's lying dead. This unit is waiting for a signal. The railroads run those diesels 365 days a year and as far as I know, the only time they go down is for repair. The hobo holiday is similar. When a train rider is in disrepair he'll get off the train and search for a nice place to lie dead. A place where he can wait for his ailment to mend. He might venture into a mountain valley—chop some wood, build a fire—make a nice camp and take trips to town every few days for supplies. This way he can live tension-free for many months.

The train rider might have greased the tracks in a dream— seen something in his sleep that warned him. Some dreams are visitations and any kind of visitation is best taken seriously. I've had many visitations and they've all changed the direction of my travels. I had my first one back at the Stockton yard, in California. I dreamt that I was rolled up in my sleeping bag real tight and I couldn't get out. I lay there in the dark and on the black sheet of my eyes I saw three white figures creep toward me. I tried with all my strength to get out my bag but it didn't work. I was tied in there. These three ghosts took to all sides of me with metal pipes and their blows had no direction. I didn't know when the next one was coming. The pipes came down like thunder and my poor body broke under the power of each one. I woke up and immediately got the fuck out of Stockton. The next day I was in a soup line at a Salvation Army and an Indian woman next to me started up a conversation. The subject matter was getting rolled— getting tied up in your bedroll and whipped up with pipes, ax handles, and muck sticks. She said a few men in those parts had been badly beaten in the last couple of days and to keep clear of the Stockton yards. She looked me in the face as clear as sunshine and said, "If you want to keep your face straight and pretty like it is now, you better stay out of those yards."

The combination of my dream and her advice sent me high-tailin' in the opposite direction. I took a good holiday. Got some brick work in Denver and lay low for many months.

The most common reason for a hobo holiday is the need to "lu lu over the ladies." You get tired of your big adventurous life on the road—you're cold, you're hungry, your ears are ringing,

mud is coming up through the hole in your boot, your fingernails are three inches long, and at the bottom of your pants
pocket sits a dollar and some Canadian change. And you ask:
"Where the hell's my frolic—my gin and my hash?"

And the most obvious answer is hidden in the neon lights of
Pleasantville—Hog Heaven—Easy Street—or in my case
Winnemucca, Nevada. Eating, laughing, and sleeping are all
best done in the company of a beautiful woman. You know your
life is honey when you get a kiss first thing—before you put
your hand on a single tool—a lady touches your face with her
soft lips. A lady can confirm dreams. She can share sunsets.
She can keep you warm. If there is anything more powerful than
love, then I am an ignorant man. I can look down a road for
miles and not see a single car or even a cactus on the side of the
road—nothing but sagebrush and power lines. I can walk two
hundred yards down that same road and a woman will appear.
She'll slam her cigarettes down on the bar. She'll take her shirt
off in the car. She'll cry when she is happy and roll up into a
ball at the bottom of the bed when she's sad. It's no coincidence
that I jumped off that train in Winnemucca—didn't see another
train yard for two weeks.

Ponce: A young man, but generally not a pimp, maintained by a woman of means as a lover or because his presence seems to rejuvenate his benefactress.

Bale of Straw: A blond woman. Very generally used in old circus and carnival circles, and obvious as to origin, the more so since the large and sturdy type of woman is the one that makes the greatest appeal to the men who follow the show and demand their play, to match their work, in large doses. A seemingly rude term.

Leprechaun: An elf or *small* mischievous fairy of Irish folklore.

12
Winnemucca, Lovelock, Reno

NOVEMBER 9, 1991—MIDDAY

When I walked out of the Winner's Casino I thought
about buying a hat. I wanted it to say **LAS VEGAS** in big gold
letters. And I would get that hat, too.

Misty's G-string separated her crotch like a plum. There
was something wrong with the windshield wiper on her car and
she was bent over the hood, shaking it. Her miniskirt was up
around her waist. Hot chocolate thighs. She drove a gold 1979
Trans Am—like the one Burt Reynolds drove in that movie
Smoky and the Bandit. The sky was clear in Winnemucca and
there were old men sitting on a porch across the street. The top
of their house had been rented out to a billboard company and
the sign had a roll of toilet paper sitting on the beach with four

beautiful bikini women. The toilet paper looked sunburned but content. It made me want to go to California.

These old men thought about the young plum on the Trans Am and licked their lips. We climbed in the car and gravel exploded out of the tires. The old men waved and we waved back. The T-tops blew her hair over the gold paint. The stereo crackled a midday sermon and like a pair of fireflies we burned hard into the night.

Highway Finger

Misty kept the T-tops off for most of the drive. Every few minutes she bent her neck and spit into the air. Her spit was the color of bubble gum. It splattered on the windshield behind us. The old couples had more windshield than anyone else, so they got hit the hardest. They pulled up beside us and shouted obscenities out the window of their recreational vehicle. Misty liked it. She'd smile and flip them off, and if it was an old man she'd put my hand on the steering wheel and lift up her shirt. Her breasts were Coppertone and hard as rocks. Her breasts shot down the guy's spine and straight out the zipper of his Rustler jeans. I was lucky because the closer we got to Reno, the closer I got to her. I watched those miles go.

We stopped at a Texaco in Lovelock, Nevada, and I pumped the gas. There was a small television in the gas pump that played advertisements. In the reflection I saw Misty walk into the bathroom with something in her hand. I topped off the tank, put the cap on, and followed her through the door. She was sitting on the toilet seat with her zipper undone. It smelled like piss and chlorine. My hands smelled like fuel. She had a diet vanilla cream soda in her left hand and her right hand down her panties. The ash from her cigarette dangled off the window sill. It broke off and fell onto her stockings. They melted like butter and she didn't care.

She slammed the soda on the floor, grabbed the cigarette, and smashed it in the sink. She stood up and took her shirt off. Her breasts stood like they do in Cairo and like they do in Las Vegas. She kneeled down in front of me, unbuckled my belt, pulled down my underwear and pushed her tits into my crotch. The bathroom smell turned into bubble gum. The mirror moved, the walls moved. I held her breasts in my hands until they got hard as porcelain and that was enough for her. She jammed her hand back in her panties—moving fast—she fell back onto the toilet and closed her eyes. Her legs spread across the seat like chocolate pudding and her crotch wet, pink, and trembling under her finger. Sunlight shot out of her eyes—she let out a moan and in the dim Nevada sunlight she rolled off the toilet seat, passed out.

I stood there with my pants around my ankles and hot-pink lipstick all over me. Blessed be. Could have blown the top off that Texaco. I picked her up and put her shirt back on. I threw her arm around my shoulder and brought her back to the car. I drove into the desert. Her hair blew in the wind. She came to a hundred miles later, in Sparks.

Reno Town

We got to Reno at sunset. There was a special smell in the air—the stench of a million dying flowers. We sat at a stop-light under a big Sundowner casino sign and watched parade floats drive by. Snow White was draped over her throne like a sack of potatoes and the seven dwarfs were sleeping. That bum in Green River had mentioned Thanksgiving so I figured it was a turkey-day parade. Misty put her chin on the door, looked up at the Sundowner sign, and started to cry. I put my hand on her shoulder.

"Maybe they'll have the parade again tomorrow," I said. She nodded. "Maybe."

We drove around the corner to a street that had a lot of motels.

"Where do you want to stay," I asked.

"The Horseshoe, I like it there."

Her eyes lit up when we drove into the courtyard. The clouds fell away, her breasts perked up, and her high heels clicked. She walked into the office and slapped two twenties on the counter. The little freckled kid wouldn't take the money.

"That's not enough," he said.

"What do you mean, the sign says thirty-six bucks."

"That's our weekday rate and today's Sunday."

She reached into her cleavage, pulled out another twenty, spit on it, and slapped it on the counter.

"Hey, Dad!"

The kid yelled into the back room and a big fat man pulled himself out of his recliner. He put his belly on the counter and snorted. A sweet breeze passed through Misty's hair over the counter and into the TV parlor. Everything stopped. The freckled shit got happy and the fat man got happy too and they just sat there with bulges in their pants and a rotating rack of Reno postcards. Imagine all those girls in swimsuits spinning on a rack. Some of them sat by the pool. Some of them straddled camels. Some of them all you could see was their ass, nothing but a big ass jumping off the Reno skyline.

Misty turned around with her hands on her hips and looked at me. The freckled kid and the fat man dropped their heads and got a load of her ass. Rivers of drool spilled out of them. I grabbed her by the arm and pulled her out of the lobby and into the street. The sun was down. A herd of jet-setters strolled by like kings without kingdoms and rolled their eyes. I knew all they had to back it up was a split-level ranch, a putt-putt lawn, and a fleet line Dodge.

The fat guy gave us the room for the weekday rate, probably because of Misty's ass. The room looked like the interior of a '64 Buick LeSabre. Clean, straight, but with worn mattress springs and infested with thirty years of Pine-Sol and Camel smoke. It was heaven. My first bed in weeks, my first toilet paper, and my first shower without a tin can and a dirty bar of soap. It was the big time.

I sang a Roy Rogers song, "Give me land, lots of land under starry skies above . . ." In the shower while Misty arranged her clothes, fluffed our pillows, and whistled her favorite song.

I felt good, so I thought thoughts about the future and about getting married and about all those little things that can make a woman believe that you really love her. The water was hot. I washed my hair, my underarms, and my butt. The whole time thinking about making love to Misty. When I walked out of the shower my towel stood up like a tent. I felt so naive.

I was a cowboy, Misty was a cowgirl, and her Trans Am was our trusty steed. We put ourselves to sleep under Reno's neon moon. I think I loved her.

Fat Boys

At two A.M. Misty and me ran out the back door. We ran past a horseshoe mural with two gold diggers panning for gold and past the hookers and pimps. We flew down Main Street—feeling big breezes from casino doorways. We drank free whisky and soda and talked to a gambling man with gold teeth. We ran through a group of conventioneers in golf shirts. One of them dropped his bowling pin full of beer, spilled it all over the side-walk. The security guard saw it and walked away. The sign above his head said BIG BOWLERS CONVENTION. They weren't kidding—wring out one of those bowlers and you got enough pig fat to deep-fry Tonto.

The two fattest ones wanted to fight and the other two laughed. I laughed too but none of them liked that. Misty stood between us and did a kung fu kick—pulled her skirt up and threw her leg around. The fellow in a Hawaiian shirt dropped his jaw at the sight of her fine snatch. She was still moist from our two-hour hoedown on the Horseshoe carpet. She busted out laughing. The old guy fell on his ass from pure delight. His buddies bubbled like champagne.

Misty rolled a cigarette out of her stocking, lit it, and smiled. We ran back down the road. The fat boys watched us go. She branded them pure and true, didn't know kung fu but gave them a flash to write home about. Thirty years old and she kicks like a mule. Thirty years old and she'll run you along the carpet like a vacuum cleaner. For thirty-six hours I dreamed Coppertone dreams and for thirty-six hours I slept four and drank more whisky than water.

We ran under a sign that said, RENO, THE BIGGEST LIT-TLE DIVE TOWN IN THE WORLD. And stopped in the door-way of a casino called O'Shanties or O'Shenanigan's O'Flenanigan . . . O'Something, I think. There was a big fiberglass leprechaun standing inside the doorway. Maybe "big" is the wrong word for a leprechaun. But he was big—too big for a leprechaun. The carpet inside the casino was purple with green shamrocks and sitting on top of it were a thousand singing slot machines. There was an old lady with a white glove tugging on three of them at once. Finally, one of them screamed and she flew off her stool like a jack-in-the-box and shook her polyester ass all over the place. That lucky slot paid her rent. Further into the room were a bunch of blackjack, roulette, and craps tables. And mirrors everywhere. Misty was hungry, so we went down the road and found a diner in the back of another casino and sat down at a booth. I picked up the menu and it had ugly pictures of food in it.

Misty looked at me while we worked on our tuna melts and said something about an aura.

"Can you see it, it's radiating from everything. Look at that palm tree," she said, "it's filling this whole casino with life."

"That's 'cause that palm tree is the only thing in here that's alive."

"And can you smell the mist? It's coming from the tree. It's pure oxygen, like at the top of Everest."

"The top of Everest? There's no oxygen up there."

"The climbers bring oxygen with them so they can breathe when they get near the top." She was starting to talk funny and it frightened me.

"Yeah, well maybe that means they aren't supposed to be up there and maybe that palm tree isn't supposed to be growing in concrete under a Budweiser sign."

"Who cares. I think it's beautiful and if it wasn't here this place would be a bore."

"A bore?" I said. "This place has everything a guy could need."

"Well, a guy needs a little nature, too, and lots of pretty things and love and money."

"Hell, I don't have none of that scratch and I'm doin' fine."

"You're all right now, but back in Winnemucca you weren't looking so good."

"Yeah, you're right." I rubbed my eyes.

"Guess I needed a friend."

She looked at me and smiled. Her cheeks got big and pink like a true Midwestern maiden—all sweet and plump on the outside and soft in the middle. She reached into her purse and pulled out her Visa Gold and slid it across the table.

"Go buy yourself a suit and some socks and a nice pair of shoes and meet me back here in a couple of hours."

I didn't feel much like arguing, so I took the card, threw a kiss on her cheek, and walked outside. The sun was bursting out of the Circus Circus Casino. The big clown on the sidewalk had stains on his bib and barf on his shoes. I walked alone until I found a western store; I walked in and put the Visa down on the counter. The salesman had a thin mustache and a pink handkerchief in his coat pocket. He spoke with a sharp tongue. He was eating a croissant.

"Is your name Misty?"

"She's my girlfriend," I said.

"This is Reno. Everyone's got a girlfriend named Misty."

He said it sarcastically and pushed the card back toward me.

"Where are you from?" I asked.

"Mexico."

"Hey, I heard they shit in the streets down there."

He got bright pink and pointed at the door and started yelling.

"Get your ass out of my shop."

"Wait a minute, look, all I want is a suit. I want to look like that." I pointed at one of the mannequins in the window. "Like the guy with the cowboy hat. The card's good."

"You smell like manure," he said.

I smelled my sleeve. He was right.

"I bet the women are beautiful down there, but you don't look like you'd know about that."

He stabbed his bony fingers into my arm and pushed me out the door. I didn't really care. I pushed him and he fell back like a skeleton. I slammed the door and kept walking. I got to another store and walked up to the counter and asked for some respect. The old man had round spectacles and a bushy mustache. He was old enough to take my shit and my dirty clothes and he got me fixed up just like a regular customer. It was nine o'clock on a Monday morning, for God's sake; the only people I risked running out of the store were pimps and bored insurance salesmen.

"Every time they come in here," the old guy said about the insurance salesmen, "all they want is a pair of socks and then they go over to Woolworth's and sit on the curb and put 'em on."

He ran the measuring tape around my waist and across my shoulders and down my legs. The whole time not saying a thing about my ratty pants. I'd stepped up in the world. I'd always thought that a suit meant something, especially a western cut with double-barreled slacks and a pair of hi-ho silver cowboy boots.

"I'll take *three* pairs of socks," I said. "And what the hell, give me one of those Stetson cowboy hats and one of those leather satchels, too."

I signed my name on the receipt and said thank you and walked across the street to the Woolworth's. I sat down on the curb and took off my old boots and my old socks and put on a fresh pair of each. I bought the boots with a walking heel and I had the old guy leave some room in the pants in case I had to start jumping fences again soon. I thought that maybe I was being too careful, but ever since I could remember I'd always had my pants cut big. The jacket had real pockets with zippers and the old guy even embroidered my name in a secret spot. I looked like Roy Rogers on acid. I made *Saturday Night Fever* look like *Saturday Night Soup Line.*

I strolled past the leprechaun and souvenir shops. And found Misty at a blackjack table. She jumped off her stool and on to my lap. I doubled down on her eleven. The dealer hit. Chocolate thighs, sharkskin slacks—blackjack!!

I stood up and swung her to the floor. In the lounge there was a big band playing like they did in the forties. I looked like a Mexican pimp, Misty looked like Xanadu, and together we burned the oak and drank the Negro Modelo. It was high noon outside and midnight on the dance floor. The old folks came to have a carefree afternoon with the band. They danced well. They danced around us in clean clothes. They smelled of retirement and just like us they had no Mondays, jobs, or worries. Just by watching them we learned to move like a waterfall, over the artificial rocks of Reno town, across the hardwood floor and around the moonlit pond. The day turned into night and the theme changed from swing to Latin. The conga band ripped the skin off a goat, strapped it to my heart, and pounded me through another sleepless night. Misty and me learned how to salsa.

★

We left the casino at four A.M. and walked down the center of Virginia Street. We stopped at the railroad tracks and sat in the gravel and watched the Union Pacific rumble through town. A jukebox was playing Roy Orbison in a doorway down the street. His felt voice mingled with the freight. I put my arm around Misty and we watched the units pass, five in all. The engineer smiled and I thought that maybe he was having daydreams of Reno honeymoons. The locomotive whistle blew, the diesel burned, and his highball disappeared into the neon haze. It was a foggy morning in a burned-down village. The natives spend their nights in the casinos and their energy on slow-moving thoughts. The cards came and went, the money never came back, but the night was well spent. It's a form of meditation that only an American can understand. You can walk into a Reno cathedral and light a candle for your prayers. It might blow up in your face or it might send you into that euphoria that everyone has been talking about.

The village may be burning down but the people still want their drinks, goddamn it! No one gets a free ride in Reno. No one gets carried out of town until the lights go down. And we all know that will never happen. So put on your favorite hat and your fireproof shirt and sit down by the fire. There's a cowboy singing the blues and an Indian turning in his grave. Because we like the bad things here. We like to swing our udders like an old woman and moisten the carpet like newlyweds. In the end we all end up on the curb anyway. We might be down and out but at least the suit *fits*.

Sunrise

The morning sun was damn hot, so we climbed out of the gravel and walked back to the Horseshoe Motel. The fat man at the counter gave us a mean look, so we packed up the car, parked it on the street, and went looking for another room. We tried the Morrison but the owner was short-tempered and short like a midget and didn't have time to show us a room. The place was a ditch, anyway—a good place to hide out, burn a few more holes in the carpet, and stare out the window.

Two blocks from the Morrison there was a vacant lot that took up half a city block. In the center of the lot were two circus tents with flags attached to their center poles. The desert wind was gentle with the flags. There was an old Greyhound bus parked in the field. It was painted primer gray and under the paint I could see the outline of the skinny dog. That greyhound was chasing a stuffed dead rabbit. I'd bet on it. The words FULL GOSPEL TENT MINISTRY were painted on the side of the bus. It was a religious side show.

The sign on the first tent said, ENTER THE EVANGELIST'S FIELD. The sign on the second tent said, FREE DONUTS. There was a line of homeless stiffs walking out of the second tent. Somehow they all managed to smoke cigarettes, sleep, and stand at the same time. I believe this is a talent you master in a soup line. Those soup lines can be so long that by time you get your bullets you could probably have gotten a job. But there wouldn't be any sense in that. The bums came stumbling out of the tent with stacks of donuts and were immediately corralled into the "Evangelist's Field." Misty looked at me and bowed her head toward the tents. I didn't know she was the religious type—I knew I wasn't, but I followed her in anyway. The donuts were evil.

Inside the Evangelist's Field tent the sun came through the yellow canopy and turned the grass a strange shade of blue. On top of the grass were lines of white chairs that circled a pulpit. There was a small stage against the back wall and on it there was a synthesizer and an electric bass. The bums sat in the white chairs. There was a little kid with the words MARK THE SPARK ironed on his T-shirt. He ran circles around the bums, hopped up on donuts and screaming. His mother was trying her best to control him but it was too late—the devil already had that poor kid by the throat. He tripped on one of the white chairs and fell face-first into the blue grass. His mom helped him up. She smiled an embarrassed smile. She was too young to be losing her teeth, but she was losing them anyway and that explained a lot.

All of the lot lice stood when the preacher man and his wife entered the tent. His wife spoke first. She had long gray hair and she was strong. She let us have it. The band played canned rock and roll between rounds. The preacher man looked Native American. He had tanned skin that wrinkled like a chief and around his shirt collar was a turquoise bolo tie. He started to blow.

"Without Christ we are aliens," he said.

"We are not able to cope with our own existence. Always unsure of who we are."

He gently took the microphone from its stand.

"I was once just like all of you.

"*Thirty* . . . seven wasted years. I had stickle burrs in my hair and huckle burrs in my socks."

He paced in front of the pulpit and put his hand in the air.

"Hell, I . . . have been there. I was a dingbat miner, a tramp miner. I moved thirty-six times. New York, Colorado Springs, Albuquerque, and finally . . . I say finally I landed in Illinois. And do you know what happened to me there?"

He paused and looked around the tent—not a word.

"*I got saved!*

"*Is that heavy duty? Is that heavy duty?* Well, yes it is."

My jaw was on the floor. "Yes sir, that is heavy duty," I thought. I did believe that one of us was crazy. I was either crazy for being here or he was crazy for trying to change these folks. He paced the tent real slow.

"Do you know who saved me? Well, Jesus Christ, of course! But do you know who went to church without me?"

He stalled for a second and his face rolled into a smile and his eyes glossed over. He shook his head.

"My wife . . . that's who. She went to church and she prayed for me. She didn't go to church and say, 'My husband's an alcoholic.' No! There is a new tactic. She would stand up in church and say, 'He is healing the sick. He is preaching the word of God. He is saving grace. He just don't know it yet.' . . . Can you believe that?"

He stopped and looked at his wife.

"My wife did that for me. And not too long after that I had a visitation. I'm not talking about going fishing or hunting. I'm not talking about the mailman delivering the mail. A visitation. I'm talking about making a new man and a new woman. I was visited by the grace of God and he made a new man out of me."

The entire tent was quiet. I could hear cars driving by on the street and the wind on the flags. The man behind me opened a pack of cigarettes, hit one out, and lit it. The sound of the lighter broke the silence. The preacher man stood completely still. His head fell to his chest. He took his right hand and made a fist.

"The corridor of life will get so narrow that the oil of sin gets pressed right out of you. Do you hear me?"

The crowd nodded.

"I said, Do you hear me?"

The crowd whispered hallelujah.

"It says I am going to test you. I am going to press on you so hard that the oil of sin gets pressed right out of you. Do you hear me?"

"Hallelujah!" we yelled. "Ha-lle-lu-jah!"

The man behind me stood up, put his hands in the air, and let his cigarette dangle there. He pressed his palms toward the sky. He pushed up on the sky and let out a cough and then a hearty hearty shriek.

"Hallelujah!"

"I want you to listen to this because I am going somewhere. There is a way out, a better way. You *are* going to go from battle to battle. Not just your own battles but the battles of the people around you. The people you love will need you and you will need them and together you will operate on faith. You will go from faith to faith and from realm to realm and from glory to glory and you will lay down your life for others. There is a dying that takes place. You are doing what you are compelled to do. Dying to the self so that you may prepare the path for others. *Yes!* The path to the Kingdom of Christ."

The canned rock and roll kicked in and sounded good. The lot lice stood from their chairs and put their hands in the air. The tent was humming and in came the local preacher man. This preacher wore a blue suit that took on the color of the Reno sky, and in all his glory he too partook in the vacuum of Christ. Christ had consumed the tent from post to post. He too, the blue-suited mission squawker, witnessed the rise of Christ for that one brief moment. The sun came through the tinted roof and shineth upon the believers and the preacher man sang with the music:

"I have paid for the price of sin . . . paradise is down there . . . but when Jesus raised from there . . . paradise raised to the third heaven . . . yes. The Paradise of God!"

"Reno," I thought to myself, "you will be with me on this day. In the dropping of the good news and the raising of the tent. You will be with me on this good day."

"And into the big book he came with ten thousand saints. All on white horses."

And everyone in the tent looked at each other and nodded in agreement.

"Now turn to your fellow man and give him a hug. Go ahead and hug whoever sits beside you."

I turned to Misty and she had fat tears popping out of her eyes. I hugged her and she put her face into my shoulder and sobbed.

"Yes, brother, I do have hope!"

The man behind me yelled and his cigarette came flying out of his mouth. His palms pressed to the sky and in all of his excitement he grabbed the old man next to him and gave him a huge hug. The old man smelled like hooch and dog fur, but he too was going to the Kingdom of God on that Greyhound bus. Hell, all of us were gonna get on that damn bus and ride it to the great ice palace in the sky. Where the chandeliers are made of sugar, the ladies dance for free, and there's enough Dago Red to keep the sober drunk and the drunk free. And the crowd stood from their white chairs and formed a line to the pulpit. In the line there was a tall white man with an afro and a high comb, a short black man in a do rag, a construction worker, and a kid named Mark the Spark. They took to the holy water like a line of roses to the morning dew. They were the believers who had pulled themselves from the streets and into the tents of God. To bow down to the puzzle of life. To accept their fate. God is a white chair. God is a black chair. God is a silver pompadour. God is a suit the color of the Reno sky. God is alive in all of us.

★

Everyone in that tent went straight. If only for a day. We went straight with God under the big top. One down! Two down! Three down! The believers fell like dominoes as the preacher man hit their foreheads. We lay in the blue grass like sheep in the hay. Even Little Mark the Spark stood a chance that day.

"Shock it to ya!"

"Shock it to ya!"

The preacher man yelled.

Misty buried her misty eyes in my chest—wetting my lapel—trying to make sense of God. The gospel and I are kin. This is true. But where does all this fit in? Where did my feelings lie on what the preacher man was saying? Is the word of one man the word of God? For I too am a preacher man—a writer of napkin poetry, a traveler and a lover and a witness to the miracle of life, raised to believe in free will and nonjudgment. But outside my understanding was all of that—great America—the land of hot dogs, women, and Jesus—a strange and beautiful heaven born of gasoline and good nature.

★

I should have covered my eyes before America took her clothes off—because once you've seen her naked ass you are bound to be her slave. America is a hooker with a purse full of dreams, a stiletto gate, and somewhere hidden in her valleys of optimism is the belief that life could be a little bit better. I've paid little Miss America too many visits to be part of any church, my religion is the country—the greasy spoons, the quarter panel from an old Mercury that kept me out of the rain that one cat-and-dog night in the howling boneyard, the free bar of rotten motel soap they gave me at the shelter, for now these things are who I am. I did it all out of necessity, so it's not my fault. I don't want to go to hell, but my home is no more than a ghost and I have nowhere else to go. I crouched down in my white folding chair, looked into the peak of that big top tent, and let all that "hooker," "America" stuff race through my head. For that moment I decided to let the Lord in.

★

After the sermon we went back to the train tracks. The apartment building behind us held the shadows of a hundred
tramps. We saw a fat man trying to piss in the gutter. His wife
held his beer and looked out for the police. He stumbled back
to her arms. They weaved down the alley and collapsed in a
doorway. We sat down in the gravel and Misty rested her head
on my shoulder.

If all the diamonds in Reno pawn were appraised at a fair
price, they wouldn't be worth one day with Misty. The way
Reno threw stars off her sunglasses. The coconut oil on her
island skin. The dew came early in that town. The Sundowner
casino sign gave direction to a passing spaceship. It hooked and
disappeared over the Sierras.

I felt like a real piece of work—sitting in that gravel in that
alley in Reno—living the dumb life. I looked over at Misty and
told her that I wanted to go. She agreed and we left Reno the
next morning.

Journal Entry # 11: The Cowboy or the Tramping Desperado

A cowboy is someone who spends his time alone on the
prairie taking in long breaths of wild sage. Cowboys don't have
homes because homes are one of the few places they can't up
and leave. And when a cowboy can't do what he wants he gets
ornery real fast—making anyone at home wish he would "just
go."

The decision between fatherhood and his responsibility to the
countryside can cause any man to meander. This decision alone
can keep a man's dick in his pants and his boots on. The loneliness he finds is painful, but once the choice to leave is made he
can never go back. The people he loved will welcome him but

they won't depend on him. He knows this and is willing to sacrifice any of the respect this may cost him. But he always knows deep down that true love doesn't judge. True love lets be. And those who truly love him will understand.

A tramp is a cowboy. He rides the open range, he sleeps under the stars, and he believes in the luck of the Golden Years. The Golden Years are not segments of time but long moments that pass without tension or confusion. They come on a "good luck train"—a train that rolls from sunup to sundown with only a few stops for fuel and crew. The luck isn't in the number of miles traveled but in the pure surprise that comes when the day has passed so beautifully. It's a sober man's morphine.

Riding trains is timeless. The trains are a well-guarded secret that cannot be bought in a hardback book. In fact, I have questioned my integrity with every written word. I'm too young to tell anyone how to do anything. I don't even know how to raise a child or love a woman right, let alone tell the story of the most powerful breed of American outlaw.

I still have a responsibility. As does every bull rider, longboard surfer, meditator, great guru of who knows what, Japanese garden builder, music maker, tattoo artist, Texas Ranger, Lone Ranger, interstate fire goddess, hot-rod top chopper, gutbucket plucker—to the family of mind workers who slave under the heavy barrel of Americana. It is our responsibility to create a place in our hearts where fear does not exist.

It's hard, lonely work and doesn't pay for nothing and earns you the respect of a wet dog. But without it we would have nothing to live for. Everyone is a pioneer. The frontier runs through our veins like a Greyhound bus. It reveals itself in the perfect flame job or on the perfect wave.

Ford Marriage: A union usually born of gasoline and good nature.

Ford Mother: The female side of a "Ford family," or a woman traveling by automobile with a migratory worker or tramp.

13

Highway 95, Reno to Las Vegas

NOVEMBER 12, 1991—ALL DAY

Since Misty lived in LA, we decided that we would go to Las Vegas for a night, then get her home to "Shakey Town" the next day. I guess she had an audition for some commercial. We took Highway 95 through central Nevada. It's a beautiful drive for anyone interested in America or at least what America used to be. There are pockets of Nevada where folks like speed, you know, CRANK! and after visiting a few of these places it's easy to see why. Highway 95 does have its fair share of speed trash. When we stopped for gas we were fortunate enough to experience these highway folks. They came in the form of high-wired mothers yelling at their kids and counter clerks who thought they were being "badly taking advantage of" and "fuckin' ripped off!" by every "fuckin' Mexican!" who passed through. I'd never seen anything like them. The only thing stupider than an entire town on speed is nothing. There's nothing stupider than that. I thought those clerks and mothers should have dressed like circus clowns. I do believe that would have been very funny.

If you really want to meet the people of the earth you have to take the slow roads. Most of Highway 95 is slower than the sun. All the towns along this road had one post office, an empty grocery store with empty shelves, maybe one or two cans of Vienna sausages, and lots of new pickup trucks. One of the roadhouses we stopped at served Budweiser in a can, out of a Frigidaire and the damn jukebox was stuck on the same song— Neil Diamond, "Forever in Blue Jeans." We went through the same town over and over again—running the double nickel and bored to death. I put my elbow on the door and my cuff links reflected the sun. Misty kept dozing off. Twice I had to grab the wheel before we drove off the road. Her eyes got heavy and when they were half closed her cigarette fell from her mouth and landed on her lap. Twice I grabbed it and threw it out the window.

The towns before Las Vegas are the places where bumpers rust, children cry, and hope is an eight-letter word—hopeless. I felt hopeless and heavy-footed and just wanted to get the hell out of the desert and into the big lights of optimism—Las Vegas. I could feel the desperation seeping in and the sky falling down on that great American farm. Sure, I grew up in the doorways, keeping out of the rain. But when the wide-open country closes in on you, like a trash compactor, you know you've got problems. When you crave the sound of falling change or the whistle of a desperate hooker and you don't care what anyone has to teach you anymore. It's all sick, polluted, and pleasing. I felt rewarded with mobility because, unlike the man serving Budweiser in cans out of an old Frigidaire, I had places to go. I could double-down in Las Vegas or I could sleep on the Astro Turf at the Double-Down trailer park in Palm Springs—if there is one. The sun beating down on our car. Racing on.

We charged Las Vegas like a bull—pushing through the red cape of sunset. A Hollywood wind floated through Misty's hair. As it turned out, she was doing a little speed herself, crank—bikers' speed—the brown stuff and that ephedrine truck stop trucker shit—mini thins—and who knows what else. She had just finished a three-day run. She was spitting a lot and calling me names. I hated her for most of that drive to Las Vegas. I hated Hollywood for making her and the rest of the world that way. Misty continued to burn the interior with her ash and her slinky little skirt. She left a wet spot every time she got up. I ran my finger through it at the Texaco. It was the nectar of the gods. It kept my foot on the accelerator and my mind on the Horseshoe Motel. All that sexual energy building up and shutting down. I needed to get my ass out of the country and into the next dirty town. I held her hand as she cried and together we punched through the storm—hoping to see lighthouse Las Vegas somewhere inside that empty black night.

On that rough day I was proud of Nevada—proud to be a child of the gambling state. Misty and me had nothing to lose—nothing to think about—just ourselves and our past and a love that could have withdrawn without notice. In Nevada you can dress like Elvis and sing like Tom Jones. In Nevada rhinestones are more precious than moonstones. And like a hobo freight, Nevada highballs at night, sets no schedules, and checks no weight. That state is home. The coin goes in but doesn't always come back out again. Las Vegas is a bar town. If the bars line up, you go up thirty floors to the heart-shaped tub. If they drop down, you sleep in the Trans Am and make love in the backseat under the blazing neon signs. Like I said—we had nothing to lose.

We didn't make it to Las Vegas. On the way her gold card turned platinum, her tears hydrated Nevada, and the quality of her driving rapidly decreased. I had no idea that Los Angeles could have such an effect on a person. All she wanted was diet vanilla cream soda and cigarettes. In fact, she was drinking those sodas at the rate of three an hour and her Misty Ultra Light 100s didn't leave her lip the entire day. She talked in long drawn-out sentences and within a few hours managed to tell me her entire life story. It was beautiful—full of passion and complete abandon. An artist's life of the highest order. She lived in a shack in a Mexican ghost town and painted pictures. She sold used cars at a car lot in Southern California. She did funny little suntan lotion ads on TV. She was prom queen two years in a *row*. But in the end her attempts to become a star had put an end to her big bad dreams. Now she worked the "wheel" or the "circuit"—Las Vegas, Los Angeles, Reno—dancing for dollars in go-go bars.

Misty was a broken angel.

She had been a starlet at one time but after one wrong turn, one bad situation, everything she worked for crumbled. That's show business. There are a million power-hungry men between a girl and stardom, and if she ends up in a room with the wrong one, all of her innocence can be taken in less than a minute. I hate all that fame stands for and more than that I hate the hungry who can't hunt for themselves. There was a pain in Misty—a gap that was widened by her desire to be a star. It blew up one night. The sparkle in her eye was replaced with a rape and a recovery and she matured into a hot-rod bitch. No room for fancy talk. No room for the man with the satin-collared shirt. No room for the next big break. She'd say, Fuck

you and your promises *and* your leather interior. Just give me
an honest smile and a nobody. A fat, greasy T-shirted, truck-
drivin' nobody. A man who don't give a flying fuck about gold
records. His movie stars are in his old lady's eyes. His soft porn
is real. His car chases are real. His motherfucking problems are
real. Turn off the TV and make love to this godforsaken world.
It needs you.

Early the Next Day

She coldcocked me. My knees buckled. I landed in the
gravel. She sped away.

"What the fuck!"

I jumped out of the ditch and threw my finger up the road.
Didn't love her anyway.

"Fuck!"

I dusted off my pants once again. In the back pocket I had
a five-dollar bill that I had stashed for such occasions. It was the
survivor in me rat-holing a gigolo's nickel. I walked four miles
before I put my thumb out. There I was walking down Highway
95 with nothing. I could either walk up the road to some cockroach town or down the road to some cockroach town. I didn't
have a warm jacket or a bedroll, so I decided to head for the
lower elevation. I tipped my hat and straightened my pants. My
suit was still presentable and pressed but I did have a new hole
in the elbow and even a bit of dried blood. I'd been wounded.
I learned that crystal methamphetamine makes little stripper
girls do little funny things. I offered to drive and that pissed her
off. I threw her cigerette out the window and that pissed her off.
I couldn't win. I went bobbing for apples and came up with a
lemon. Oh well!

A '67 Ford Galaxie 500 slowed down beside me. There
was an old guy driving and a fat guy in the passenger's seat.

I folded back the seat and crawled in. The backseat had a wooden box the length of it and when I sat down on top of it my head was higher than the windshield. They didn't say a word. We drove off at the devil's speed. I was too broken to talk anyway, so I held onto my hat real tight as we barreled down the highway.

Those miles were what you would call "the cold back tracks." The steps you take to get back to where you were before you met her. I was sitting in a booth at the Winner's Casino in Winnemucca minding my own business—watching a good fight and figuring on Mexico. And she walked in. Now I was trigger-shy, prideless, and my dick had turned into an icicle.

Riding in the back of a convertible is like riding a horse. I thought about the Lone Ranger. I figured that if it was him in the back of that Galaxie, he wouldn't have to hold his hat on. It would just stay put. I couldn't figure out how the hell I was supposed to ride in the back of that thing with my hat on, so I just held it on my head.

Those two guys looked like they should have been out hunting rattlesnake or maybe just going into hibernation for the fucking winter. They looked tired. The old guy shifted at any passing lights. He looked in the rearview mirror more than he looked at the road and he shifted and shifted again and then the young guy started shifting and within minutes they were act-ing like bad actors in some bad cops and robbers movie. Obvious is what they were.

So, there I was coming down off a one-week love affair— nailed down to a wooden box waiting for my forehead to splin-ter the windshield. Finally the old guy spoke. I should say he yelled. The wind was mighty loud at 110 mph.

"I gots a Latin girlfriend in Vegas and I gots to see her by tomorrow. Dick's liable to fall off."

That was it. That was all he said for the entire ride. I sat back with my hand on my hat and looked up at the mighty stars. That night they were introspective stars. The ones that palm readers look at and tell you if the odds are in your favor. I was once again on my way to Mexico, so I figured that my destiny was in good hands. At that moment I didn't care for my past as much as I did for my future. I knew that these two were subject to the same scrutiny, but my future had more possibility, so I went with it. What had just happened to me was a free man's biggest fear. I had fallen in love with a broken angel.

All that time on love's slippery highway—behind me. All that time on trial with Cupid's wicked bow—behind me. I hadn't had that much heartache in my entire life but it was a kind heartache and it was for the better. I could have checked into the Depression Motel but I didn't. I let my letdowns be bygones and appreciated the fine desert air. I guess life isn't always kind. I guess love doesn't always express itself through beauty. It can flower, all right, but can it regenerate itself after it's dead? That was my wonder. I hadn't gone and fucked up my love for Misty, someone did that before me. And through all her pain I couldn't see it coming back again. But I'll tell you one thing. If love can be stolen it can also be restored. But that will take a man more patient than myself. I'm sorry, Misty, but I have fortunes to tell and stars to gaze and I can't see your love returning without a fight. I'll look up at the same moon as you every night. I'll have wet Horseshoe dreams. I'll shoot a Hollywood star. But I won't fall in love with a fight.

★

The other passenger looked like a greased-up horse. He had a long mane of hair slicked back with axle grease. I could smell it in the backseat. Both of his index fingers were bent to the trigger. He looked like he held his guns more than his ladies. Prep cooks, fence menders, carnies—no way. These two had to be criminals. They had that two-month grin. That "just got outta jail and I wanna fuck" grin. I felt all glamorous and worthless at the same time, so I didn't care if they were child molesters or candle makers—I just wanted to ride.

Criminals don't like to be called criminals. Purple Hearted soldiers, outlaws, vigilantes—anything but criminals. They've stepped out of the circle and learned to furnish their lives with secrets. It's safer that way. The rules have changed, my friends. A criminal has found his freedom. A criminal is self-employed, and once a man starts turning his own tricks he don't want Uncle Sam pimpin' his spirit. What he desires is the ability to go and do whatever he wants whenever he wants, and there isn't anyone who can tell him otherwise.

The old snake pushed on the 390 V8. It shifted hard. At 60 mph we popped up to 110 mph in two seconds. A shift kit. George liked it. His fat trigger finger grabbed the dashboard. I nearly fell off my box. That box I was sitting on. What the hell was in that box? I didn't want to know. The floorboards under my feet rattled like a busted guitar. I looked down and there was a pile of empty beer cans a foot deep. They were covered up with whisky-soaked army fatigues. If we got pulled over the cops would *surely* ignore the stench and *surely* have no idea that under that mountain of army pants and coats was enough aluminum to build a small shack. My drivers were too dumb to litter. Buried in the corner was a five-gallon glass bottle. It had a light fog on it. I bent down to see what was in it. It was dark, but in the bottom of it, I could make out the shape of a snake. I looked closer and sure enough it was a goddamn rattlesnake. I think it was sleeping. That's when I knew those two had to be from Texas. Texans are the only folks I know of who get a kick out of pissing off rattlesnakes—some kind of big man sport thing. I made sure the bottle was plugged up good by pounding down on the huge cork in the top of it.

The driver was having a Latin BBQ in his pants. He was dreaming of a hot set of legs falling out of a miniskirt and a rose tattoo with his name circling the stem. He was driving for the same reason every man on that highway was driving. He was driving for love. And there I was sitting on that goddamn box waiting for Vegas glitz to smack me in the face. I needed a blow job right that second and I had five bucks with her name on it. I didn't care about the teeth. I didn't care about tomorrow. I want a split second to peek up Vegas's lovely skirt. I know it's sad below the belt. I know that a man is a waste of innocence. But I'm not a man. I'm a stunt man.

There we were, strolling down Highway 95, and there I was in a parallel universe thinking of myself as a charming bull-fighter. I was daydreaming that I had made it to Mexico. I had a perfect señorita girlfriend. A true lady. The kind of lady that will tell you when she just wants to be fucked. I like when I can look behind a lady's eyes and see a strong pair of legs. The kind that will walk out of a restaurant if the food ain't right. She puts her ass in one direction and keeps it there. She doesn't wash the clothes, then complain about equality. She washes her panties, then puts them on and moistens them with reality. She knows what she wants and she knows where to get it. She wants it hard. She wants it in. She doesn't want slobber on her neck. She doesn't want a word in her ear. She's the brown-skinned woman of my Mexican dreams and she wants it *in*.

★

We drove 110 into the sunrise. The snake rattled and the car purred and those two bank robbers continued to drink that hard, cheap beer. The tires on the front of the car must have been out of balance. It was swerving from line to line. We'd be riding the guardrail one second and pounding our coffin nails the next. I had heard about Mexican drivers and I'd even had dreams about a few, but I'd never had the pleasure of pissing my pants. It was a warm stream but it got cold right away. I had to hold on to my hat. I could wash my pants but there's no way I could replace that hat. There was a cloud of dust with every curve and then finally—thank God—a set of red lights came over the hill behind us.

"Oh, shit! Oh, fucking shit!" the Mexican yelled.

"Push on it! Fuck it, push on it, fuck it. Goddamn it, George, push on it!"

The old snake pushed. The wrinkles in his face folded and his blood started pumping. At that point the sun was stabbing the windshield. The wind plastered my eyelids shut and all I could do was listen to the screaming tires and the siren fading in and out. Those cop cars have muscle. The 390 V8 was happy on the straightaways but it couldn't handle the curves. Too much weight. The wind was pure and all of my childhood days screamed past me and I had another vision of Mexico. The dirt from the Mexican road pouring in the windows. The Federales smoking cocaine and chasing the poor gringos out of town. I kept my eyes closed and kept daydreaming.

I think the only way to get away from your dreams is to give up. Those two wouldn't have stopped for Niagara Falls. They would have thrown their hands in the air and fell into the great season of opportunity. Death is the chance you take when you cross the border. Death is the chance you take every day, so you may as well have a side of adventure and shot of stupidity to go along with it, that was my thinking. My head felt like a needle splitting the wind—reading the prisoner's blues.

Those two were looking through prison bars or Mexican palms, whichever came first. I ducked my head down and opened my eyes. When we turned the next corner the passenger opened the glove box, grabbed a brown paper bag, and threw it out the window. They rummaged through their pockets, pulled out odd pipes, rolling papers, and other paraphernalia and threw it all out of the car after it. When they agreed they were clean the snake slowed down to the side of the road. At this point the cops weren't taking any chances. They stood at the back of the car with their guns out.

The snake and the horse both had outstanding warrants. The cops took my information and, after realizing I was just a hitchhiker, let me go. The snake and the horse were cuffed and taken away in the back of the squad car. They left me and the Galaxie on the side of the road. They told me to walk to the nearest overpass—about a mile down—and catch a ride from there. I thought about it and decided it would be best to retrieve the brown paper bag before I tried to catch another ride. I waited for the squad car to disappear, then walked back up the highway. I found the bag at the bottom of the drainage ditch. It had torn open and lying on the ground next to it was what looked like an ounce of marijuana. It was dried-out High Mountain Mexican. I smelled it and decided to hold on to it— maybe try to sell it when I got to Las Vegas. I lifted up what was left of the bag and underneath it was a small roll of ones and fives—about fifty dollars all together. I put all the booty in my pocket and walked back up the highway. I passed the Galaxie and made my way toward the exit ramp. I thought about that wooden box and wondered what was in it. The police didn't say anything about it. They would find out when they came back to impound the car. Maybe I should have gone back just to satisfy my curiosity, but something inside told me that whatever it was, I didn't need—I had enough trouble as it was. Bad days can domino into bad weeks if you aren't careful, and I didn't want to take any more chances.

I figured I was about two hundred miles north of Las Vegas. I walked up to the overpass and hitched a ride to the next town with a turkey farmer. It made sense. I felt like a turkey. I was a turkey. The town was typical, small and isolated. There was no sign telling the name of it. The wind didn't blow. The neon sign on the service station was covered in buzzing bees. I couldn't read it. There was a small sticker with a greyhound dog on it. I figured the bus must stop there so I walked in. The overhead doors on the garage were open and inside there were three homeguards sitting on stools. They had completely dismantled the front end of an Oldsmobile Cutlass Ciera and sat there thinking about how they were going to put it back together again. Two of them were men with dirty-blond beards and the third was a woman with dirty-blond hair and a cigarette. I think they were related in a "far away from anyone else" kind of way. There was an animal that looked like a Brillo pad rolling around in an oil stain on the floor. It was a potbelly pig. A pet pig. The kind you see on late-night TV and think how cute it would be to order one—there's no sense in it—just cute. This particular pig wasn't a cute pink one with a curly tail. It was a half-hairy one with a rope hanging out of its ass. The thing stunk. It strolled around the garage like a vacuum cleaner—tracking motor oil in and out of the place.

The lady loved her pig. She resembled her pig and when it squealed she thought it was her maternal call. The responsibility of a suckling tit hanging from her sweater. She coughed up cigarette butts and stale smoke and wiped her face away. The lipstick covered her sleeve.

"He's my best friend," she said.

"He's my husband, my children, my brothers and sisters rolled up into one."

"There's a problem here," I thought.

"Is he sick?" I asked.

"Oh, no, those bumps on his back are left over from a bad attack. One hundred bees came out of nowhere and attacked him. Poor rascal got bit so bad he had to sit in a tub of oatmeal for two days." A tear welled up in her eye. I was trying not to laugh because part of me really felt bad for the thing.

"So, let me get this straight," I said. "A swarm of bees came into the garage here, right through the door, and just attacked the pig?"

"Yup, and then they up and left. I haven't seen a bee in here since."

One of the bearded men told me the bus was due in a couple of hours. I sat there on one of the stools and watched them put the Oldsmobile back together. It took thirty or forty "fuck!"s and about ten "shit!"s to really get it right, but even then they had to take it apart again.

"Damn foreign cars!" the first bearded men yelled.

"It's an Oldsmobile, Jack—made in America," said the second one.

"Damn Japanese parts!" said the first one.

"Damn Japanese parts!" said the second one.

I sat on the stool. The bus came and I got on it. I sat in a seat by the window and took time to think.

I decided that the events of the last week had proven my inability to cope with the real world. I was still a young man—too young to see the warning signs of a heartbreak. I was learning but not fast enough. I figured that every man must fall in love at least a hundred times before he can understand it and even then he won't understand it. Broken hearts are as common as the rain and must be addressed when telling the tale of an American man. I had time while walking on that highway— time to think about things. There was that Mexican salesman who wouldn't sell me a suit. I reacted harshly to his insult—to the point of pushing him away. What was I thinking? I had forgotten about more important matters—like hi-ho let's go to Mexico and ain't nothing going to get in my way. But there I was—out of the train yards for less than a week and I had already forgotten about it. After Misty, the snake, the horse, the full gospel tent ministry, frozen blue fingertips, Pork Pie, Bobby Blue, and all those blistering days in the sun all alone in this great enchanted land—I had had enough.

I would be in Las Vegas in a few hours. I decided that when I got there I would get a room for a night and further evaluate my travels. Maybe call my pop and let him know I was all right. I was thinking of Denver for the second time since I left, and going home had become an option.

Journal Entry # 12: Soap Rivers and a Stetson Hat

A good hat. The main thing a hat does is keep the sun off. A hat can also be used when approaching a brakeman or engineer for information. A tip of the hat will render you harmless, and if it's a nice-looking hat it might earn you some respect. If it doesn't help to tip your hat you can take it completely off. This will increase your chances of getting an honest answer as to the destination of the next train.

A bar of soap. A hobo and a slow river are soul mates. There are a few rivers left in faraway places—train places— where the water is clear and clean. It's usually stone-cold mountain water but it's medicinal and it used to be snow, so it's fresh. Mountain water can take that horrible train noise away. I just sit

there and listen to the snow roll over the rocks and wait for a
bird to chirp or a fish to jump—maybe skip a rock to the other
side. I throw water on my face and take a hobo shower and let it
all pass. When I'm done I put my clothes back on, build a little
fire, and lie down on the ground. I watch the night sky dance
between the trees.

Some hobos call this boilin' up. Defined as: A period of rest,
usually beside the railroad right of way and near a stream of
some sort, with an oppurtunity to wash the clothes and person,
repair clothing, et cetera. The true "hobo" is a cleanly individual and welcomes any opportunity to keep his person clean and
neat, since a good "front" is essential in looking for work.

It could be time to streamline, fly light—get rid of everything
and not even try to understand the world. You might be a down
and dirty tramp but the sun won't get you because you still got
your hat. They can have everything else but they can't have the
hat. When the sun is burning down and you're still moving
on—with or without her—that hat will be worth its weight
in gold.

Hot Spring

China Camp

Click: To succeed. No doubt from the "click" of a roulette ball when it drops into the division of the wheel, and by which someone is lucky enough to win. The term is widely used by actors and stage folk.

Carrying the Banner: Walking the streets all night to avoid arrest as a vagrant or to keep from freezing.

Las Vegas

Pacific Rail Road

14
Las Vegas
NOVEMBER 14, 1991—3:00 A.M.

Aloha! from Las Vegas

Driving into Sin City. The first four things I saw from the bus:

A roadrunner gliding across the highway.

A black man with big white lint in his afro and all of his possessions rolled into a bedsheet and thrown over his shoulder—walking out of town.

Three teenage Indian girls hitchhiking out of Henderson.

A station wagon filled to the ceiling with plastic Coke bottles.

Greyhound let me off at the Plaza Hotel on Main and Fremont in downtown Las Vegas. I walked off the bus with no baggage in my hand. The drunk little Indian in the back of the bus wondered about this. He stumbled off the bus and the second his boot hit the sidewalk he had a cigarette on his lip. He looked at me some more. He wondered if I was rich or poor— did I have a boot full of payroll or was I just a minimalist.

I was coming to Las Vegas the way most people left— with nothing. I figured this meant something. That maybe I would leave strong and wealthy like a Texas longhorn or better yet I was going to prove that town wrong and give it a royal lesson in luck. The little Indian sucked on his Kent and looked up Main Street one way, then turned and looked up Main Street the other way. The lights of the Plaza hung over our heads and put a golden shine on our boots—American sunshine. Bold and useless is how I felt. We stood there looking up and down Main Street. It was obvious that neither of us had a plan past the end of that cigarette. He flicked the butt on the ground—put the spark out with his toe and decided on down the road.

I walked down Fremont Street. The city spread itself before me like the yellow brick road, and like the many miles before, I found myself walking through town alone. Fremont Street was covered in a cathedral of lights and every half hour they would turn themselves into dancing ladies and spaceships. They call it the "Fremont Experience." There was a twenty-foot-tall neon cowboy standing on the roof of a casino. He would take his cowboy hat off and put it back on again. He was tipping it to the twenty-foot cowgirl across the street. She sat on the roof of a go-go bar—smiling. She was real pretty but not too bright.

As I walked I was hit by the presence of God. He was

tangled in my hair and hardened to the soles of my cowboy boots. The lights of Las Vegas are like small angels that protect you from the night. No matter where you are in that city it never gets dark. Sin City runs hard and tough like a boxer. It's a fire pit for the gods. A furnace for burning speed trash and brain cells. I was in the middle of Vegas—alone—four in the morning—an ounce of weed and a twenty-dollar bill. The only thing I could think to do was keep walking. It was cold so the walking kept me warm. I figured that I would walk till noon, then check into a motel room with the twenty dollars I had left, try to sell the pot, and use the money to get a meal.

Where Las Vegas Boulevard turns into the Strip is where all of the wedding chapels, head shops, and tattoo parlors are. The first chapel I passed had an Astro Turf lawn—bright green and glowing. It softened the steps of a nervous groom. He was wearing patent leather shoes and a black tuxedo. He stopped, peeked through the chapel doors, bowed his head, and paced across the Astro Turf lawn. Inside the chapel was a Liberace in pink pumps holding a Bible the size of Texas— hard as Texas and meaner than a Texan in-law. I could hear a Casiotone playing a wedding song. The music drifted out of the door, into the desert air, and settled onto the Strip like a dead flat cat.

On the next block I passed a head shop/tattoo parlor. There was a kid in the window sitting on a dentist's chair with a tattoo artist hunched over his arm. The gun buzzed—the pin shot into his arm and the ink mixed with his blood. The little tattoo said something about a punk and suburban decay and nothin' else. The kid was real ugly and blue like a punk ought to be. The man with the gun was forty-five and still alive—better than most. I walked in and bought some rolling papers, then went around the back, sat down against a fence, and rolled a joint. I was wedged between a Dumpster and a Cadillac. I smoked half the joint, then put the other half in my jacket pocket.

"What the hell am I doing in Las Vegas?" I thought. I stood up and tilted the mirror on the Cadillac so I could see my face. I took my hat off and shoved my fingers through my hair. It was tangled and dirty.

"What in the hell am I doing in Las Vegas?"

My face was beat down. I had more wrinkles than I should've had. I thought about how I felt when I looked in the mirror at the Cafe El Toro in Missoula. I was beat down and cold but there was no problem in my heart. For some reason my reflection looked different in Las Vegas. My cheekbones were hard as granite and there were deep blue rings under my eyes. I felt all right. My energy was good but my heart was tragic. It burned for clean love—some sweet experience that would remind me of my big dreams and remind me of Mexico. I had forgotten completely. The only light I saw in the mirror of that Cadillac was a reflection from the White Cross drugstore across the street. The young boy that had pounded out of Denver a month earlier had disappeared and in his place was a poet—a vigilante with no law and no home. I was now made of dirt and buffalo grass—train smoke and tar. I had learned to see love and honor in that old hard face of time, and if that old hard face of time would allow me one more day, I swore I would use it sparingly.

★

I stood outside the head shop and managed to sell the weed for a fair price. I kept a little for myself. The kid who bought it guessed the weight and I agreed. He left happy and so did I. I continued walking down the Strip. I went to a place called the Fashion Show Mall and got a slice of pizza and a drink. I had

a good chunk of money, so I went to a department store and
bought six pairs of socks, three T-shirts, three red bandannas, a
tube of Brylcreem, and a cheap suitcase.

I sat on a leather couch in the center of the mall. There
was a huge skylight above me. The sun poured through it and
onto the marble floor. There was a silk palm tree on either side
of the couch and in the sunlight they almost looked real. I took
the plastic off the shirts and socks and neatly placed them in the
suitcase. I threw my old bandanna in the garbage and replaced
it with a new one. The suit Misty bought me had faded. The
sharkskin had lost its shark. I latched my new suitcase, straightened my pants, and walked outside into the warm desert air.

Not having a bedroll meant that I would have to sleep
under a roof every night. I was prepared to do whatever it took
to accomplish this. I'd have to meet someone new in every town
I visited or stay in a shelter or dig a ditch. I wasn't climbing the
social ladder. I wouldn't dream of that. I was making myself
available to a finer class of lady. I found a barber who was open
late and he put a pompadour on my head. I slapped the
Brylcreem into my hair, ran a comb through it, and ventured
into the laughing Las Vegas night.

I stopped at this place next to Circus Circus called Slots
O' Fun. I went into the gift shop and bought a hat that said
LAS VEGAS in big gold letters. The Circus Circus in Las Vegas
has a different clown than the one in Reno. It wears these awful
polka-dot pajamas and holds this round thing that looks like a
lollipop. The Vegas clown has a huge electronic billboard in its
stomach that shows video clips of cats pushing shopping carts
and dogs wearing dresses. I didn't like the clown or the shopping cart or the dancing dog. None of them made sense to me.
Slots O' Fun had free popcorn and cheap beer, so I went in,
grabbed a bucket and a bottle, walked back outside, and sat

down on my suitcase. Packs of tourists rushed by me. They had cameras around their necks and those funny little purses around their waists—all of them—all two million of them wore these things. I was enjoying watching them hustle in and out of the casinos—like kangaroos—they hopped and stopped— hopped—looked around and stopped. I drank my beer.

A man exploded out of the crowd. He was six feet tall and his arms had to be three feet long—they danced around him like a windmill. He wore a western shirt that had long red tassels hanging off the sleeves. When he took his long steps the tassels swished through the crowd. His cowboy boots were made of snakeskin leather and they had silver buckles over the top and silver stirrups shooting out the back. He wore gold sunglasses with small statuettes of Caesar carved in the side. He was all walk and talk and there I was right in front of him eating popcorn and smiling. I liked him the minute I saw him. He was bare-ass outrageous and in Las Vegas it doesn't get any better than that. It's the most ridiculous place on the planet and all the people look the same. This man was an outcast. The kangaroo tourists didn't know if he was a movie star or a loony tick. Two hours later I was sitting on a pink couch in his designer apartment off Maryland Parkway.

Buckthorn Superstar

I'd like to introduce you to Buckthorn Superstar. He lives in Las Vegas in a Miami flat with a small electronic typewriter that he uses to edit what he calls "gambling systems." The idea is that you buy this system and it teaches you how to win at various casino games. They are masterminded by professional gamblers who spend a lot of their time testing the "systems." Buckthorn Superstar was an apprentice to a pair of these gamblers. And just like them he had a bankroll set aside for gambling. The professionals he worked for made between fifty and three hundred thousand dollars a year. They were curly-haired guys who wore tennis shorts, drove Lincolns, and lived in high-rise buildings with names like the Marie Antoinette; you know, white Roman statues, mirrors and glass, covered parking, high-top basketball shoes—shit like that.

It's not the amount of money that you make that defines you as a professional gambler. It's simply whether or not you can support yourself and your habits by doing it. A smart man will walk out of a casino with fifty dollars of the house's money. If he did this every day, he would have fourteen hundred dollars by the end of the month. A gambler goes to work whenever he pleases. And if his luck holds up he'll happily support himself with his earnings.

The best thing about Buckthorn Superstar was his cowboy shirts. He bought them at a Salvation Army off the Strip. This place specialized in winning-day leftovers—mostly gaudy golden rope stuff that Texans buy in casino gift shops when they win and throw out when they lose. These muraled shirts and polyester pants keep the radical afloat on the sea of common folk. Buy an electric shirt, plug it into the wall, throw on your sunglasses, and *stroll, MAN! Stroll.*

The second best thing about Buckthorn Superstar was his furniture.

"*Look* at this stuff," he said, throwing his arms across the room.

"Can you *believe* those hotels just *throwing* out all this designer furniture?"

He fell into his chair and shook his head.

"Can you believe *that!?* No holes, nice colors, and all for nothin'. *Nothin'!* Not one cigarette burn in any of it. *What a deal!*"

There was a tall window in his living room that faced the Strip. He turned his chair and looked out of it.

"*Look* at that."

I looked out the window and there were golden lights shimmering through the branches of a tree.

"This town is about as meatless as hot dogs," he said.

We sat there for five minutes staring through the tree. Buck jumped up, flew into his bedroom, and came out with a red leather jacket on. A tapered Michael Jackson thing with tassels all over it.

"Are you hungry?" he asked.

"Not really."

"How 'bout a beer?"

"That would be great."

He opened the door and flew down the stairs.

There was a phone sitting under a lamp next to the sofa. I stood up, walked to the window, and looked out at the city. So golden, so tempting. The broken heart part of me wanted to give in and start a beautiful life of habit and sin. I was in the right place, and it was the right time to do it. In Vegas a man's roots lose strength in the desert sand and if he comes in busted he'll timber like wood. And that's just how I felt. What I needed to do was get out. And the more I thought about it, home was the only place I could think to go. I walked back to the sofa, picked up the phone, and called Denver. After three long rings I got the answering machine.

"You've reached Eddy and Wild Bill. We're both temporarily away from home. If this is you, Eddy, there's plenty to eat in the pantry. I brought in enough wood for a couple days and there's ten bucks under the bed. If you need me I'll be out on the highway looking for you. It was the only place I could think to look. I talked to some fella who swore he saw you in

Winnemucca. If you need a couple more weeks alone I understand. Take care of yourself. I love you."

I dropped the receiver on the hook, put my head in my hands, closed my eyes, and cried. Tears fell and my back broke. I crumbled into the couch and lay there for ten minutes. The tears kept coming and I had to let them go. I reached into my coat pocket, pulled out the rest of my money, and shoved it in my boot.

"What about Mexico?

"What about finishing what I started?"

After hearing my father's voice I didn't have the nerve to go on.

"What's a dream?" I thought.

"Just a bag of bones that weren't even mine to begin with. I've learned enough from these gadabouts and drifters. Like they say—maybe 'it's not about getting there but what you learned along the way.'" I've never been one to abide by cliché, but something about Las Vegas made it all right, just this once.

★

Buck came back from the liquor store with a six-pack. We sat on his balcony and drank. He laughed and chugged on his bottle and talked about New Orleans. I threw my head between my legs and let my beer hang off my arm. I was bum-tired and pistol-whipped. Buck looked over at me.

"What's wrong?" he asked.

"Heart's broken."

He put his right elbow on his knee.

"What about?"

"A lot of things. Homesick. Lovesick. You name it."

He shook his head.

"Know that feeling."

Traffic passed on Maryland Parkway. The Russian man in the apartment below us yelled at his Russian wife in Russian. Buck was concerned about me but didn't know what to say.

"Are you thinking about going home?"

"Yeah," I pointed at my boot. "Seems like the best thing to do. Think I got enough here for a ticket."

I pulled the Mexican postcard out of my back pocket and handed it to him.

"That's where I've been trying to go. It's somewhere in Mexico. But it hasn't worked out. It's been one thing after another, complete insanity the whole way."

I dropped my shoulders.

"Buck, America is a goddamn loony bin. I saw it myself and that's all it is. I don't think anyone knows it, either. The way we carry on—like we ain't all gone monkey nuts or somethin'."

I leaned back and closed my eyes.

"All I wanted to do was get to that beach. That was it."

I closed my eyes and a hundred dirty towns thundered through my skull. *Clickety clack, clickety clack.* A boxer freight two miles long. *Clickety clack.* A million ears of corn. *Clickety clack.* Crumpled notes from a Vietnam vet with a broken jaw— dead and gone. Three grand miles of metal flake. Sunburned diesel eyeballs. A man stone-dead at the bottom of a muddy river. A runaway kid with a golden grin. *Clickety clack, clickety clack.* Love and money. A waitress with hard hips and sweet movie-star lips and always that gospel music with its *clickety clack, clickety clack.* Pockets full of motel matchbooks and you wish you could—but you know you can't—ever go back. *Clickety clickety clack.*

"You know what, Buck?"

"What?"

"America's probably the most glamorous tragedy in all the world. All history. And you know what else, Buck?"

The Strip sparkled.

"I love her. I really do. Like my own flesh and blood."

BMX Boy

Buck had two old BMX bikes. A pink one with Barbie all over it and a blue one with lightning bolts. He wanted to show me the Sex Pistols slot machines at the Hard Rock Casino. So we rode bikes there. I got on the pink one, he got on the blue one, and we peddled down Maryland Parkway. Before we left he tied bandannas all over himself and they flapped all over the place when we rode. My new suit was trashed. It had motor oil on the sleeves and the joint in my pocket had burned a hole in it. I push extra hard to keep up with him. We passed weekly motels, big concrete canals, and tall power lines. When we stopped at Paradise and Flamingo a jeep full of college guys pointed and laughed at us. Buck didn't care and peddled away. I kicked my boot out and flipped them off.

"Take that, cushion head!"

I followed Buck up Paradise and threw my finger back behind me again. I was peddling so hard that the chain grabbed my pant leg, tore it, and threw me into the handlebars. The bike fell on top of me. Buck turned around and helped me up. We got grease all over our hands trying to pull my pant leg out. When we got to the Hard Rock Casino we ditched the bikes in the bushes, threw our sunglasses on, and strolled in rich.

Hard Cock Casino

The Hard Rock Casino is built on LA bedrock. It was laden in Hollywood boys in satin-collared shirts and shallow

smiles. They fly in for the weekend, unbutton the top two buttons, and become Las Vegas. Too bad it doesn't work that way.

The place was crawling with these rich twenty-five-year-
olds and it made me want to puke. The TV girls with their TV
haircuts, tart music, and all that hot ass in tight black pants.
They were looking for a star. The boy who could be something.
And all the boys were searching for the girl who would look
good on the trophy shelf beside the picture of their favorite football player. About as deep as a baby pool.

Buck only noticed the good things. The Sex Pistols slot
machine. The Jimmy Hendrix sport coat and Prince's famous
words about simple girls. The ones that don't have to be rich.
The ones that don't have to be cool. I wondered if Prince really
meant it.

The ladies were Coppertone like Misty but as timeless as
cheese. I wanted to ejaculate into the nearest slot. I wanted to
cut the skirt off a TV girl and eat her designer stockings.

We went to the bar and ordered Mexican beer and the
whole time we were sitting there Buck didn't acknowledge any
of the stares. After a few minutes the TV folks stopped staring
and some of them even talked to us.

The satin-collared boys weren't so bad. Talking to them
was like watching a soft porn. A mist passed through their sentences. Their words had been dulled by fantasy. The one
beside us was all neck and muscle. He was whispering something to his friend. I caught his last sentence and it wasn't very
nice.

"Where are you fellas from?" he asked.

"Vegas."

"What do you do for a living?"

"I'm a lover, a thief, and a tramp. My friend here's a gambler."

The satin-collared boys laughed, thinking I was joking. I took my hat off and leaned into him.

"You're an actor?" I asked.

"How'd you guess?"

"You smell like one."

He leaned back. He wasn't sure if he should laugh at me or punch me. He let out a little chuckle.

"What's that supposed to mean?"

"It means you've got too much chrome and not enough muscle."

"For a bum kid you sure got a lot to say."

"I'm just offering you some friendly advice, that's all."

"And what's that." He stood up, put his nose right up to mine, and cringed like a bull. I put my middle finger into the air and pushed up on it.

"Take your longest finger and stick it up your ass, take your right thumb and stick in your mouth, now close your eyes and dream. That's Hollywood. It's like a twelve-year-old trying to suck his own dick."

He sat there shaking his fat neck.

"Oh, boy!" I thought. "This is gonna get good."

I stood up, stepped on my toes, and backed into a boxing stance. I had assumed those would be the last words of the evening. You know when a midget gets called short or a cop gets called a pig. Words turn to fisticuffs real fast, real quick. The satin-collared boy looked down at me. I was bouncing around like Muhammad Ali. He pointed, grinned, and said the stupidest thing I'd ever heard.

"I drive a Harley."

He looked over at his friends for approval. They stabbed their elbows into the bar and slammed their beers down on the wood. They was ready to rumble. I looked around for the nearest exit. Buck stood off his stool and casually looked around the room. The music was Bob Dylan. The slots stopped burping, no one was winning, no one was talking. It was quiet. A tide of people shifted from the entrance and we had a clear shot for the door. I pulled my arm back as far as it would go and in one foul streak of genius swung, missed, and stumbled down the stairs and out the door with Buck right behind me.

Those fit and hungry boys would have eaten us for lunch, so we didn't have a choice. The doors swung open, our boots knocked over the sidewalk, past the valet, the ground turned to black top, and we were running down the street under the shifting light of sunrise. Buck's bandannas flying in the wind. My suit ripping in new places. Our toes fit perfectly into the chain-link fence and we disappeared into the future site of the Las Vegas Love Canal. It was a construction project that never had been completed and had been long abandoned. We climbed down into the canal and hid and laughed like two overzealous pirates. There was nothing left to steal. We shared a few words about the fight and our fabulous timing and how they thought they were gonna get the best of us. We patted each other on the back. Buck pulled out a flask of home-spiced rum and we got drunk in the dirt. We decided to change the world one sucker punch at a time. And we talked with pride as the city came to life.

Buck put his finger up to his mouth and perked up his ears.

"Quiet," he said, and rolled his eyes toward the embankment. I heard the straight pipes of a Harley-Davidson and the snap of a kickstand. We looked up and looming with the sun was the herd of bulls from the Hard Rock Casino—holding bottles of imported beer. Upside down and empty.

Dolly Parton

We dragged our bikes into the living room. I took a shower and went to sleep in Buck's extra room. The bed had red satin sheets and heart-shaped pillows and smelled like roses. The walls had been dedicated to Dolly Parton—pictures of her everywhere. There was a pinup on the ceiling. Her God-given gifts falling from the sky like papayas. On the wall in front of me was a poster of her sitting under a willow tree in a red-rodeo mist. I fell asleep with her in my arms. Turned out Buck was a member of her fan club.

I woke up at sunset and walked into the kitchen; Buck was in there. There was a large, smooth egg-shaped stone in the sink. He washed it off, then stuck it in a Tupperware container and poured distilled water over it. It was a Shiva lingam—the rock that Krishna sent Shiva into outer space to retrieve. Buck took it into his room, put it on his bed, and lay down next to it. I closed his door and went back into my room. Dolly was bright and country high.

★

The next morning I packed up my suitcase and went with Buck to the Greyhound station. He was going to Los Angeles to see his girlfriend. I gave him a hug and put him on a bus with all the hopefuls. As he drove away I thought that he might see the boys in satin-collared shirts and that maybe they would get him this time.

I walked outside, sat on my suitcase, and considered all of the time one could spend becoming a movie star and about poor Misty. I even considered catching the next bus to Hollywood. I pictured myself on the silver screen in front of the world and swimming in a rich lady's pool and sipping expensive gin and forgetting the point. I decided that I liked wide-open spaces, open road cowboy hats, and women who live for love, not for fame. A woman who wants fame bad enough will cheat for it and I didn't have time for that. I hailed a cab. The first two didn't stop on account of my suit. The third guy wore a turban and gladly took me to the airport.

Journal Entry # 13: Skid Row Downtown—Ice Palaces Uptown

> Chicago was at this time (and still qualifies) the down-and-outs' capital, the center of hobo-hemia, the temporary port of vagabonds and fugitives and hands for hire, the driftwood—the moochers, stewbums and dingbats—as well as the job-hunters and the working stiffs. West Madison Street is the slave market area, Clark Street is the Rialto of the slum—In Zorbaughs' description the "Zone of instability and change—the tide-lands of city life . . . an all-night street which harbors the criminal, the radical, the bohemian, the migratory worker, the immigrant, the unsuccessful, the queer and the unadjusted."
>
> KENNETH ALLSOP, REFERRING TO CHICAGO'S SKID ROW, PAST AND PRESENT, IN *HARD TRAVELLIN'*: *THE HOBO AND HIS HISTORY* (1968)

Skid road is an old logger term. It was the road down which they dragged all the trees and tree trunks. If a tramp was a tree trunk and pawn shops, hook joints, and tattoo parlors were woods, it would be the same situation. A tramp mooches the stem, he drags himself down the main drag, and everyone that sees him thinks "what a drag."

In the old days skid road was the place where you could get a room for a nickel and a shot of whisky for the same. There was usually a barrel house on skid road where you could buy cheap

hooch from the bottom of the barrel. It was the leftovers from
the finer drinking establishments, but it was cheap, so it didn't
matter where the hell it came from. Skid road has turned into
skid row and it's now the place where you'll find the homeless
shelter. I've visited homeless shelters from El Paso to Missoula
and they are all the same. The food sucks but tends to taste
good if you haven't eaten in a while. The beds suck but tend to
feel good if you haven't slept in a while, and the showers—they
just suck. A shelter is a social environment made up of the finest
bums, tramps, and the occasional hobo. They're a good source
of information. If you are unfamiliar with the train yard in a
town you can go to a shelter and there is usually someone there
who will know about the yards.

There is nothing finer than sleeping under the stars in an open
field. It's a sweet feeling. The temperature is right, the crickets
are conversing, and nobody in the entire world knows where you
are. But sometimes you get stuck in a big city during a snow-
storm and your clothes are wet and your bedroll is wet and
you're hungry and at that point there's only one place to go—the
Sal (Salvation Army). There is usually a brief sermon by the
resident salvation rancher, hallelujah peddler, mission squawker,
or preacher man, but he won't force it on you and if he does you
don't have to listen. If you do need a little God, he's tucked into
all the corners—painted on the walls in the form of murals—
hanging in the bathroom on little plaques of wisdom—mixed
into the gristle soup along with bullets and uncooked beans. I've
never been to prison but I believe a shelter is similar in many
ways. If you do sleep in a shelter it's important to rise early and
get some good walking in before sunrise. This will feel good in
the lungs and remind you of your freedom.

When you visit a shelter, remember this—the people who run
them are doing the work of God and they are also doing you a

favor, so they deserve respect. They will give you a blanket or a jacket if you need one and they will even sit down and talk to you about the road or the weather. They're folks who happen to spend their days with the crust of society, and through all of their ideals and beliefs they still understand that Jesus was a drifter and that we all came from the dust with nothing and that we will all return to the dust with nothing. They tend not to judge a man down on his luck.

The other option to a shelter is night travel or carrying the banner. In places such as the desert where it's real cold at night and hot during the day, it's better to travel at night. It's a simple way to avoid arrest or keep from freezing. The walking keeps you warm and when the sun comes up you find a nice bed of grass under a tree and get your sleep in during the day. A man who travels by night is called a nightcrawler. The nightcrawler is similar to Tokala the fox (a totem we'll talk about later). He doesn't care to be seen—he might not have anything to hide and he might not be running from anything. But he still wants to be left alone. Criminals and illegal Mexican field workers travel this way because they have the veil of night to protect them from the law. If the law can't see you, the restrictions of everyday life do not apply.

If you're not careful, skid row will beat you down and stick you to the ground like bubble gum. On the Strip, I looked in the mirror of that Cadillac and I knew I had troubles. I took my capital (a couple hundred bucks from selling the pot) and invested in myself. All I'm saying is that it is very important to take to the stem once in awhile. Pour that ink in the gutter—go to a nice diner—order a short stack of buttermilk flapjacks— trade your dirty shirt for a new one—buy a bow tie and butter- fly over to the Fireside Lounge in Las Vegas.

The ice palaces are uptown. Away from skid row. They have

soap in the bathroom and in Las Vegas there's a fellow standing
by the sink with a towel and a bottle of cologne. Give him a
couple coins and he'll hand you the bottle *and* the towel. The
bottle is usually green and it stinks. It's high octane Sin City.
It's not much—I know—but for that second you're a high
roller—a chance man—you can smell the roses again. Like it
used to be.

When I stepped off that Greyhound in Las Vegas I didn't
know what to do with myself, so I walked slow—like a nightcrawler. It was well after midnight, anyway, and I didn't want to
pay thirty dollars for three hours in a room. I carried the banner.
I walked the stem—Las Vegas Boulevard—and in the morning
I had my revelation. I had to get clean and tall again before I
fell into another bad situation. I was lucky—I had an ounce of
High Mountain Mexican and a full head of hair. I had capital.

Blow Off: In circus cant, the *end* of the show, when the concessionaires come out. In the carnival, specifically, when at the end of a show, the crowd (sometimes just the men) is often offered an extra added attraction for an extra fee, something you can pay to see (if you have a strong enough stomach or perhaps a strong enough desire to see a lady you think might be naked). The "blade box" (see glossary) is a classic carnival "blow off."

15
McCarren International Airport, Las Vegas
NOVEMBER 16, 1991—MORNING

Airports are the places where people are reunited. I watched a three-hundred-pound woman run into the arms of a three-hundred-pound man. They hugged like they hadn't seen each other in years. They both cried.

I was trembling. I pictured myself walking off the plane in Denver and seeing my father. He would cry and I would have to explain to him why I needed to do what I did. An airport security guard kept his eye on my nervous shuffle. I walked back and forth in my dirty suit. I kicked the leg out and dusted it off. I fixed the collar and stood tall.

The gate finally opened and a fine-voiced lady came on the intercom.

"Flight Four-Eleven now boarding for Denver."

I let out a tear. It landed on the toe of my boot. I watched it dry as I walked down the ramp. I could hear the dinner bell of home ringing and smell the wood stove burning and feel the grease building between my fingernails, and there in Denver I could see the leaves falling. I turned around. The fat couple walked alongside me.

In Denver it's always time to go. The town was cursed by the Indians a long time ago and the people who call it home only do so because they have to. The electric doors opened and I was blasted by the sun. I tilted my hat and walked like a cowboy into the sunset of the world's loneliest town. Las Vegas.

I would go home when I was broke. I know that a broke man is usually a single man, but a single man can go and do whatever he pleases. I was nineteen years old and strong and that alone was reason enough for me to keep trying. A broken heart wouldn't be enough to put me on that plane.

"Things become important when you go out and see them."

So I walked up Tropicana and found a pay phone. I called my father and got the answering machine again.

"Dad, it's me. I'm in Las Vegas. Man, I can't even start to tell you everything. I love you. I thought you should know that. I really do, might not seem like it, but I do. I'm all right. Last month ain't been easy, it's been harder than hell. But I did good. I felt things I've never felt before and I've seen things I've never seen before. I'm torn up but my spirit's still good and strong. Vegas is real freaky. I met this gambler named Buck. Don't worry about me, okay? I'm going to Mexico, I didn't think I'd make it but I'm gonna and I bet there's a lot of other places we could go to. I just can't come back to Denver right now—seen too much. I'll call again in a couple days. Don't worry about me, okay? I love you."

I hung up, straightened my jacket, and headed up Tropicana. I walked three miles to the Boulder Highway, sat on my suitcase, and stuck my thumb in the breeze. I'd take it south to Kingman and from there nail a hotshot to the border.

Journal Entry # 14: Laredo; The Rainbow

There's a junker that goes from San Antonio, Texas, to Laredo, Texas. I figure that it runs once every two days. If you ever find yourself in San Antonio I would recommend taking this train. There's an air force base outside of town—which direction, I can't remember, but the yard is near it. There's a little hobo jungle over the fence from the yard and when you sit in the trees with the bugs and snakes the fighter planes blast directly overhead. The ride to Laredo from San Antonio will only take seven hours and you'll be rewarded with beautiful scenery. Laredo is the rainbow—the gateway to Mexico. It's a border town and a border town is a place of transition. A place where you leave any concept of security you had behind.

I would compare crossing the border into Mexico to walking into a freight yard for the first time. The smell of diesel is replaced with the smell of tortillas but the sense of helplessness is the same. The fear is the same. The first few days are always difficult but eventually you *are* rewarded. In Mexico you get beautiful people and sunshine. In the train yards you get a trade and a step-by-step introduction to the most immense feeling of lawlessness that exists. A dangerous freedom.

If you really want to get away, you have to go to other countries like Mexico, Belize, or Guatemala. And maybe find the mescal man. You can buy mescal in the little tiendas or you can buy it direct and dirty from the mescal man himself. He sells the cheap stuff—bottom of the barrel hooch. He hustles his third rail smoke out of a gasoline can. If you want to have a real blast, bring your own bottle down south and bathe in the tropical sun with all the other mescal muchachos. They're the men with leather skin, loose muscles, and well-fed stomachs who sleep in the midday sun. They lay on the corner and let the Coca-Cola trucks blow diesel down their throats. They have all the time in the Mexican world, mescalitos in dreamland busted like an American tramp. You can sail swift *along along* the Caribbean coast like a pirate—grab some shade under a palm tree and not worry a bit about how tired or busted you are because everyone down there is busted down and dirty in pink handmade dresses and Mexican pompadours. Busted but happy to be alive.

★

I have cried alone in Mexico and I have cried alone in America and the pain is the same. It's that of a young man trying so hard to find a place to call home. The funny thing is that I grow more in three weeks on the trains than I do in six weeks off of them. Off the trains I feel like a dime on a dirt road—like if I don't keep rolling I'll get pushed deep into the mud. I'm in Las Vegas now looking at these damn notebooks and wondering how the hell I could ever get this story into words. The tears don't write themselves down. I told myself I wouldn't leave until they did.

I can hear wedding bells from my motel room. Elvis got married seven times right here on Las Vegas Boulevard and where did that get him. Dead. No, I'm not any closer to home. But I am out here on the range breathing that sage and daydreaming. Reliving the three weeks that changed my life forever. Buckthorn Superstar is with me. His apartment is just down the road from here. If you enjoyed this story at all you can thank him for that. He is a very wise man and his knowledge of life and words made part of this story possible. Before I had a con-

tract or money he let me camp out in his extra room and write. I
stayed with him for three weeks and during this time we went
through my manuscript with a fine-tooth comb. I love him for
that.

The golden gates do come.

No matter what I have witnessed with cynical eyes and no matter what I have written about my observations—I still see diamonds on the horizon. I see my dimes turning to quarters and
my old ways finding retribution in the pine-cone air.

I found a home in Reno for two days with Misty and a home
in the heart of Alabama and a home under that willow tree in
Green River. The last I heard, Alabama was dead. He got
stabbed in some dispute over squatters' land in New Mexico. If
he is dead, then this book is for him too, and if you aren't dead,
Alabama, look me up for God's sake.

Now that I'm done with this book I'm going to go to the
Midwest, find some dirt track, and race old Fords. I'll peel
around that track like a jackrabbit. Kind of like my grandfather
Don. Next time you see me, I'll be a fluent mechanic with
bloody knuckles and I'll have another lowbrow story about
dumb little towns with no names.

Or maybe I'll join the 400—go straight and become a family
man. I don't know. It's not my job to know. For now you can
find me here in downtown Las Vegas. I'll be the one drooling
on the coffee counter—sneaking naps and sipping sorrow. My
girlfriend's gone, left a few weeks ago—guess her "real" world
didn't approve of me. I regret to say that it is with a broken
heart that I give this to you.

If you think that it's so very important to be a responsible man or a responsible woman, then you should be prepared to do whatever it takes to accomplish a sense of place and respect. The first step is knowing what responsibility actually is—is it being a Christopher Columbus, discovering new lands and ripping off Indians with pretty beads? Or is it driving an eighteen-wheeler and sleeping in the cab with a small television set and a VCR? It has to be one or the other. So, until someone tells me the right way to live, I'm going to sit by this river with my self-caught fish, my wood flame, and a felt-tip pen.

If you see me standing in the drainage ditch on the side of the road—pick me up and bring me with you to wherever you're going, I don't care. And if you know something about living that I don't—let me in on it. I am just like you. I need to feel as much love as humanly possible before my time runs out. We all deserve more than this.

Just like me, you probably know of a nice roadhouse on the horizon where the laughter flows and the love resides. And just like me, you know what it actually takes to get there. You get what you ask out of life and that's just an old simple truth. A truth that's as real as the book that you are holding in your hands. But watch out, because if the sun gets a hold of this book it'll dry up, the cover will fade, and the binding will melt—so there goes all that truth changing again and there we go looking into the neon horizon with sunset eyes—hoping for the best and sharing all the rest.

Epilogue: Sunset Road

A tramp does his homework.
The cowboy, the Indian and the tramp
A brief hobo history

My story ended in Las Vegas and that's where I am right now. I walk up and down the Strip a lot. I ran into that same nail punch the other day. The one in the beginning of the book who said, "A house is not a home if love does not reside there." He was sitting under a palm tree at this business park near my apartment building. This time he was drunk. After a handshake and a hug he looked me straight in the eye and said:

"Dice dope dames. Man! Hobos built the damn railroad. Hobos! They blew their payroll on dice dope dames. And when the railroad was done, they were as broke as when they started so they had to hop a damn freight. Those were the first hobos."

I went to the Las Vegas public library that very same day and checked out every book I could on the subject of trains and train riders. I wanted to figure out when this train riding business started and what it really meant to be a hobo. A hobo isn't *just* a hobo. Part of a hobo *is* born that way but the other part of him learned it. I wanted to know where he learned it from.

The Indians

"They were hoboing before hoboing was hoboing and you just can't argue with that."

> WINTER LINCOLN, RAMBLING PHILOSOPHER, REFERRING
> TO NATIVE AMERICAN INDIANS, SALVATION ARMY,
> SAN ANTONIO, TEXAS, FALL 1993

Last fall I was riding a northbound out of Denver. It was a cool night—there was ice in the air and I could see my breath. The train drifted west through Boulder and turned north toward Fort Collins. Outside of Boulder there's a turnout where the coal trains disappear into a power plant. There's a lake in front of it and it is very pretty at night. I looked out the other side of the grainer and saw a large fire burning in the trees. There was tin roofing on the west side of the pit to shelter it from the wind and inside, covered in blazing cinders, were a hundred red-hot river stones. The men that tended the fire had no idea that I was sitting on the train. They were hunched over long-handled shovels and wearing baseball caps and cowboy hats. I'd have sworn on all my holy Bibles that it was a hobo jungle and that these men were preparing stew and coffee while waiting for a train to take them somewhere else. They had the perfect spot

to catch out, the perfect batch of trees to hide in, and the perfect black pearl sky to sit under. But they were Indians. To the
east of the fire pit was a circle of rocks. In the center sat a buffalo skull circled in sagebrush and tobacco ties. Three feet past
the skull was a small sweat lodge that was wrapped in blankets
and old carpet. In the light of the fire and the moon the lodge
looked like a globe of the earth.

★

I went back to that spot three weeks later. The Indians were still
there. They were Lakota Sioux from North Dakota and they let
me take part in their sweat lodge ceremony. This experience
changed me in ways it would take many books to explain. The
ancient smell of water on hot stones and sagebrush burning
brought me closer to the land that my tired bones had been
tramping over for many years. The medicine man who led the
ceremony told the story of Tokala. "Tokala" is the Lakota word
for fox, and the fox is one of many animals that they consider
sacred. In the book *Animals of the Soul: Sacred Animals of the
Oglala Sioux* by Joseph Epes Brown, Brave Buffalo (a late
nineteenth-century Teton Sioux medicine man) said this:

> Let a man decide upon his favorite animal and make
> a study of it . . . let him learn to understand its
> sounds and motions. The animals want to communi-
> cate with man, but Wakan Tanka does not intend
> they shall do so directly—man must do the greater
> part in securing an understanding.

The fox is a gentle animal. Tribes that identified with the fox
concentrated more on camp life and hunting and less on war-
fare. The fox's power was in underground things such as herbs

and roots, and by sharing this knowledge with people, he showed them how to use their natural resources for healing. The fox is clever and swift. During the sweat lodge ceremony the medicine man told us the story of the fox who lived outside the village. He would protect the village but rarely take part in its function. Tokala was a mystery—a shadow. He ran from view when the light of the campfire was cast in his direction. You might see him out of the corner of your eye but if you turned to look he'd be gone. I immediately thought of a comet.

A comet is a hobo who rides the high 48s, the hotshots, or any train just for the pure scenery of it. He's there on a flat car freight rolling slowly through your town—you might see this hobo out of the corner of your eye but if you turn to look he'll be gone. A comet understands the ways of underground things. He keeps his camp outside the village. He doesn't enter the village but for grub and stake[10] and no matter the town or the people in that town, he will—with all his broken heart and mangled hand—protect it. He might clean the alleyways of aluminum cans or he might give bad directions to a grifter who wanted to "do business" in your town.

A hobo's joy comes while sitting on a park bench, watching his brothers and sisters work toward their great American dream. If the need in him arises, he might go for a jog around the park—run side by side with the folks in high-tech shoes. He might run two miles—hard and heavy in old boots. But eventually the hobo will tire and disappear.

The hobo lives off the land. He's patient. He takes time

---

10. Grub and stake is a term derived from "grub stake," which is defined as: A sum of money for food and outfit, given to a prospector by a storekeeper or another who then shared in whatever minerals the prospector might discover. It is also closely related to the term "road stake," which is defined as: Money to live on while traveling, or with which to secure transportation.

for reflection. When the hobo wanders—drunk from his tears—he feels the earth's heartbeat through the hole in his boot. And that simple connection with the earth is what the hobo has in common with the Indian. Tokala the fox is gentle and strong. His interest is in underground things. He is always there but will only appear when the need for him arises. The hobo needs a totem and the fox seems to fit him best.

The Cowboys

"You find sympathy between shit and syphilis in the dictionary."

—FROM *RIDING THE RAILS* BY MICHAEL MATHERS

In the late 1700s the western part of America was the land of the free selector. Squatter's land, the Wild West. There were fur traders and scouts and Indians and hunters, and under the big ponderosas they all lived hard and free. No trains or milk-shakes—just a pair of feet and a gun. If I were alive back then, that's where I would have lived. I'd have gladly wrestled a rabbit into the stew and slept in a cold cave, like an icicle in the land of milk and honey. The Wild West was one of the first hobo jungles as near as I can figure, a fur trapper sending embers into the sky and stinking up the frontier with burnt rabbit fur and gunpowder. I figure you don't need a train or a broken tooth or a big head full of resource to be a hobo. No, I figure the first cowboy who could keep himself from the temptation of responsibility and out of the crosshairs of society—he was probably the first hobo. Unless, of course, you consider what my friend Winter Lincoln said about the Indians.

The hobo is an American original. I think all the Pilgrims who flew the European coop and came to America were a bit loose in the boots to begin with. They came with diamonds in their eyes and managed to spread their restless seed across the continent. They created a land of bums and hot dogs. A star-freckled land of make-believe. America. When they got here they called themselves "settlers" and ran into the frontier like a pack of hound dogs, sniffing and barking and drooling all over the place. Some of these settlers went completely loony tunes out there and became an active part of the food chain—others came back with their tails between their legs. Whatever fate a man or woman of the frontier chose was completely self-made and all the tramps that have ever been or who will ever be are a direct reflection of those first American decisions. The tramp is what America found in bed with herself after a hard night of drinking. We're all still just a bunch of windbags, anyway—tramping through the land, looking for the pot of gold or a heel of bread, whichever comes first.

By the late 1800s America was cut up by fences and fences don't mean anything when you're on a train. The railroad came along in the late 1820s and changed everything. Soon the cowboy hero in dime-store books traded in his saddle for steam, and the romance of the cowboy cavalier was stuck on the back of a freight train. Trains rumbled through backyards. Trains rocked baby cradles. Kids grew up wanting to work on the railroads. Wherever those trains were going, kids wanted to go.

The Civil War

The old-time American tramp was recruited largely from the ranks of the Civil War veterans who found it hard to settle down to a humdrum existence, or who failed to find employment after the war; these men in turn drew others from the street gamins, who then knew no higher entertainment than listening to the exciting tales of tramp life told them by the oldsters.

—GODFREY IRWIN, REFERRING TO CIVIL WAR VETERANS IN HIS
BOOK *AMERICAN TRAMP AND UNDERWORLD SLANG* (1930)

When the Civil War ended in 1861, many soldiers from both sides found themselves on the road. They looked to the railroads for work and became part of the labor force that built the American railroad system. In his book *Hard Travellin': The Hobo and His History,* Kenneth Allsop also refers to these men:

There was a short hectic boom. The transcontinental link was made by the crashing hammers of Irish and ex-convicts and mule-skinners and men still in scraps of blue and gray uniforms thrusting inland from the East, and the Chinese and Mexicans thrusting inland from the West.

On May 10, 1869, the Central Pacific and the Union Pacific joined at Promontory Summit in Utah—completing the transcontinental railroad. This moment was celebrated by pounding the "golden spike." Before the railroad was complete a man on horseback could expect to spend six months crossing the continent and take the chance of being one in ten travelers who died trying. This same trip took six days by train. After its completion the transcontinental railroad would be blamed for taming the Wild West.

In 1873 the railroad boom ended and the work ran out. The railroad workers—including gandy dancers, graders, gaugers, bolters, and spikers—were stuck in devil's country, unemployed, so they hopped freight—the same freight they laid track for. They tramped around the country looking for work. There was a depression at the time, so many of them ended up staying on the rails for years—beating from town to town—bumming food at back doors and sleeping in the dirt.

The advent of the huge agribusiness-based tract farm in the late 1840s also facilitated the hobo, as Kenneth Allsop wrote about here:

> The commitment of almost all the Middle West to wheat during the second half of the nineteenth century killed the American tradition of the small, compact, diversified family farm, and set in motion the process toward the huge agribusiness prairie tract. It also created the short-term harvest hand. The man for whom the need was urgent but brief, a beautiful person in the sight of God when the wheat ears hung heavy but whose absence was required in short order, as soon as the single stupendous crop was in.

This need for seasonal help created the migratory worker. There are still tramps who follow these same harvests—mostly Mexicans. In the old days they carried a hoe and a bedroll and they were called hoe-boys, which probably turned into hobos but no one knows for sure.

By the late 1800s the tramp was proving to be a real pain in the ass for the rich folks. He was sleeping in their dirt, stealing their chickens, and crowding their city streets. So they came up with ways to get rid of him.

On July 12, 1877 the *Chicago Tribune* printed this method for dealing with hobos:

> The simplest plan, probably, where one is not a member of the Humane Society, is to put a little strychnine or arsenic in the meat and other supplies furnished the tramp. This pro-

duces death within a comparatively short period of time, is a warning to other tramps to keep out of the neighborhood, keeps the Coroner in good humor, and saves one's chickens and other portable property from constant destruction.

And nine years later in 1886 the supervisors of Westchester County, New York, published this:

Hundreds of this class flock to this county from New York and the adjoining State of Connecticut. . . . These tramps are a source of great danger and great nuisance to our citizens. . . . The expense, directly and indirectly, to the tax payers of this city, caused by this tramp raid, has reached the enormous sum of 75,000 dollars per year.

In this same report the superintendents of the poor and asylums were instructed:

To erect a building in a suitable place on the county farm, which shall be so situated and constructed that it can be flooded with water to the depth at least six feet, and so arranged with apartments and platforms that all persons com-mitted as tramps and vagrants can be placed therein and thereon, and when the water is turned on to be compelled to bail or be submerged thereby.

This shelter for the homeless was never built.

The IWW

And on him, as he wanders forth in a world that is a wilder-ness to him, are heaped the sins of society. About the only consolation left the truly unfortunate tramp is the thought that

Christ was a tramping vagabond whom the world crucified to
get rid of, and all honest men suffer for the sins of the world.

—*THE WEEKLY WORKER*, AUGUST 14, 1875

In 1905 the hobo got pissed off. He was sick of being treated
like shit and working for shit wages, so he organized a union.
It would be called the Industrial Workers of the World, or the
IWW. Members called themselves Wobblies and their mottos
were "to push back, pull out, or break off the fangs of
Capitalism," "to fan the flames of discontent," and "he who
travels lightest, travels fastest." Their song and lifestyle contained the philosophy of travel and the need for radical action
against a system that did not nurture the free man.

Wobblies tore through the country with propaganda, beat-
up guitars, and broken fists—rambling from campfire to campfire—unionizing labor. They carried red cards that granted
them hassle-free travel on many train lines—mostly in the
Pacific Northwest—where they were accepted by the agrarian
Populists who also believed that the real enemies were the
"money barons," "lords of industry," and "the vested interest
who threshed the real profits out of America's crops."

In the opening campaign for the IWW Agricultural
Workers' Organization, one of the Wobbly job delegates, or
"rigging packers," explained it like this (also from Kenneth
Allsop's *Hard Travellin': The Hobo and His History*):

With pockets lined with supplies and literature we left
Kansas City on every available freight train, some going into
the fruit belts of Missouri and Arkansas, while others spread
themselves over the states of Kansas and Oklahoma, and
everywhere they went, with every slave they met on the job,
in the jungles or on the freight trains, they talked IWW, dis-

tributed their literature and pointed out the advantage of
being organized into a real labor union.

The outcome was rarely peaceful and the wheat belt
became a battleground—fighting between union members and
land barons raged hard and heavy.

At this point the federal government saw the IWW as a
serious threat to their system and did everything it could to
break up their unions. They flooded the wheat belt with sur-
plus men in order to replace any of the strikers. When the strikers had control and the harvest was in jeopardy railroad police
busted into jungles with rifles in hand, rounded up every bindle
stiff in sight, and brought them to the government employment
office. If they accepted the wage offered they were sent to work,
if they refused they were put on a passenger train and made to
pay their own way out of town. Regardless, the IWW blazed
through the wheat belt like wildfire and made the working class
think about themselves and their situation. Between 1915 and
1918 the IWW managed to recruit fifty thousand members into
their agricultural branch, in turn raising the daily wage from
three or three and a half dollars a day to four dollars. By 1920
IWW members were rejecting employment at seven and a half
dollars a day. That same year in Aberdeen, South Dakota, four
hundred bindle stiffs marched through town protesting the
offered wage of sixty cents an hour and chanting the IWW slo-
gan: "We don't want an honest day's wage for a day's toil. We
want the abolition of the wage system." At this point the IWW
was getting too powerful—the flames were getting too high, so
the government began putting Wobblies in jail for inciting
rebellion against the state. In California more than five hundred
Wobblies were indicted in a cleanup called the "Big Pinch."
This more or less busted the IWW to pieces and in the process

gave the anti-tramp folks new artillery. Now hobos weren't just bums that should be poisoned, they were political outcasts, revolutionaries, traitors of the state. They were opposed to the war, big-money interest, the wage system, and capitalism. All of the things that supposedly made America great. The Wobbly's ability to stand up for himself made him an enemy to the state and the rich and therefore he needed to be destroyed. In *Hard Travellin'*, one Wobbly leader explained his situation like this:

"If you were a bum without a blanket; if you had left your wife and kids when you went West for a job, and had never located them since; if your job had never kept you long enough in a place to qualify you to vote; if you slept in a lousy, sour bunkhouse, and ate food just as rotten as they could give you and get by with it; if deputy sheriffs shot your cooking cans full of holes and spilled your grub on the ground; if your wages were lowered on you when the bosses thought they had you down; if there was one law for Ford, Suhr and Mooney, and another for Harry Thaw;[11] if every person who represented law and order and the nation beat you up, railroaded you to jail, and the good Christian people cheered and told them to go to it, how in the hell do you expect a man to be patriotic?"

More Thoughts on the Wobbly

A hobo can use his hands. That's his pride. America needed the hobo to harvest and labor. The Wobblies defended the hobo from America's "land barons" and "lords of industry."

---

11. In this sense, Harry Thaw refers to any man living outside the constraints of "normal" society (including a Wobbly himself), and Ford, Suhr, and Mooney refer to men afforded higher civic and political luxuries because of their economic and political standing.

And in that war for labor rights, the hobo, the Wobbly—the overworked hand of America's laboring class—was hammered and chiseled into history. In every jungle and at every division point along the line there is the ghost of at least one hobo who died trying to find his bread and his liberty. When there's a fire burning in the jungle, he is recognized not in words or prayers but in the eyes of the men who still ride. On a freight train history is frozen. The hobo has been living the same way for over a hundred years. He still ties up his bedroll with old belts and he still picks up odd jobs in odd towns. The jungles aren't what they used to be. The freight is faster. America is faster. But hobos and tramps are still the same. You can look in the eye of a young train rider and still see the frustration of a Wobbly.

Thoughts on War

War equals post-traumatic stress disorder—Alabama had it and lived with it. Life in the United States of America wasn't the same for him when he got back from Vietnam. When we traveled together we hardly talked about the war at all. Alabama smoked cigarettes when he could get them and he built fires by the railroad tracks. That was his therapy. His heart was broken and probably wouldn't get fixed. I was his friend but I didn't ask him about his past. It's not something train riders talk about. It's over. Men who fought in the Civil War built railroads and tramped the same track they built. They fought like dogs and got put out. War puts men on trains. Most tramps who have taken lives in the name of liberty don't want to talk about it—therefore, offering a fellow tramp a swig of your wine is a substantial gesture of compassion—no matter the wars he has fought or the burdens he has lumbered. Beautiful, lifelong friendships can flower from this one silent and simple gesture.

The American Indians were victims of war. The cavalry raised hell with them and they got murdered or put out. The descendants of these Indians have survived and some of them ride trains. The Indians got put out, along with the Civil War vets, the Vietnam vets, the drunks, the confused, the uninspired—all the men and women of "moronic" or "inept" personality. They are the railroad hobos and the turnpiker tramps.

> These men are the new cowboys
> And when these bridgers pass away
> "Take the westbound" as they say
> Their offspring will safeguard the cannonball secrets
> carry the tradition,
> to a land far far away
> And no matter which vice they stop to please
> they will always know their place—
> in the trees
> out of sight
> a whisper below the breeze.

> Yours Truly,
> Eddy Joe Cotton

That is the core of trampdom. It's what I learned from talking to tramps and from sitting in the Las Vegas Public Library for three days studying the history of hobos. A hobo is an outlaw spirit, either man or woman, who takes the law of freedom above all other. And that is my only conclusion:

> A clown in the rain
> He thinks about having a nice home
> A place that would keep him out of the hard
>   weather

But he knows that would break him down—
Trying to keep up and feel right
Fly straight, think straight in a crooked world
Easier to catch a cold and a freight
Stay free
Like a clown in the rain

Glossary

ACE *CENTER FLOW* — See "Grainer."

Alley Apple — A stone or piece of brick or paving used as a missile in street fighting.

Artist — Any skillful crook or confidence worker who inspires respect in his work by other, less gifted criminals.

Bad Road — A train line rendered useless by some tramp's bad action. A train line, train car, or train track that is in disrepair. A "flat wheel" + "bad road" = a bad day.

Bale of Straw — A blond woman. Very generally used in circus and carnival circles, and obvious as to origin, the more so since the large and sturdy type of woman is the one that makes the greatest appeal to the men who follow the show and demand their play, to match their work, in large doses.

Barrel House—Originally, and before prohibition, the cheap Bowery resorts where the dregs from liquor barrels were served at as little as a penny a drink. Any cheap-lodging house, speakeasy, or brothel of the lowest, filthiest sort, where the money to pay for a drunken sleep is all that is asked of a patron.

Barrel Stiff—An old, worn-out bum, living in a barrel house, eating whatever may be salvaged from garbage cans or cheap lunchrooms, and absolutely without hope or ambition. Starlet (see) + Barrel Stiff = "a union born of gasoline and good nature."

Beachcomber—A tramp or bum who hangs about waterfront saloons and the docks and begs food from sailors. Adopted from the correct usage to indicate a tramp in the tropics.

Beezer—The nose.

Big Top—The main tent used for a circus performance.

Bindle—A bedroll carried by tramps and migratory workers, and no doubt a corruption of "bundle."

Bindle Stiff—A tramp or worker carrying his bedding or "bindle."

Biscuit Shooter—A waitress or short-order cook. The average tramp and migratory worker is not used to restaurants where the food or service is of the best, and the manner in which the dishes are "shot" at the diner is reflected in the term for the person responsible.

Black Strap—Coffee, so called from the blackstrap molasses with which the beverage is sweetened in logging camps and on tramp ships in lieu of the more expensive refined sugar.

Blade Box—A carnival act in which a performer (on most accounts a woman) stands or lies in a wooden box while swords are carefully pushed through it, creating the illusion that the woman is impossibly contorting her body. At the completion of the performance the woman will remove what scant cloth-ing she has on and the men in the audience will be coerced into paying an extra fee to peek into the box, usually to be disappointed by the sight of a G-string or swimsuit. The blade box is a classic carnival "blow off."

Blowed-in-the-Glass—Genuine; to be trusted. From the old-time liquor bottles and other containers, which had the name of the maker or the product blown in the glass to ensure the quality. A "blowed-in-the-glass stiff," then, is one who never works, is in the know, and is able to take care of himself in any situation.

Blow Off—In circus cant, the *end* of the show, when the concessionaires come out. In the carnival, specifically, when at the end of a show, the crowd (sometimes just the men) is often offered an extra added attraction for an extra fee, something you can pay to see (if you have a strong enough stomach or perhaps a strong enough desire to see a lady you think might be naked). The "blade box" (see) is a classic carnival "blow off."

Blind—An old term for the front end of a baggage or mail car on a passenger train; more especially and more correctly when the door is locked and when there is no platform. A dangerous place on which to ride, but one much favored by the younger, more daring tramps. Also used in the plural.

Bonehead—A dolt or simpleton. A stupid error or faux pas, in this connection usually a "bonehead play." In both instances the term is apt, for no one whose head was not thick, or largely of bone, would make the mistake.

Bone Orchard—A graveyard. To most vagabonds the material things in life far outweigh any other consideration, and the one crop a graveyard may be depended on to yield is certainly bones.

Boneyard—See "Bone Orchard."

Brakeman—Train crew member responsible for track and car management. Also referred to as a "brakie." See "Switchman."

Breeze—Idle chatter; talk of no importance. False information.

Bridger—A train rider who has ridden both steam and diesel trains. Hence "bridging" the two eras of railroad technology.

Bull—An armed private employee of the railroad who is hired to protect the railroad's land, equipment, and freight. Also referred to as "railroad police," "special agents," or "railroad detectives."

Bullets—Beans, often served so poorly cooked that they are as hard and as indigestible as their namesake.

Bull Horrors—A morbid fear of the police, usually the result of a previous ill-treatment at their hands, or from the realization that an arrest would mean a long term of imprisonment.

Bum—The tramp who does not travel and who will not work; one who lives on charity from choice, although in many cases able to earn a living. One of the most generally misapplied definitions in underworld and tramp argot, but clearly explained in the words of an experienced hobo: "Bums loafs and sits. Tramps loafs and walks. But a hobo moves and works, and he's clean."

Bums on the Plush—The idle rich. Although the true "bum" is one who "loafs and sits" and neither works nor wanders, this term is given those members of society who need not work for a living and who are able to travel about on "the plush," that is, in passenger coaches and Pullman cars, the tramp's idea of luxury. Of IWW origin. The hobo's idea of the "bum on the plush" and his responsibility for social misery is well put in the verse that declares:

The bum on the rods is a social flea
Who gets an occasional bite,
The bum on the plush is a social leech,
Bloodsucking day and night.

Burlington Northern—A railway (freight) company.

Business—Actions by a performer intended to establish atmosphere, reveal character, or explain a situation. (A guy comes on stage, looks off left, leans against the lamppost, looks at his watch, sighs, and lights a smoke.) A vaudeville term.

California Blanket—Newspapers, when used as bedding or stuffed inside the clothing to keep out the cold. So called since much of the southern part of the state has a climate that allows sleeping out of doors with but scant covering.

Calling In—Visiting; using another's campfire for cooking or to warm the person.

Can Moocher—A tramp or bum, filthy, lost to hope and ambition and often demented, an exile from everything worthwhile. Originally the tomato can was used as a container into which were drained the dregs from beer kegs outside of saloons; later the same receptacle came to be used as a catchall for begged or salvaged food.

Cannonball—A fast, scheduled freight or express train. A note or other message sent by one in jail through a trusty, or the other way around. In both cases the question of speed is responsible for the word.

Canvas Joint—A carnival game housed in a portable canvas-on-wooden-frame shack.

Carny—Someone who works in a carnival. The term is also applied to the carnival itself. Used by some in the business and disliked by others, because it can imply that the person or attraction is less than reputable.

Carrying the Banner—Walking the streets all night to avoid arrest as a vagrant or to keep from freezing.

C, H, and D—Cold, hungry, and dry. The tramp "calling in" at a jungle fire will declare he is "C, H, and D" to indicate he wants food and drink, with an opportunity to warm himself. A play on the initials of the old Cincinnati, Hamilton, and Dayton Railroad.

Chopper—A machine gun or the man operating such a weapon with a gang of racketeers or robbers. A custom motorcycle with an elongated front fork; also, a "coffin"-shaped fuel tank (usually adorned with a cryptic mural, painted in a high-gloss "metal flake" paint), a backrest or "sissy bar," and highway bars (especially high foot pegs to allow the rider a "laid-back and far-out" riding stance).

Cinder Bull—An older term for "bull." (See "Bull.") More specifically, a bull who patrolled "over the road" or the "right of way."

Click—To succeed. No doubt from the "click" of a roulette ball when it drops into the division of the wheel, and by which someone is lucky enough to win. The term is widely used by actors and stage folk.

Comet—A high-class tramp or a hobo who rides only fast trains, and for long distances, even though there is no reason for such moves.

Conductor—Crew member who rides with engineer in the front unit. A "train boss" who orders movements such as cutouts and pickups. See "Engineer."

Coupler—The large steel clasps between freight cars that hold them together. See "Knuckles."

Cover with the Moon—To sleep in the open.

Creepers—Felt or rubber-soled shoes worn by prison guards and sneak thieves; sneakers or tennis shoes.

Cut Out—To drop off one or more freight cars on a siding or in a freight yard. Usually for the use of a customer, to be filled and "cut in" to another train later.

Daddy—A Cadillac automobile.

Dago Red—Cheap red wine, such as that usually drunk by Italian laborers.

Deadheading—Driving a truck (an eighteen-wheeler) without cargo, an empty trailer. Also, "hauling sailboat fuel" or "hauling a load of dispatcher brains."

Dingbat—A tramp or bum of low degree.

Ditch—To hide; to secrete; to desert; to put off a train by force or threat. In the first three instances, from the fact that anything placed in a ditch is not readily seen; in the last, from the ditch along the right of way, into which one falls when thrown from a moving train.

Division—Any location "over the road" where railroads change crew.

Do Rag—An elastic or Spandex fabric with two attached tie-downs. Used with a curl-activating hair product to promote a healthy Jheri Curl.

Double Down—A gambling term (specifically blackjack). The players' option to double their original bet in exchange for receiving one more card. Usually but not always a player may only double down after receiving the first two cards. The amount of the additional wager can be less than the original one, though this is not common. In some casinos the additional card is dealt facedown and not exposed till the end of the round, hence "double down." In blackjack it is wise to double down if your first two cards add up to eleven—considering that when you hit, the odds of getting a face card are good.

Double Nickel—Traveling at 55 mph; a 55-mph speed limit. A trucker term.

Double Sawbuck—A twenty-dollar bill; a twenty-year jail sentence. In both cases, from the double X, indicating twenty in Roman numerals.

Drag—Influence; a slow freight. Influence because it is often through this "pull" or "drag" that one is often able to obtain a desired end or to secure preferment; a slow freight, always so called on a railroad, since these trains drag their way over the road.

Drifter—A person who lacks aspirations, goals, or enterprise. A "drifter" is mostly associated with the interstate or a lost soul who travels aimlessly. Can be seen walking alongside most any American roadway.

Driftwood—See "Drifter."

Elevated—Under the influence of liquor or drugs; from the fact that one is then high-spirited.

Engineer—Crew member who drives the train and is also the crew boss.

Fag—A cigarette.

Faker—One who shams or pretends; one who "fakes" or improvises an excuse.

Fence Mender—One who fixes broken fences, especially on a ranch where barbwire is often in need of repair.

First of May—Properly, anyone newly employed by the circus, where the season starts about the first of May. By adoption, any tramp, but one newly arrived in a "push" or new to tramp life and as yet inexperienced.

Flame Job—A paint job on a custom car or hot rod that displays a graphic representation of flames, usually starting at the front of the car and working toward the back. The flames are traditionally painted in a place where actual flames could manifest under "too fast and too hard" racing conditions. Possibly borrowed from similar graphics on World War II fighter planes.

Flatbed—See "Flats."

Flatcar—See "Flats."

Flats—A flatcar; a freight car with no walls. They have wood floors that can be used to nail down "load blocking" to prevent a load from shifting and "stake pockets" on the side if vertical staking is necessary. This was a commonly used term in a railroad eating house, where "a string of flats, plenty of pin grease, and a tank of murk" would mean an order for a plate of pancakes with plenty of butter, and a cup of coffee.

Flat Wheel—See "Flatwheeler."

Flatwheeler—A freight car with one or more flat wheels. Caused by a brake clamping down too hard, freezing rotation and causing the wheel to slide down the rail on a braking train. The wheel is ground flat, thus creating a violent jerking and bouncing motion. A bad ride for a tramp.

Flip—To board a moving train. The act of a rider being flipped or flirted against the side of the train as he boards it.

Flop—A bed, or a place to sleep. From the fact that one drops heavily asleep, or with a dull thud when falling. Also used to indicate a fall. A failure.

Flying Light—Hungry; without food; traveling without any excess impediment such as a bindle. From the railroads, where a light engine is one traveling over the line without a train, and so able to move swiftly and without needless delay.

Ford Marriage—A union born of gasoline and good nature. The man and woman continue to live together, traveling about the country from job to job in a car until the man tires of his consort, or until she becomes pregnant and seems likely to be a burden, when she is deserted. If the two get along well together, or if the man is "easy" or has a sense of responsibility, a "Ford family" results.

Ford Mother—The female side of a "Ford family," or a woman traveling by automobile with a migratory worker or tramp.

48 or 48s—See "Hotshot" and "High 48."

Frog Sticker—See "Sticker."

Fruit Tramp—A migratory worker who travels from orchard to orchard or from one fruit-producing region to another, according to the crops that are to be gathered or packed. The word "tramp" is almost a misnomer here, since many of these men are well-to-do, steady workers.

Gadabout—One who wanders about looking for fun, excitement, or gossip.

Gandy Dancer—A railroad section hand or worker; a laborer who, while working along the tracks with a tamping bar or pick, tends to take on a waddle, similar to that of a gander or goose.

Gas—To talk; idle chatter. Much as in English slang, except that in America there is no sense of "brag" to the conversation. Impure liquor, such as doped cider or wine, "needle beer," "smoke," and the like.

Ghost Story—A story or long tale of woe to gain sympathy; a begging yarn. Like fashions, those ghost stories in vogue and "just the thing" this year are soon out of date and must be altered to meet changed conditions, and it is a matter of pride with every real tramp to have a good string of stories at his command.

Glad Rags—One's best clothes, or those worn on occasions of recreation or to give an air of prosperity and wealth. Clothes generally worn when a tramp needs to present himself as respectable, especially if the acquisition of work is in order.

Glass Packs—A straight-through muffler that uses fiberglass packing in the expansion chamber to muffle noise. Louder than stock mufflers. They create a distinct rumbling noise that is sometimes coveted by hot-rodders and bothersome to police.

Go By—A slight or "cut." Take no notice. An evasion, as "I gave him the go by," meaning, "I took no notice of him," or "I evaded him."

Gondola—A roofless (with minor exceptions), low-walled, flat-bottomed freight car designed to haul coal, steel, pipe, recyclables, etc.

Grabbing Scenery—Looking from a boxcar or other place of concealment on a train, a procedure that, marking the inexperienced tramp, is frowned upon by the older, wiser ones, since it is likely to lead to detection and a consequent "ditching" by the trainmen.

Grab iron—A handrail on the side or end of a railroad car, near the steps or ladder.

Graft—A term for most any outlaw activity or exercise in which the power of the law does not inhibit one's decision to procure a meal ticket or execute a said business endeavor. A specific trade or craft, as in "What's your graft?"

Grainer—A "bulk commodity" freight car designed to carry heavy loads that need protection from the elements (e.g., corn, wheat, sorghum, malt, beans, salt, phosphate, lime, cement, and soda ash). The "Ace *Center Flow*" (as stenciled on the side of the car) grainer is noted as the most "rideable" by tramps. An "Ace" can be recognized by its cylindrical shape, as opposed to flat-walled grainers, which are mostly unrideable. A tramp will also note that a grainer has a platform on the front and on the back, the back platform being the premium choice. There is a small cubbyhole on these platforms which a full-grown man can tightly fit into and be unseen. Also referred to as a "closed hopper."

Grease Joint—A dirty restaurant or lunchroom, or the cook tent on a construction job. In show circles, a hamburger or hot dog stand, and to those who have seen these eating places the word is apt.

Grease the Track—To be run over by a train. To commit suicide by leaping in front of a train.

Grifter—The crooked game operators, shortchange artists, clothesline robbers, shoplifters ("merchandise boosters"), pickpockets, and all other types of criminals associated with carnivals. Used in tramp circles to describe a thief of similar "carnival" caliber.

Grind—A speech given in front of a carnival or tent show to draw a crowd, or "tip." Most of the time a set speech that is delivered poetically by the pitch man or "grinder" with the intention of stimulating a response from the crowd or from a specific member thereof.

Grinder—The man or woman who "grinds." A good grinder must have more than a voice that can be made to express every nuance of expression; he must be a keen student of human nature and know just when to stop his grind and enter upon the exhortation.

Gumbo—An old coffee can or soup can used to heat water or stew in or in any other way made useful by a tramp. See "Can Moocher" and "Gunboat."

Gump—Chicken; scrap of meat. An ancient and frequently used word, yet one with a long forgotten origin.

Gunboat—An empty tin can, used in the jungles for cooking, carrying water or liquor, or for any other practical use. An old term for a coal car. See "Gumbo."

Gut Bucket—A washtub bass. A musical instrument fashioned out of a washtub by securing a clothesline to a broom handle and also to the tub, whereupon the clothesline is "plucked" to attain a sound. Used to make "hooch music."

Handle—A nickname used by a trucker for fast and easy self-identification, specifically while talking over the road by CB. See "Moniker."

Harness—The equipment or "rigging" worn by gamblers to hold cards up the sleeve until wanted to cheat with.

Hallelujah Peddler—A minister; one who tries to "sell" salvation.

Heater—A pistol or revolver, perhaps since it is from the weapon that the proverbial "hot lead" is discharged.

Highball—(v) To travel swiftly; to go away; a swift-moving train.

Highball—(n) A "proceed" signal on the railroad, in the old days, in which the hand or lantern is raised or swung about the head as a command to the engineer to start the train. Also commonly, a drink of whisky and soda.

High 48—The speed at which a "hotshot" travels, a hotshot sometimes being referred to as a "48."

Hobo—A migratory worker, especially one who will work whenever he finds an opportunity; a tramp who works. According to some the word is from the Latin *homo bonus*, or good man; others say that the word was first used after the Civil War in the United States, when soldiers walking home through the country replied, "homeward bound," when questioned as to their destination. Another source for the word could be the fact that migratory workers often carried hoes and bedrolls and were known as "hoe-boys." The usual dictionary gives an entirely incorrect definition, since a hobo is not by any means a "professional tramp."

Hog—A locomotive; a "hog" for coal.

Hoghead or Hogger—An engineer, the one who handles the "hog."

Homeguard—A possible union term. A man who travels little, maintains a steady job, and tends not to strike. One who sustains a home base for his more indecisive and scatterbrained friends. Thought up by the old-time tramp to facilitate his illusion of superiority over those who remain idle in one-tank towns while he procures a life of fancy while becoming "a man of the world."

Hooch—Booze, drink, beer, whiskey, grog, moonshine, devil water, and any other term used to describe spirits of the intoxicating variety.

Hooch Music—Music influenced by the consumption of distilled spirits or "hooch" (see "Hooch"), therefore instilled with the internal drama and heartache of the performer's most recent love and loss.

Hoofer—In theatrical circles, a dancer, and usually one working on a cheap circuit; on the road, any cheap actor, the word originating from the classic joke that pictured the unfortunate members of a stranded show walking home.

Hook Joint—An old term for a house of prostitution.

Hopped Up—Under the influence of opium or any narcotic or stimulant.

Hopper—Roofless (open hopper) or roofed (closed hopper) freight car designed to haul heavy bulk commodities such as grain, coal, sand, or cement. Equipped with sloped V-shaped floors or "gravity shoots" for easy bottom unloading. See "Grainer."

Hoppins—Ingredients.

Hotshot—A fast freight. A train that carries piggybacks (flatbeds with tractor trailers) or container cars (sunken flatbeds with a single or double stacked containers). Also referred to as the "48s" because many of the wells in container cars are 48 feet long. A hotshot can cover five hundred miles in eight hours, as opposed to a regular manifest freight, which will cover only two hundred to three hundred miles in the same time. See "Red Ball," an older term for high-priority freight.

Hump or The Hump—The summit of a railroad grade, especially over a mountain pass. (The train finally "humped" the Rocky

Mountains.) Also, the artificial hill in a classification yard over which cars are pushed to travel by gravity to their proper places in the lower yard, where they are made up into trains; the middle of a prison sentence, in this case the prisoner feeling the worst is over; sexual intercourse.

Hustler—A criminal, drug dealer, or street woman. In all three senses, one who "hustles" or hurries, who works quickly and in fear of detection. The street is usually their place of operation.

ice Palace—A high-class establishment, a saloon, or a brothel, so called from the many mirrors and cut-glass chandeliers found in these resorts.

ink—Cheap red wine. See "Dago Red."

Jack—A generic term for any tramp or other man. Generic also for money. Both of these applications are seemingly without reason. A locomotive, possibly because the engine "jacks" or forces a train over the road.

Jack Roll—A roll of money. See "Jack."

Jack Roller—A town crook who fleeces the workers; one who "rolls" them of their money. (See "Roll.") A tramp thief or "yegg" who robs his fellows, especially when they are intoxicated.

Jamoke—Old term for coffee, and without a doubt from the two words indicating the sections of the world, Java and Mocha, from which much of the coffee came from.

Johnny-Come-Lately—A tramp with but scant experience on the road. Another term borrowed from the circus, where it indicates a clown starting his second season "under canvas."

Join the 400—Go straight. To reintroduce oneself to "normal" life after having disappeared into the underworld, both physically and mentally, for an extended period of time.

Jug—A jail or prison.

Juke Joint—Any musical hangout or gathering place, and not always a "low resort" in the estimation of the underworld, although it is sometimes used in a slighting sense.

Jungle Buzzard—A tramp or yegg (see) preying on others of his kind; one who holds up the unarmed men gathered at the jungles, robbing them of food and drink. Also one who begs for food and drink at jungles and makes no attempt to contribute to the communal store.

Jungle Stiff—One who rarely leaves the jungles to travel. A bum who lives in the jungles instead of in a town.

Jungle Up—To rest, wash, and eat in the jungle.

Junker—A local work train. A junker's main purpose is to pick up and deliver short-range freight. Also, a rather slow and boring freight; an old term for a drug addict.

Kelly—A hat.

Kick—A turbo rush of physical and spiritual exhilaration, as a football is "kicked" and therefore in relation to the mind "elevated" to a purely righteous and heavenly state of affairs.

Kid Show—A sideshow or annex to the main circus tent or "big top." Also a job on which the majority of the workers are young and without experience.

Knuckles—The movable parts of a freight car coupler that fold and lock around each other. Also called "glad hands."

Lam—A hasty getaway or escape; to run; to escape. Possible explanations may be found in the lamb's nervous habit of running from anything strange.

Lamps—The eyes.

Lead Joint—A shooting gallery such as those found in amusement parks and at fairs, carnivals, and the like.

Leprechaun—An elf or *small* mischievous fairy of Irish folklore.

Library Bird—A tramp who frequents libraries in order to avoid bad weather, or from an honest desire to read and improve his mind.

Lillies—The hands, probably an ironic reference to their lack of cleanliness.

Lizzie Stiff—A tramp who travels from place to place in an auto. Thus "riding high" for the time being. The Ford car, popularly referred to as a "tin lizzie," was the vehicle most often used, hence the name.

Loony Tick—An erratic individual. Applied to anyone who seems not quite right.

Lot Lice—Local townspeople who arrive early to watch the unloading of the circus and stay late. An unsavory audience or "tip." Also circus and carnival hangers-on who follow the show but are not a part of the salaried staff. They are vermin in every sense of the word, and a thorn in the side of every well-conducted show, although tolerated by the smaller, less reputable establishments.

Lot Lizard—A prostitute who frequents truck stops, sometimes "servicing" up to ten trucks in one lot in one night.

Low Pitch—A sales pitch delivered from the ground. The act of speaking about oneself in a less than flattering manner.

Luey—A circus clown, and apparently a corruption of "Joey."

Lump—A package of food given a tramp. A proper lump, to a tramp of discernment, is one that contains not only the food for sustenance but some pastry or cake as well; hence a "bald-headed lump" is one with nothing but bread and meat.

Lu Lu—Anything unusually worthy or desirable. A coined word of no readily traceable source, but widely used by the older tramp and crooks.

Lying Dead—A tramp or criminal who is in hiding or temporarily out of the life, living quietly on money begged or stolen. Also—and this is where it was found by the tramp—a train or engine that has pulled off the main line and is lying quiet, or "dead."

Main Drag—The main street of a town or city; the best street on which to beg; the street most frequented by tramps and hobos; the main line of a railroad. See "Drag."

Manifest—A fast freight train, from the "manifest" of the goods carried.

Meal Ticket—A woman supporting a lover; any free source of income. From the card or ticket issued by a restaurant on the payment of a certain sum, and good for a certain amount of food or number of meals, until the value has been canceled by punch marks.

Megaroll—The act of covering a lot of miles in a short period of time on a long stretch of highway. Possibly a trucker term.

Michelin—Boot soles.

Mini-Thins—Ephedrine tablets. Also called "trucker's speed."

Mission Squawker—An evangelist, one who not infrequently "squawks" or raises his voice to unnecessary heights when exhorting his flock. See "Hallelujah Peddler."

Moniker or Monicker or Monica or Monniker—A name or nickname of an individual; occasionally a signature or artistic symbol chalked on walls or boxcars as a guide or as proof of a tramp having visited a certain location, thus called a "tag." Most of the time comprised of a tramp's proper name and his general characteristics and relating to his place of origin or to a place in which he had an especially rigorous or spiritual experience, such as "Laredo Slim," "Short Stop," or "Piss Whiskey." See "Handle."

Mooch—To beg; to stroll about; to walk away from.

Moocher—A beggar, one who "mooches."

Mooching the Stem—Begging on the street.

Muck Stick—A long-handled shovel, one in general use by ditchdiggers and others working in the earth, as opposed to "banjo" or short-handled "scoop" shovel for coal, grain, etc.

Mud Floor Show or Mud Show—A smaller tent circus. Also one in which the spirit of the crew must outweigh their desire for financial retribution. A gypsy show "thrown" in the dirt under lowbrow conditions. See "Rag Tag" and "Rag Front."

Mulligan—The great tramp stew, composed or thrown together, depending on the ability of the cook, from anything and everything that is obtainable by theft, begging, or purchase. The base of the proper mulligan is always meat of some kind, the cooking utensil varies from a stewpan rescued from a dump to a stolen pot, and the dish is served in anything that will hold it, from a large leaf to a salvaged tin can.

Mugging—Making faces—on stage as a means of creating a laugh, in criminal circles to give silent warning behind another's back or to warn. Also, artificially presenting one's social "stature" as respectable.

Nut—An insane or erratic individual; one out of the ordinary and therefore a "hard nut" to crack for the rest of society.

Oil Rig—See "Tank Car."

Oiled—Intoxicated; "well oiled."

On the Bum—Literally, broken in pocket and spirit. See "Bum."

On the Hog—Penniless; down and out; forced to accept anything, much in the way a hog roots for whatever it can find.

On the Lam—Avoiding the police; running at top speed. See "Lam."

One-Tank Town—See "Tank Town."

Open Hopper—See "Hopper."

Over the Road—Any train track outside of the yards.

Padding the Hoof—To travel by foot.

Pickets—The teeth. A playful reference to the "picket fence," in which a series of "pickets" or upright palings, generally painted white, are used to enclose a lawn or yard.

Pick Up—To "pick up" a freight car from a customer or freight yard.

Pimp—A hustler who lives on the earnings of a street walker or prostitute. Man who solicits the trade of his woman or lover for compensation. The woman might then be referred to as his "meal ticket" (see "Meal Ticket").

Pink Lady—Wood alcohol, specifically wood alcohol strained from the paraffin in a can of Sterno and mixed with soda. So called because of the pink color of the paraffin and of the drink itself.

Pirate Stew—Any soup or stew fixed in a gumbo over a small fire, particularly with hoppins of the stolen or pilfered variety.

Pitch—Selling merchandise by lecturing and demonstrating. Candy pitches often included promises that valuable prize coupons would be found in certain boxes. Medicine pitches often have a life of their own, in carnivals and also in medicine shows. The medicine show would travel rural areas, offering free entertainment and repeated opportunities to buy the sponsor's "medicine." Also to "sell" or articulate one's idea or philosophy.

Pitch and Business—Simply a combination of the terms "pitch" and "business." Once the philosophy, or "pitch," is delivered it must be followed by the action, or the "business."

Player—One who schemes or gambles on success; a race car driver or competitor who tests his skills and his machines against rivals, either on or off the track—"race car spelled backwards is race car" is common philosophy of said enthusiast. Also, a man who frequents the company of more than one woman at any one time.

Plush—A stuffed animal, specifically a carnival "prize" of the cheap and stuffed variety.

Ponce—A young man, but generally not a pimp, maintained by a woman of means as a lover or because his presence seems to rejuvenate his benefactress.

Possum Belly—To ride on top of a passenger train, in which the rider must remain flat on his belly to avoid being jolted off. Taken from the habit of the possum, which carries its young on its back. Also, a circus term meaning a storage box attached to the bottom of a passenger car or work wagon to carry cable, stakes, rigging, etc.; at times, a place for a quick nap by a worker or temporary homes for their unauthorized women. This box was also a common place for tramps to ride and in which, at one time, it was common practice for cheap carnival bosses to require some of their laborers to sleep on the road.

Pullman—A train car. Named after George M. Pullman of the Pullman Car Company.

Push—A crowd; a gang or clique, usually of tramps or criminals, but especially applied by "pitchmen" to the crowd attracted by the "spiel" or "bally" at a carnival—probably since the crowd pushes or presses about the "pitch."

Rag Front—A tent show, circus, or carnival, or more strictly the canvas banners and signs erected in front of the show as advertisements. See "Rag Tag."

Rag Tag—Small circus that travels the rural circuits; a tattered and ill-kept show.

Rambler—A high-class tramp or hobo, one who rides only fast passenger trains, and usually for long distances; one who wanders aimlessly.

Rambling—Traveling at high speed, afoot, or by rail or other means of conveyance.

Rat Holing—A gambling term meaning to remove checks or chips from the table before cashing out of the game. Typically this is done to hide a player's winnings from the pit boss to avoid suspicion.

Rattler—A passenger train or fast freight, both of which rattle along the tracks when traveling.

Red Ball or Red Ball Manifest—A fast-as-hell freight, one operating on a schedule and with timetable rights over other trains. So called in the old days because cars for dispatch in such a train are "carded," or marked with cards bearing a large red ball to indicate at once the importance of the car and its contents. See "Hotshot."

Reefer—A refrigerator car.

Riding the Rods—An old term meaning to ride on the braces beneath a car. See "Rods."

Rigging—A gambler's "harness" (see "Harness"). IWW propaganda or literature, very probably in the sense that the use of such material will ensure harnessing a convert into the movement.

Rigging Packer—An IWW organizer, one who "packs" or carries the "rigging."

Right of Way—The strip of land over which facilities such as highways, railroads, and power lines are built; the right to pass over property owned by another.

Ringtail—A grouchy individual. No doubt from the name of some especially vicious or dangerous animal that happened to have a tail marked with a ring of different colored fur.

Road Stake—Money to live on while traveling, or with which to secure transportation.

Rods—On old boxcars (no longer used), the braces running lengthwise beneath a freight or passenger car. By the means of a short, cleated board, or in many cases without his "ticket," a tramp can ride on these rods, the body being supported diagonally across the two rods, the arms and legs hooked around them to prevent the motion of the car from hurling the rider off.

Roll—(n) Money, as one would say "roll of bills."

Roll—(v) To rob a drunken or sleeping person of his "roll," or by rolling him to one side or the other to secure his money or valuables. A more violent method is to secure the said victim in his blankets and beat him with pipes, shovels, or any blunt and heavy objects.

Roughies—Temporary help hired to erect or tear down a carnival.

Roustabout—A circus workman, laborer.

Rube—A farmer; an outsider; a stranger to any circle of life. From the once generally accepted idea that nearly all farmers were named Rube or Reuben. In show circles, an outsider to show business.

Rum Dum—Intoxicated to the point of foolishness, but still able to walk, even if unable to talk with any intelligence. Merely a variation of "dumb from rum."

Running the Front Door—A trucker term. Front door is the lead truck in a convoy of trucks. Running the front door is the act of "leading." In truth, a risky position if the convoy happens to be traveling at a speed higher than the law allows. Trucks in a convoy will usually take turns in this position.

Sal—The Salvation Army.

Salvation Rancher—A preacher; a mission evangelist.

Scenery Bum—A tramp who is continually talking about the glories of nature, or who persists in "grabbing scenery" (see "Grabbing Scenery").

Scratch—Money, banknotes, or other assets.

Sea Stiff—A sailor tramp, or a tramp or hobo who has been to sea.

Shaky Town—A trucker term for Los Angeles.

Shock Joint—An old term for a lowbrow saloon or speakeasy where the booze was hard enough to "shock" the drinker into submission for an extended amount of time.

Sidekick—A partner or friend. An old, old term in vagabondia.

Sky Pilot—A minister. Taken from the sea, where the chaplain is so called, and since the 1880s in general use ashore as well as afloat.

Slack—"Play" or "travel" built into a train's coupling system to soften impact and ease starting and stopping. See "Slack Action."

Slack Action—The tendency of a train to jolt violently while the "slack" (see "Slack") in the line is being pulled out by the locomotives. Mostly caught approaching by an experienced tramp, since the radical action and sound begins at the locomotives and is thrown backward. Can also occur along the road while the train is traveling en route. Also more of a problem on a "bad road." (See "Bad Road.")

Smoke—The cheap and sometimes poisonous booze that was once served in "Shock Joints" (see "Shock Joint"). Derived from shellac and other commercial alcohol or solvents, also from distilled garbage. So called because of its smoky appearance when water is poured into it.

Snipe—A cigarette stub; an old term for a railroad section hand. In the former instance, so called since the hobo or tramp who retrieves the smoke from the street does so in a furtive manner, much as one hunts the wary bird of the same name.

Snipe Shooting—Picking cigarette stubs from the street or sidewalk.

Spiel—A speech. Used by tramps, hustlers, or pitchmen to peddle goods or to promote tent shows.

Sterno—Portable cooking fuel that comes in a silver can. A mix of paraffin and wood alcohol.

Stew Bum—A drunkard, usually a drunken tramp or hobo, and especially an individual almost continually sodden with drink.

Sticker—A knife.

Stiff—A generic term for the worker, such as a "lumber stiff," a woodcutter, or a "bindle stiff." Also, an alternative term for any tramp or hobo on the road or at work.

Streamline—To travel light.

Switchman—A freight yard worker who assists in assembly of trains and alignment of tracks as ordered.

Tag—See "Moniker."

Take the Westbound—To pass away; to die. A hobo "takes the westbound" to a warm and tranquil land.

Tank Car—Freight car that hauls liquids such as chlorine, oil, corn syrup, or herbicide.

Tank Town—A small and relatively unimportant town on a railroad, one at which most trains in the old days stopped, if at all, merely to take on water from the tank.

Third Rail or Third Rail Smoke—Strong, cheap liquor, stuff that seems to galvanize the drinker much as would touching a "third" or electrified rail in a subway. See "Smoke."

Thousand-Mile Paper—Thick brown paper used in freight cars for packing.

Tip—Advice; a bit of information; in carnival or pitchman's slang, the nucleus of a crowd, especially that attracted by the "ballyhoo."

Tokay Blanket—Drinking booze to keep warm.

Towners—Townspeople, especially when they are, or seem to be, massed against a "mob" of tramps, or against a circus or carnival crowd.

Tramp—One who loafs and walks. In America the word covers practically every unfortunate on the road or off it, yet there are thousands who have no membership in the real tramp fraternity. Some of these outsiders are "hobos" (see "Hobo"); some are mere adventurers, youths who pay their way so far as food and lodging are concerned and "steal" rides; while others are mere gypsies. The real tramp is a man unto himself, one who "wanders and never works."

Turnpiker—A tramp on the road or highway.

Unit—A locomotive. A train will have from two to five units, depending on the length of the train. The front unit will be the only one occupied by the crew, therefore making it possible for a tramp to ride in one of the empty back units. An engineer or conductor will be more apt to throw you off a unit than any other car. When a hobo rides a unit, he has access to the crew and this can make the crew nervous. Kind engineers have been known to offer tramps rides in units. But this privilege is reserved for only the most respectable and upstanding train riders. If there are no units on the front of the train, then the train isn't going anywhere.

Westbound—See "Take the Westbound."

Windcheater—Any burlap bag, feed sack, or similar found object worn and used as protection from the elements.

Winter Stake—Money acquired and hoarded during the summer or working season to carry one through the winter or slack season.

Wheel—Burlesque circuit.

White Cross—Amphetamine or methamphetamine. Over-the-counter ephedrine tablets. Identified by the cross stamped into them. Referred to as copilots or black Cadillacs by truck drivers. Also the name of a drugstore on the Strip in Las Vegas.

White Line—Raw alcohol, probably from the line of color to be seen when water or fruit juice is added to the liquid beverage. Also, by extension, any poor liquor. See "Pink Lady."

White Line Fever—The "fuzzy" feeling a trucker or highway man gets in his head from staring at passing white lines on the interstate, a rather addictive sensation; vertigo. Merle Haggard referring to said affliction: "A sickness born down deep within my soul." Possibly related to the old underworld term "white line." "White line fever" is the outcome of too much "white line" (See "White Line.")

Yard Dog—A small locomotive used only in the train yard to build trains. Also, a "goat"; a fellow prisoner or confidant on whom a prisoner will depend for protection; in Florida: an alligator.

Yegg—A tramp thief or criminal, to be found mainly along railroad lines and specializing in burglary and the robbing of poorly protected and flimsy safes in country towns, or railroad cars and freight houses (good sheds). Originally a criminal too wise, too cautious, too old or too cowardly to risk crime in a city, where police and private detectives were alert, and who took to "the road" for easier "graft."

Resources

Works Cited

Allsop, Kenneth. *Hard Travellin': The Hobo and His History.* New York: New American Library, 1967.

Brown, Joseph Epes. *Animals of the Soul: Sacred Animals of the Oglala Sioux.* London: Harper Collins UK, 1997.

Irwin, Godfrey. *American Tramp and Underworld Slang.* New York: Sears Publishers, 1931.

Littlejohn, Duffy. *Hopping Freight Trains in America.* Los Osos, Calif.: Sand Rivers Press, 1993.

Mathers, Michael. *Riding the Rails.* Boston: Houghton Mifflin Company, 1979.

Websites

http://www.goodmagic.com/lingo

http://www.layover.com